Sound and Form in Modern Poetry

Sound and Form in Modern Poetry

HARVEY GROSS

AND

ROBERT MCDOWELL

ॐ

Second Edition

Ann Arbor Paperbacks

THE UNIVERSITY OF MICHIGAN PRESS

First edition as an Ann Arbor Paperback 1968
Revised and expanded edition 1996
Copyright © by the University of Michigan 1964
All rights reserved
Published in the United States of America by
The University of Michigan Press
Manufactured in the United States of America
⊗ Printed on acid-free paper

1999   1998   1997   1996   4   3   2   1

A CIP catalog record for this book is available from the British Library.

LIBRARY OF CONGRESS CATALOGING-IN-PUBLICATION DATA

Gross, Harvey Seymour, 1922–
    Sound and form in modern poetry / Harvey Gross ; revised and
expanded by Robert McDowell. — Rev. and expanded ed.
        p.   cm. — (Ann Arbor paperbacks)
    Includes bibliographical references and index.
    ISBN 0-472-09517-X (hardcover : alk. paper). — IBSN 0-472-06517-3
(pbk. : alk. paper)
    1. English language—Versification. 2. American poetry—History
and criticism. 3. English poetry—History and criticism.
4. English language—Rhythm. 5. Literary form. 6. Poetics.
I. McDowell, Robert, 1953– . II. Title.
PE1505.G7   1996
821.009—dc20   95-52355
                                                                        CIP

Acknowledgments

Acknowledgments are extended to the following authors, publishers, and agents for kind permission to quote copyrighted materials.

To the Estate of Richard Aldington for "The Faun Sees Snow for the First Time," from *Collected Poems,* 1949.

To Random House, Inc. and Faber and Faber Ltd. for excerpts from:
"Doom is dark and deeper," copyright 1934 and renewed 1961 by W. H. Auden. Reprinted from *The Collected Poetry of W. H. Auden.*
"Hearing of Harvest Rotting," copyright 1937 by W. H. Auden. Reprinted from *On This Island,* by W. H. Auden.
"Look, Stranger, on This Island Now," copyright 1937 by W. H. Auden. Reprinted from *The Collected Poetry of W. H. Auden.*
"Musee des Beaux Arts," "The Unknown Citizen," and "In Memory of W. B. Yeats," copyright 1940 by W. H. Auden. Reprinted from *The Collected Poetry of W. H. Auden.*
"For the Time Being," copyright 1944 by W. H. Auden. Reprinted from *The Collected Poetry of W. H. Auden.*
"Under Which Lyre," copyright 1946 by W. H. Auden. Reprinted from *Nones,* by W. H. Auden.
"The Shield of Achilles," copyright 1952 by W. H. Auden. Reprinted from *The Shield of Achilles,* by W. H. Auden.

To Robert Bly for "The Great Society."

To the Clarendon Press, Oxford for "The Growth of Love," "The Downs," and "Trafalgar Square" from *Poetical Works of Robert Bridges,* 1953.

To Liveright Publishing Corporation for *The Collected Poems of Hart Crane,* copyright © 1933, 1958 by the Liveright Publishing Corporation.

To the University of California Press for "A Counterpoint" and "The Way" from *Collected Poems of Robert Creeley, 1945–1975,* copyright © 1983 by the Regents of the University of California.

To Harcourt, Brace & World, Inc., for 1 and 13 from E. E. Cumming's *No Thanks;* for 13 and 40 from *XAIPE;* from *Poems, 1923–1954,* copyright 1935, 1950 by E. E. Cummings.

To Little, Brown and Company for Emily Dickinson's "After Great Pain, a Formal Feeling Comes."

To Harvard University Press and the Trustees of Amherst College for Poems 258 and 1695 from *The Poems of Emily Dickinson* edited by Thomas H. Johnson, copyright © 1951, 1955, 1979, 1983 by the President and Fellows of Harvard College.

To Harcourt, Brace, and World, Inc., and Faber and Faber Ltd. for excerpts from T. S. Eliot's *Collected Poems 1909–1962,* copyright 1963 by T. S. Eliot; from *Selected Essays,* copyright Harcourt, Brace, and Co., 1932, 1936, 1950; from *The Family Reunion,* copyright 1939 by T. S. Eliot; from *The Cocktail Party,* copyright 1950 by T. S. Eliot.

To Farrar, Straus & Company and Faber and Faber Ltd. for excerpts from T. S. Eliot's *On Poetry and Poets,* copyright © 1943, 1945, 1951, 1954, 1956, 1957 by T. S. Eliot; from *The Elder Statesman,* copyright © 1959 by T. S. Eliot.

To Charlie May Fletcher (Mrs. John Gould Fletcher) for excerpts from John Gould Fletcher's "The Green Symphony" and "The Skaters."

To Holt, Rinehart and Winston, Inc., Jonathan Cape Ltd., and Laurence Pollinger Ltd. for excerpts from Robert Frost's *Collected Poems of Robert Frost,* copyright 1930 by Henry Holt & Co.; copyright 1936 by Robert Frost.

To Henry Holt and Co., Inc. for "The Draft Horse" from *The Poetry of Robert Frost* edited by Edward Connery Lathem, copyright © 1962 by Robert Frost, copyright © 1969 by Henry Holt and Co., Inc.

To The University of Chicago Press and Faber and Faber Ltd. for "My Sad Captains" from Thom Gunn's *My Sad Captains,* © 1961 by Thom Gunn.

To The Macmillan Company (United States), The Macmillan Company of Canada Limited, and St. Martin's Press for excerpts from *Collected Poems of Thomas Hardy;* by permission of the Trustees of the Hardy Estate, Macmillan & Co. Ltd., London, and The Macmillan Company of Canada Limited.

To the Grove Press, Inc. for excerpts from H.D.'s *Selected Poems,* copyright © 1957 by Norman Holmes Pearson; from *Helen in Egypt* by H.D., copyright © 1961 by Norman Holmes Pearson.

To George Hitchcock for "Solitaire."

To the Oxford University Press for excerpts from *Poems of Gerard Manley Hopkins,* Third Edition, copyright 1948 by Oxford University Press, Inc.

To the Viking Press, Inc. and The Society of Authors (London) for a passage from James Joyce's *Finnegans Wake,* copyright 1939 by James Joyce.

To Weldon Kees for "Farrago." Reprinted from *The Collected Poems of Weldon Kees*, edited by Donald Justice, by permission of the University of Nebraska Press. Copyright © 1975, by the University of Nebraska Press.

To Jane Kenyon for "Let Evening Come" copyright 1990 by Jane Kenyon. Reprinted from *Let Evening Come* with the permission of Graywolf Press, Saint Paul, Minnesota.

To Maxine Kumin for "Grace" from *The Privilege,* copyright © 1965 by Maxine Kumin. To W. W. Norton & Company, Inc. for "Hay." "Hay" is reprinted from *Looking for Luck: Poems by Maxine Kumin,* by permission of W. W. Norton & Company, Inc. Copyright © 1992 by Maxine Kumin.

To Farrar, Straus & Giroux, Inc. for "Compline" and "Days." "Compline" and "Days" from *Collected Poems* by Philip Larkin. Copyright © 1988, 1989 by the Estate of Philip Larkin. Reprinted by permission of Farrar, Straus & Giroux, Inc.

To The University of Chicago Press for excerpts from Richmond Lattimore's *Greek Lyrics,* copyright 1949 and 1955 by Richmond Lattimore; all rights reserved; copyright International Copyright Union, 1955.

To New Directions Publishing Corp. for "The Dog of Art" from Denise Levertov's *Collected Earlier Poems,* copyright © 1959 by Denise Levertov.

To Houghton Mifflin Company for excerpts from *Selected Poems by Amy Lowell,* copyright 1922, 1925, 1926, 1927.

To Harcourt, Brace, and World, Inc. and Faber and Faber Ltd. for excerpts from Robert Lowell's *Lord Weary's Castle,* copyright 1944, 1946 by Robert Lowell.

To Farrar, Straus & Company, Inc. and Faber and Faber Ltd. for excerpts from Robert Lowell's *Life Studies,* copyright © 1956, 1959 by Robert Lowell.

To Houghton Mifflin Company for Archibald MacLeish's "Frescoes for Mr. Rockefeller's City," from Archibald MacLeish's *Collected Poems, 1917–1952,* copyright 1952 by Archibald MacLeish.

To Faber and Faber Ltd. for excerpts from Louis MacNeice's *Collected Poems 1925–1948,* all rights reserved.

To The Macmillan Company and Faber and Faber Ltd. for "The Monkeys" and excerpts from Marianne Moore's *Selected Poems,* copyright 1935 by Marianne Moore; for excerpts from *What Are Years,* copyright 1941 by Marianne Moore. To the Viking Press for "In the Public Garden" from *O To Be a Dragon,* copyright © 1956, 1957, 1958, 1959; copyright © 1958 by The Curtis Publishing Company.

To Frederick Morgan for "After Shen Zhou," copyright © 1991 by Frederick Morgan. First published in *The New Criterion,* September 1991.

To Grove Press, Inc. and Faber and Faber Ltd. for excerpts from Edwin Muir's *Collected Poems 1921–1951,* copyright © 1957 by Edwin Muir.

To Maureen O'Hara for "Poem" by Frank O'Hara.

To New Directions and Chatto & Windus Ltd. for excerpts from *Poems of Wilfred Owen,* all rights reserved.

To Molly Peacock for "Dream Come True" from *Take Heart* by Molly Peacock, copyright © 1989 by Random House.

To New Directions, to Mr. Arthur V. Moore (agent), and to Mr. Ezra Pound for excerpts from *Personae, the Collected Poems of Ezra Pound,* copyright 1926 by Ezra Pound; *The Cantos of Ezra Pound,* copyright 1934, 1937, 1940, 1948 by Ezra Pound; from *Section: Rock-Drill,* copyright 1956 by Ezra Pound; from *Thrones* © 1959 by Ezra Pound.

To Alfred A. Knopf, Inc., Laurence Pollinger Ltd., and Eyre & Spotteswoode Ltd. for excerpts from *Selected Poems by John Crowe Ransom,* copyright 1924, 1927, 1934, 1939, 1945 by Alfred A. Knopf, Inc.

To The Macmillan Company for excerpts from *Tilbury Town: Selected Poems of Edward Arlington Robinson,* copyright 1925, 1953 by The Macmillan Company.

To Doubleday & Company, Inc. for excerpts from *Words for the Wind (The Collected Verse of Theodore Roethke),* copyright 1958 by Theodore Roethke.

To Doubleday & Company for excerpts from Delmore Schwartz's *Summer Knowledge,* copyright 1959 by Delmore Schwartz.

To Random House, Inc. for excerpt from *Essay on Rime,* by Karl Shapiro, copyright 1945 by Karl Shapiro.

To Alfred A. Knopf, Inc. and Faber and Faber Ltd. for excerpts from *The Collected Poems of Wallace Stevens,* copyright 1923, 1931, 1942, 1947, 1954 by Wallace Stevens.

To Alfred A. Knopf, Inc. and Faber and Faber Ltd. for "Valley Candle" from Wallace Stevens's *Collected Poems,* copyright © 1923, 1951 by Wallace Stevens.

To Harcourt, Brace, and World, Inc. for excerpts from Ruth Stone's *In an Iridescent Time,* © 1959 by Ruth Stone.

To New Directions, J. M. Dent & Sons, Ltd. and the Executors of the Dylan Thomas Estate for "What Is the Meter of the Dictionary," and other excerpts from Dylan Thomas' *Collected Poems,* copyright 1953 by Dylan Thomas.

To New Directions and Faber and Faber Ltd. for excerpts from Vernon Watkins's *Selected Poems,* 1948, all rights reserved; from Vernon Watkins's *The Death Bell,* all rights reserved.

To New Directions and MacGibbon & Kee Ltd. for excerpts from *The Collected Earlier Poems of William Carlos Williams,* copyright 1951 by William Carlos Williams; from *Paterson, Book II,* copyright 1948 by William Carlos Williams.

To The Macmillan Company, The Macmillan Company of Canada, A. P. Watt & Son (agent), Messrs Macmillan, and Mrs. W. B. Yeats for excerpts from *Collected Poems of W. B. Yeats* and *Collected Plays of W. B. Yeats.*

Contents

Prologue: The Moon through the Trees

The prosodist attempting the hazards of modern poetry finds the way blocked by four significant and confusing problems: no general agreement on what *prosody* means and what subject matter properly belongs to it; no apparent dominant metrical convention such as obtained in the centuries previous to this one; no accepted theory about how prosody functions in a poem; and no critical agreement about the scansion of the English meters.

We must first consider the problem of terminology. Classically understood, prosody was part of grammar and, like grammar, concerned itself with rules and paradigms. Prosody explained the classical meters, their nature and structure. Prosody was the grammar of metrics; its precision was such that dictionaries still gave as its first meaning that science which treats of versification. Far from naming a science or being subsumed under grammar, prosody has now a number of descriptive and evaluative meanings.

The word denotes not only the study of a poet's versification, but that which is studied, the versification itself. This is an accepted meaning of the word. When Saintsbury titled his *History*, he called it a *History of English Prosody*. He did not intend it as a history of the theory of versification; he meant it primarily as an account of the poetry itself. Thus we speak here of "Yeats's prosody" or "Eliot's prosody." Perhaps it would be clearer if we relinquished this use of prosody to describe the technical abilities a poet shows in versification, and speak only of a poet's *metric*. Unfortunately *metric* suggests meter, and it seems absurd to discuss the *metric* of lines like these:

(im)c-a-t(mo)
b,i;l:e

FallleA
ps!fl
OattumblI

sh?dr
IftwhirlF
(Ul)(lY)
&&&

away wanders: exact
ly;as if
not
hing had, ever happ
ene

D

                                   Cummings, 57 from *XAIPE*

Here is our second problem: the "prosody" of nonmetrical verse.
The lines above are an extreme example, even for cummings, but the
rhythmic structure of much modern poetry is seemingly without metri-
cal basis. We say seemingly because a true nonmetrical prosody is
difficult to sustain in English: Whitman again and again falls into
"English hexameter"; Eliot often writes in strong-stress meter. But we
must recognize the typographic rhythms of cummings (and the later
efforts of Concrete and Language poets) as characteristic nonmetrical
prosody. In the poem above, prosodic shape exists for the eyes alone;
the poem's rhythms are visual rather than aural. We cannot, however,
write a grammar of cummings's visual prosody; we can locate the
ground of his rhythm, but not the measure by which it moves.

Our third problem combines with the first: understanding what
prosody *is* depends on how we conceive its function. Our first chapter
describes the way rhythmic structure works in a poem. We venture that
rhythmic structure neither ornaments conceptual meaning nor pro-
vides a sensuous element extraneous to meaning; prosody is a sym-
bolic structure like metaphor and carries its own weight of meaning.
This concept of prosody is possibly too broad; it might be the cannier
strategy to restrict *prosody* to exclusively metrical matters. But we would

have to discard, as being without rhythmic structure, the unmetered sections of *The Bridge* and *Four Quartets,* the *Song of Myself,* nearly all of the poems of D. H. Lawrence, and a good deal of the poetry written in English from 1950 to the present day.

Prosody is an evaluative as well as a technical term. We tend to use the word qualitatively: if not precisely as an honorific, certainly with a charge of special meaning. A prosody is something a poet achieves— distinction in the movement of an individual language, a style with deep historic roots growing up from the bedrock of shared speech. And perhaps the title of this book should be *Examples of Style in Modern Prosody.* Style in art, as Whitehead remarks, "is the fashioning of power, the restraining of power"—in other words, control. Such control is always the result of an equilibrium: the balancing of idiosyncrasy with tradition, personal freedom with restraint, revolt with conformity. To be idiosyncratic, however, presupposes the existence of tradition; to revolt presupposes the presence of a conformity, a convention, against which revolt is possible.

In English verse syllable-stress (frequently called accentual-syllabic) meters establish the normative convention. Against this convention, or against the memory of it, poets achieve distinguished prosodies. Mere metrical regularity, of course, does not produce distinctive pros- ody; it is more apt to produce doggerel. But when we turn to the poetry that evokes the deepest feelings, we often find metrical struc- tures strongly influencing the rhythms, making thought clear and emotion precise. This is even true of the many varieties of nonmetrical prosody—where rhythm hardly runs down the "metalled ways" of iambs or anapests. Whitman's prosody is largely a matter of syntactical parallelism, but many memorable lines move to a hexameter lilt:

> Oh how shall I warble myself for the dead one there I loved?
> And how shall I deck my song for the large sweet soul that has
>   gone?
> And what shall my perfume be for the grave of him I love?

Those often-quoted passages from Pound's *Cantos* reveal the smoothest, most limpid meters:

> Hast 'ou seen the rose in the steel dust
>   (or swansdown ever?)

so light is the urging, so ordered the dark petals of iron
we who have passed over Lethe.

Canto 74

We now encounter our fourth difficulty: the scansion of the English meters. "Very few can mark the scansion from a line of Shakespeare's sonnets," Yvor Winters remarked with characteristic gloom.[1] Proof of his observation might be found in a book by Robert Hillyer on "the enjoyment of poetry":

And trou | ble deaf heav | en with | my boot | less cries.[2]

This scansion compounds insensitivity with ignorance. *Heaven* is monosyllabic in Elizabethan verse; to scan the second foot as trisyllabic, placing a heavy stress on *with,* distorts the rhythmical beauty of the line. The trisyllabic foot is conspicuously absent in the Shakespearean sonnet line; but the inverted foot, at strategic points of rhythmical tension, is often very much present. The line scans:

And trou | ble deaf | heaven with | my boot | less cries.

We might expect to find metrical ineptness in popular books of appreciation. However, when a scholar with the stature of Herbert Grierson scans the final line of Donne's "A Nocturnall upon St. Lucies Day,"

Both the years | and the days | deep mid | night is,[3]

we wonder if anyone understands the nature of English syllable-stress metric. Grierson uses the inappropriate macron (—) and breve (˘) of classical prosody and marks approximate speech stress rather than the metrical pattern. He is *phrasing* the poem, not scanning it. This practical confusion is quite common even today, especially among American poets and critics; some no longer recognize meter, and some cannot adequately describe it. Our reading of the meter is:

Both the | years and | the days | deep mid | night is.

Grierson's scansion, following as it does his own performance of the line, does not discover the crucial variation from the metrical norm: the inversion of the rhythmically sensitive second foot.

Since polemic is not our intention, we need not multiply examples of the mistakes and misconceptions that plague metrical theory. It is enough to say that generations of scholars, critics, and cranks obscured simple but basic principles. From about the middle of the nineteenth century to the publication of Saintsbury's *History* (1906–10), prosody developed into a war of contending theories, and on various fronts, skirmishes of this conflict continue in our time.

Many of the "revolutionary ideas" developed and promulgated now seem so wrongheaded that we wonder how anyone could have seriously entertained them. The musical scansion of Sidney Lanier's *The Science of English Verse*, praised by T. S. Omond, Harriet Monroe, and others, remains a dismaying example of a theory ridden sadly beyond the limits of good sense. A scansion that gives this sort of thing is worse than useless; it flings sand in the eyes and pours wax in the ears:

We might, for the moment, oppose Saintsbury to Lanier. *The History of English Prosody* is in the great tradition of three-volume scholarship. But Saintsbury dodges fundamental theoretical questions, talks about "long" and "short" syllables, and heroically resists the idea that stress has the crucial role in determining the English metrical foot. We are, of course, impressed by Saintsbury's vast acquaintance with the texts of English poetry; we may be irritated by his chauvinism, and sometimes appalled by what can be only deliberate or convenient ignorance in elementary matters:

> Is it not a rather more reasonable theory that we Englishmen talk very much as our ancestors talked when first the blend of "Saxon and Norman and Dane" historically established itself in our race and, to say the very least, historically coincided with these first appearances of our poetry?[5]

This in the face of the philological and linguistic evidence painstakingly gathered by Saintsbury's contemporaries!

His faults are also his virtues. To modern scholarship his lack of method may seem frivolous and irresponsible; in our cynical age he may seem naive and unprofessional—an English don who relishes poetry. Yet carrying no great burden of theoretical preconceptions, he rarely stumbles into self-contradiction. He relies on his ear to tell him what is good or bad prosody. Unhindered by set formulas, he can approve of Walt Whitman's "versicles" and acknowledge that the prosodical ideas of a yet unpublished poet, Father Gerard Hopkins, deserve special notice.

An ideal prosodist would combine Saintsbury's taste and enthusiasm with a comprehensive theory of English metric. But what theory? Many contemporary writers and readers, arguing over the revived interest in narrative and formal verse so much at the center of the skirmishes we may call, for lack of a better term, the Poetry Wars, ask this question with renewed vigor. The issues are all familiar: quantity versus stress; foot prosody versus musical scansion; the linguists versus the aestheticians; even rhythm versus meter itself!

On this battlefield of prosodical inquiry, some recent contributions have helped clear the air. Timothy Steele's *Missing Measures* reminds us that the current debates over form and meter must trace their lineage back to ancient texts in order to grapple with centuries of shrewd misreadings that have combined to give us, whether we know it or not, our own understanding of these matters;[6] Paul Fussell's *Poetic Meter and Poetic Form* is, in our opinion, the most useful handbook currently available;[7] *Strong Measures,* an anthology of poems and critical commentary, is a generous document that not only attempts to call attention to traditional forms as they are employed by contemporary poets, but also gamely tries to define some free verse in terms of nonce forms—new forms spun from the fiber of old ones.[8]

If Steele reminds us of the scope of this centuries-long debate, if Fussell aims to provide a concise guide for poet and reader, if Dacey and Jauss seek to validate free verse by describing it in the terms of traditional forms, we find, for our purposes, common ground in Wimsatt and Beardsley's "The Concept of Meter."[9] They would return metrical study to its classical concerns with law, with figures of grammar—not matters of taste or interpretation—on which general agreement can be reached. Consequently, these authors recommend the traditional foot prosody and its traditional nomenclature for scanning syllable-stress meter.

These views, which we believe correct, have no general currency. The journals reecho with noisy polemics and learned confusion; the writer on prosody should take nothing for granted. Our terminological confusion can be best handled by clear statements about prosody, metric, and versification, and the consistent use of these words in similar texts. The prosodical nature of modern poetry will challenge us throughout the book, but it is the whole intention of this study definitively to include and comprehend it in our discussion. But the howling disagreements about the function of prosody and the nature of the English meters must be addressed before we can proceed.

Harvey Gross

Robert McDowell

I

Prosody as Rhythmic Cognition

Our understanding of prosody's function is based on what a poem is, and how we conceive the nature of rhythm. Without launching into extended aesthetic theory, let us scrutinize briefly the ontological terrain. A poem is not an idea or an experience rendered into metrical language; still less is it an attitude toward an experience. A poem is a symbol in which idea, experience, and attitude are transmuted into feelings; these feelings move in significant arrangements: rhythmically. It is prosody and its structures that articulate the movement of feeling in a poem, and render to our understanding meanings which are not paraphrasable. Prosody enables the poet to communicate states of awareness, tensions, emotions, all of humanity's inner life that the helter-skelter of ordinary propositional language cannot express.

Rhythmic structure, like all aesthetic structure, is a symbolic form, signifying the ways we experience organic processes and the phenomena of nature. We speak of the rhythm of life: the curve of human development up from birth, through growth, and on to decay and death. These are not elements in a pattern of simple recurrence. They form patterns of expectation and fulfillment; birth prepares us for each succeeding stage of human development, but no stage merely repeats the stage that precedes it. All process, human or natural, thus has characteristic rhythm. We experience life not only by clock and calendar; we live by another kind of awareness. We shall, let us say, be taking a trip in a few months. We chafe with expectation; the day

8

comes to leave and the tensions of expectation disappear. Our calendar has told us a certain period in time has been traversed; our "other awareness" has told us a certain passage of time has been experienced. The period is a series of separate events, which we can measure and date; the passage of time itself is experienced as a continuum, a mounting tension and its resolution, a rhythm.

It is rhythm that gives time a meaningful definition, a form. "[If] the feeling of rhythm must be granted the status of a genuine experience, perhaps even of a cognition, then what is experienced in rhythm can only be time itself."[1] In the arts of time, music, and literature, rhythmic forms transmit certain kinds of information about the nature of our inner life. This is the life of feeling that includes psychological response as well as what psychologists term affect. There is often difficulty in distinguishing between affect, or emotion, and certain kinds of physical sensation. Those who attempt the neurological explanation of human experience see the difference between physiological and emotive behavior as one of degree and not one of kind. Wild anger or mild irritation depends on how much current flows along the nerves and across the synapses.

Rhythmic sound has the ability to imitate the forms of physical behavior as well as express the highly complex, continually shifting nature of human emotion. The rhythmic form of the following lines is imitative; we hear the rise and fall of feet keeping time to the beat of a drum:

Stone, bronze, stone, steel, stone, oakleaves, horses' heels . . .
T. S. Eliot, "Coriolan"

Prosody here is onomatopoeic, or nearly so. It sounds and "feels like" bodily movement, the flexing and unflexing of muscle. Prosody functions more subtly in these lines:

Daughters, in the wind's boisterous roughing,
Pray the tickle's equal to the coat tearing,
And the wearing equal to the puffing.
Ruth Stone, "Vernal Equinox"

Prosody does not imitate the noise of the wind, but gives a curve of feeling, the shape of an emotion. Prosodic elements include the formal patterning of syntax and stress, the quantities of vowels, and the alliteration of consonants.

As we see it, then, prosody—rhythmic form in poetry—has a more crucial role to play than most theoreticians have previously discerned. The function of rhythmic form in poetry has been treated almost exclusively as a matter of meter and meaning. John Crowe Ransom believed that meter offers a phonetic surface independent of meaning; we enjoy metrical textures for their own sake. Yvor Winters agreed that meter has an expressive function, and in a highly suggestive passage pointed out the possible relationship between emotion and rhythmic structure:

> In the first place, music is expressive of emotion. I do not understand the relationship between sound and emotion, but it is unquestionably very real: the devotional feeling of Byrd or of Bach, the wit and gaiety of much of Mozart and Haydn, the disillusioned romantic nostalgia of Franck, these are perfectly real, and it is not profitable to argue the point. The correlation between sound and feeling may have its origin in some historical relationship between music and language, or it may, like the capacity to form ideas, have its origin simply in human nature as that is given to us.[2]

But Winters shies away from what might have been a theory of rhythm and feeling; his insistence that a poem is a species of rational discourse and not a symbolic construct leads him back to the belief that meter is primarily a means of semantic emphasis. Regular or irregular metrical structure, in continual interaction with the poem's propositional sense, points up or submerges words, ideas, and attitudes.

Our view is that meter, and prosody in general, is itself meaning. Rhythm is neither outside a poem's meaning nor an ornament to it. Rhythmic structures are expressive forms, cognitive elements, communicating those experiences that rhythmic consciousness can alone communicate: *emphatic human responses to time in its passage.* Our view does not contradict the theories of Ransom and Winters but supplements them. Prosody, as meter, does offer a texture, an "aesthetic surface"; meter unquestionably brings into special prominence words and ideas. But neither theory stresses that it is through rhythmic structure that the infinite subtleties of human feeling can be most successfully expressed.

The theories of Ransom and Winters, restricted as they are to metered verse, cannot account for the function of rhythmic structures in nonmetrical verse or in well-written prose. Rhythmic structure offers the means by which a work of literature achieves its peculiar reality, the illusion that what we are reading is quickened with a life of its own. This life is perceived in mental performance as well as in oral recitation; any good prose written for silent reading has significant movement, a "prosody." We do not ordinarily speak of the "prosody of prose," but certainly the rhythmical elements of well-wrought prose offer themselves to aesthetic analysis. Two novelists, far apart in technique and point of view, reveal themselves masters of prosody:

It is a truth universally acknowledged, that a single man in possession of a good fortune, must be in want of a wife.

Stately, plump Buck Mulligan came from the stairhead, bearing a bowl of lather on which a mirror and a razor lay crossed.

Jane Austen creates "a motion of meaning" by exercising the most loving care for grammatical arrangement. By dispossessing the adjective from its normal position ("truth universally *acknowledged*"), and delaying the predicate of the modifier group with information of crucial interest to middle-class mommas ("in possession of a good fortune"), she fashions a prosody of wit. The movement of her language is quick with "the feel of thought"—the powers of abstraction, of generalization, of perceiving and confronting ideas. Joyce's language moves on different principles. His prose is dense with heavy stresses, alliterative effects, and a careful placing of long and short vowels. He is not concerned with the presentation of an idea but with *things* and arrangements; and, as we learn from the context, with symbols.

It is clear that Joyce's prosody is achieved by devices characteristic of poetry: stress, alliteration, and quantity. But how can Jane Austen order *by syntax* the sounds of language into rhythmical meanings symbolic of feeling? The logic of grammar sets up a pattern of expectation, and the expressive delays, the departures from usual word order, and the surprising repetitions all form an articulating rhythm representing the liveliest intellectual activity. It may be the rhythm existed in Jane Austen's mind even before she fully worked out the ideas; the feeling of a thought may take shape in consciousness even before the thought can be adequately formulated.

All expressive rhythms are variations upon a pattern of expectation. The prosody of prose functions first as those departures from the normal grammatical structures of the language that set up lesser or greater impulses of meaning. When phonetic patterning increases, as in the example from Joyce, prose is shocked into verse. We may think of the difference between prose and verse as a matter of meter; this is partially true. But the difference lies in the ability of poetry, through all the organizing devices of prosody, to achieve a higher expressiveness. The overlappings and concurrences of meter, quantity, and syntax can symbolize the movement of many simultaneous physical or psychological tensions. The tensions of life are never felt singly, in a straight line, as it were; they cross and overlap each other. They exist in depth and are felt in many dimensions. As one tension resolves, a second begins, and a third or fourth may be in yet another stage of development. Prosody transmits the intricacy of the life of feeling—an organism where systems of bone, blood, muscle, and nerve often work on different frequencies, cross rhythmically.

ও *II*

The function of prosody is to image, in a rich and complex way, human process as it moves in time. On the lower level, prosody can be a direct representation of physical activity. Numerous theorists have pointed out that iambic pentameter resembles simple human physiology: the systole and diastole of the heartbeat or the inhalation and exhalation of breathing. But human process, even in its more basic physiological aspects, is enormously complicated. Growth, fruition, decay, stasis; the process of maturation and decay: all have movement that prosody can image. Prosody can also trace the curves of psychological process: perception, sensation, and affect move in time and have their characteristic rhythms. The rhythmic structures of prosody reveal the mind and nerves as they grow tense in expectation and stimulation and relax in fulfillment and quiet.

A short poem of Emily Dickinson shows, in a highly dramatic way, prosody's functions; the poem's subject is the very nature of the inner life of feeling:

After great pain, a formal feeling comes—
The Nerves sit ceremonious, like Tombs—
The stiff Heart questions was it He, that bore,
And Yesterday, or Centuries before?

The Feet, mechanical, go round—
Of Ground, or Air, or Ought—
A Wooden way
Regardless grown,
A Quartz contentment, like a stone—

This is the Hour of Lead—
Remembered, if outlived,
As Freezing persons, recollect the Snow—
First—Chill—then Stupor—then the letting go—

A prose paraphrase (a deliberate heresy) tells us that profound suffering leaves mind and body in a curious state of detachment. The mind sees the body from a great distance; feelings of depression, inadequacy, indifference afflict consciousness but cause no tremor of emotion. Life has been arrested; the soul has crossed over to the country beyond despair.

Our paraphrase is inadequate, of course. The experience is rendered in the movement of the lines, and part of what the poem "means" is the movement itself. Syntax, meter, quantity, and pause articulate feelings of formal detachment, stupefied indifference, and ceremonious numbness, and rhythmic structure conveys these "ideas."

The poem opens with an abstract assertion of feeling in a syntactically complete proposition. At the fourth line the syntax becomes fragmentary, and the soundless rhythm of meaning falters on an unresolved grammatical ambiguity. A similar ambiguity arrests the meaning of line 8. Metrically, the lines are of uneven length, although iambic movement dominates. In the second stanza the meter beats metronomically:

Of Gróund, | or Áir, | or Óught.

The quantities of the vowels are nearly equal. The poem ends with a slowing down of rhythmic energy as consciousness dwindles into coma: the otherworldly calm that comes after terrible suffering.[3]

We have gradual expansion and relaxation, ending not with the final syllable, but continuing into the silence of the final dash—which we read as a held rest. The effect is hesitating; the line slows down and subsides into nothingness. Prosodic movement carries over beyond the final sound in much the same way that a Beethoven adagio slowly progresses into the silence of apparent time.

We approach the crux of the problem, and we can formulate a working definition of what prosody is and how it functions in poetic structure. It comprises those elements in a poem that make concrete for perception the flow of time. This time, experienced in a passage of verse, is not chronological time, measured by metronomic pulse, but *felt* time, musical "duration." If we understand this, the widely used term "the music of poetry" becomes more than an empty honorific—a facile way of complimenting a poet for smoothness of texture or skillful use of verbal color. Prosody is the musical element in poetry because it reveals time in its passage and the life of feeling that moves between points *then* and *then*. Prosodic structures are akin to musical structures because phonetic patterning and syntactical expectation constitute a semantic system, a language, as it were. Like music, the language of prosody rises out of abstraction; at first it represents nothing, but may come to suggest everything. But nonverbal "languages" are meaningful; few modern aestheticians are prepared to assert that the abstract art of music is purely formal, devoid of human qualities and human import.

To insist on "prosody as music" neither denies that prosody develops out of, or emphasizes, conceptual meaning nor asserts that rhythmic and phonetic elements are autonomous structures. We stress here that a poem's prosody cannot exist apart from its propositional sense. Prosodic rhythm and propositional sense work as identities in poetic language. Phonetic patterning creates meaning in language; rhythm in linguistic structure is itself *sense*. Most of us have experienced conversations with nonnative speakers whom, despite their polished English grammar and vocabulary, we could barely understand. They speak English to a rhythm that makes no *sense* to our ears. Prosodic structures, which are a heightening of the ordinary rhythms of English, are created by the meanings of words and the logic of syntax. The elements of prosody work in the closest possible way with the poem's propositional sense—even when that sense is ambiguous or seemingly nonsensical.

Lewis Carroll's "Jabberwocky" provides a good example of a poem in which prosody functions in seeming isolation (it does not, really), and hence we can analyze the poem's rhythmic structure somewhat apart from its paraphrasable meaning. "Jabberwocky" is not, however, meaningless. Carroll conceals, parodies, ornaments meaning; there is more "sense" than the mind can readily detect:

> 'Twas brillig, and the slithy toves
>   Did gyre and gimble in the wabe:
> All mimsy were the borogoves,
>   And the mome raths outgrabe.

Although what is going on is not clear, the controlling rhythms of syntax and meter give an illusion of denotational meaning as well as the tenor of feeling. Precise grammatical structure creates a soundless syntactical rhythm, a skeleton of meaning without lexical sense. Carroll preserves word order, inflectional endings, and empty words; consequently we can diagram the lines without knowing what the words mean. Meter is regular until the fourth line; here trimeter breaks the prevalent tetrameter movement. The feeling is one of hollowness and sinister vacancy; we are reminded of Keats's "And no birds sing."

We respond to prosodic structure, to metrical and syntactical rhythm. Because Carroll maintains English syntax, we feel that we understand the qualities of "brillig" and "slithy," the actions of "gyre" and "gimble." Syntactical rhythm gives the *feeling* of thought, the forms of mental activity. The closely patterned metrical rhythms elicit generalized affective responses: mystery, confusion, pointless activity. Rhythms of syntax and meter articulate relationships among objects, qualities, and actions that are never precisely denoted. Carroll, we remember, was a mathematician; mathematics deals in pure relationships, devoid of "content." Using the rhythmic structures of language to indicate pure relationship is the essence of Carroll's nonsense— and is the "meaning of his meaning."

The full meaning of a poem involves a great deal more than its paraphrasable conceptual content. This is a truism of contemporary poetics, yet little critical attention has been paid to rhythmic structures that are the direct conveyers of feeling. Indeed, Richards, Empson, and their disciples were contemptuous of the "emotive" aspects of language; the party-line New Criticism largely concerned itself with the poem's paraphrasable content (ambiguity, paradox, semantics) while maintaining a piety toward the notion that poetry is unparaphrasable. The meaning of a poem includes the meanings its rhythmic structures communicate to the nerves and brain. Obviously we must expand our concept of "meaning" to include rhythmic cognition if we admit prosody as an important structural element in poetry. Like metaphor, prosody is a symbolic structure and is not merely perceived in a poem; its meanings are understood through the symbolizing activities of human consciousness. The mind interprets prosody as feeling, whether we name as feeling crude sensation, violent emotion, or the most delicate of responses to the outside world.

We see the futility in using scientific instruments to interpret the phonetic patterns of poetry. It is true, of course, that prosody orders into special patterns phonetic values: the sounds and silences of language. As a formal element in poetry, meter is an immediate perceptual given: we have the demonstrably audible and measurable facts of stress, quantity, pause, and number. But, we insist, the sounds and silences of meter are not perceptual entities as such; we do not respond to metrical texture as we do to fine silk or highly polished wood. The acoustic arrangements of meter are images of time shaped and charged by human feeling. The machines used in prosodic analysis show what happens in an arbitrary temporal sequence. The oscillograph knows nothing of *durée*, of time grasped and understood by human awareness; the machine can record but it cannot perceive in psychological depth. It cannot translate the symbolism of stress and pause, quantity and pitch, into feeling. The results of the machine are a tautology because no machine understands the uniquely human import of symbolic structures; the machine returns a set of symbols still requiring human interpretation.

We object to the linguist's analysis of prosody on the same grounds. To assume that the description and measurement of a poem's phonetic features account for its prosody is to believe that phonetic texture has no symbolic value and consequently no human relevance. Linguistic science can detail every physical minutia in a line of verse; it can show us phonetic structure but no prosodic function. Seymour Chatman believes "that sound symbolism as such—the assumption that individual phonemes have expressive functions in morphemes— is either without objective foundation or is too subliminal to be very useful in linguistics or stylistics."[4] This may be true for individual sounds or words; it is not true for rhythmic structure in poetic contexts. Linguistic analysis ignores the effect of rhythmic structures in poetry; its approach is statistical, counting and measuring phonetic elements isolated from their rhythmic functions. Like the oscillograph, its results are tautological; the symbols of linguistic analysis do not interpret for us the emotional significance of prosodic structures. Like symbolic activity in general, rhythmic cognition is a function of human consciousness.[5]

❧ *III*

The analysis of poetic structure must show the identity of content or idea and the rhythmic conveyers of feeling. But the poet's private experience of the rhythms of nature and human process *must be accessible,* through the senses and intellect, to the reader. The poet makes them accessible by providing a primary "aesthetic surface":[6] an unbroken texture of phonetic values and patterns. Poetry exists in a sensuous realm of sound; we cannot feel a poem's rhythms until our ears have engaged its aesthetic surface. In many poems this surface is its meter—heard in spoken performance or imagined and felt in silent reading.

Some poems present this surface so obviously that we are aware of little else:

> Before the beginning of years
> There came to the making of man
> Time with a gift of tears;
> Grief with a glass that ran.

Prosody, if it is a valuable part of poetic structure, must create the illusion of experienced or durational time and what we experience in those fictitious intervals—the movement, stress, and tensions of our emotional life. Swinburne's verse creates little more than an illusion of automatic physical activity; we hear marching men or galloping horses.[7] The higher purpose of prosody is not imitation of physical process, though we can, if we like, do sit-ups to

> Strong gongs groaning as the guns boom far,
> Don John of Austria is going to the war.

These examples return us to an earlier question: what is the relation of a poem's prosody to its referential meaning, its paraphrasable content? Certainly prosody has, or should have, mimetic value; there should be some correlation of idea and rhythm. If we sense a disparity between thought and movement—if the meter sounds incongruous to the idea—we have valid grounds for making negative judgments about the poem's value. Swinburne's rhythm, with its catchy swing, seems inappropriate to humanity's making and the tears of time. We should have rhythms expressive of mystery and grief; not a quick march tempo. We feel muscular exhilaration: scarcely what the subject requires.

We do not believe that every emotion has a precise symbolic form, and in the case of poetry, an exact rhythmical equivalent. The rhythms of poetry belong to the "non-discursive forms" of human symbolism.[8] Rhythms are highly connotative structures, and we cannot say the meter of Swinburne's poem denotes anything more than its patterns of stress:

$$\breve{\ }\,\acute{\ } \mid \breve{\ }\,\breve{\ }\,\acute{\ } \mid \breve{\ }\,\breve{\ }\,\acute{\ }$$
$$\breve{\ }\,\acute{\ } \mid \breve{\ }\,\breve{\ }\,\acute{\ } \mid \breve{\ }\,\breve{\ }\,\acute{\ }$$
$$\acute{\ } \mid \breve{\ }\,\breve{\ }\,\acute{\ } \mid \breve{\ }\,\acute{\ }$$
$$\acute{\ } \mid \breve{\ }\,\breve{\ }\,\acute{\ } \mid \breve{\ }\,\acute{\ }$$

Swinburne's meter does not fulfill his denotational content. It is as if a composer were to write a funeral march *presto giocoso* in one of the more brilliant major keys. There is no absolute aesthetic demand that funeral marches be written in minor keys or in tempi suited to an actual procession of mourners. We feel, however, that speed and brilliance do not connote grief and dignity; they are not the proper forms for emotions we normally associate with funerals. Swinburne's galloping meter is not an emotional form suitable to his subject.

If prosody is itself meaning, meaning also forms prosody. Rhythmic structures grown out of patterns of rhetorical emphasis: patterns that sometimes move against or across the meter. We find in Donne's poetry many startling instances of expressive rhythms emerging out of ambiguities of emphasis: where meter pulls the propositional sense in one direction, rhetorical emphasis in the other. In "A Valediction: Of My Name, in the Window," the poet imagines that his mistress might take another lover; he hopes that his name, scratched in the window-glass, will blot out the name of his successor:

> And when thy melted maid,
> Corrupted by thy Lover's gold, and page,
> His letter at thy pillow'hath laid,
> Disputed it, and tam'd thy rage,
> And thou begin'st to thaw towards him, for this,
> May my name step in, and hide his.

The last line presents a metrical crux. If we follow the meter closely, we scan and read:

May mý | name stép | ín and | hide hís.

"My" and "his" are thrown into rhetorical balance; the parallel is between "my name" and "his [name]." The poet feels reasonably secure that his name will cover the name of her new lover. But if we follow the "prose" stresses of the words, we scan:

Máy my | náme step | ín and | híde his.

The meter breaks down, and we do not even have a regular final foot. "May" is stressed; it now seems highly conditional that the image of the poet's name can keep his mistress faithful. The stressed "hide" tinges the whole line with interrogation—and the poet dissolves in doubts. Although the poet never says he is anxious, his rhythm gives him away.

Whether the patterns of rhythm and meter genetically precede conceptualization; whether they are formed after the idea has been formulated; or whether rhythmic form and conceptual meaning are conceived simultaneously seem matters of individual poetic genius. Supposedly Yeats wrote his lines out as prose and counted the meters off on his fingers; it is also said that he always had a "tune in his head" when he composed. Eliot remarked, "I know that a poem, or a passage of a poem, may tend to realize itself first as a particular rhythm before it reaches expression in words, and that this rhythm may bring to birth the idea and image."[9] However the poet works, the meaningful structures of language can form rhythms and meters. The grammatical function of a word can determine whether it is metrically stressed or unstressed:

Thís is | the énd | of the whále roád | and the whále . . .

Tíme that | with *thís* | strange éx | cúse . . .

The individual word also has characteristic rhythm, depending on its pattern of stress, and isolated words may form cross-rhythms with basic metrical structure. Here is the opening of *The Waste Land:*

> April is the cruellest month, breeding
> Lilacs out of the dead land, mixing
> Memory and desire, stirring
> Dull roots with spring rain.

These lines achieve rhythmic distinction due to Eliot's bold use of the pause in lines 1–3. Trochaics ("April," "cruellest," "breeding," "Lilacs," "mixing," "stirring") predominate, and the falling rhythm they create weaves itself about the underlying stresses, while symmetry in the three trochaic participles contribute to the poem's rhythmic distinction.

The manifold ways in which sound and meaning coalesce in poetry are, of course, the subjects of our inquiry. It is perhaps sufficient, at this point, to say that neither meaning nor sound can operate independently. It is also important to distinguish between what we term the primary and secondary devices of prosody. The articulations of sound in temporal sequences, rhythms and meters, present us with "aesthetic surface"; it is this surface which our perception immediately engages. Prosody is an aural symbolism, a significant arrangement of acoustical phenomena. But since poetry has been written, and more importantly, *printed,* visual qualities have contributed to prosodical arrangement. Line endings, stanzaic shape, the general appearance of the poem on the page—all contribute to rhythmic effect. These visual elements, however, are, and *should* be secondary—in the way that written directions in a musical score are in no sense the music but only useful guides to realizing an accurate or satisfying performance. Visual elements are aids to performance—remembering that performance includes the mind's silent re-creation of a poem as we read to ourselves.

To multiply the visual elements in a poem reduces for perception the available aesthetic surface. Through the agency of sound, poetry makes imaginative facts out of the deepest, most elusive feeling. The poet who substitutes visual tricks for a surface of articulated sound limits the range of feeling; he or she gives up the primary means by which feelings can be symbolized and apprehended. A poem must sound; it is sound that we first experience as pleasure (or pain) in the reading of poetry. Nursery rhymes, children's game verses, primitive charms: all appeal through the movement of sound. Prosody offers in the basic forms of metrical structure a continuous articulating surface that makes rhythmic cognition possible. It is to these forms that we now turn.

II

The Scansion of the English Meters

❧ *1. Strong-Stress and Syllable-Stress Meter*

We should say, of course, the *scansions* of the English meters. The curse of metrical theory has been prosodical monism: the notion that there is a single law governing the behavior of all English verse, from *Beowulf* to Elizabeth Bishop. *Beowulf* is composed in the old Germanic strong-stress meter; Elizabeth Bishop may count syllables as the French do or forge a prosody relying on grammatical structures. But no one "law" of English metric controls the prosody of all poems. Our basic policy in scansion is to scan the verse according to the system of metric it is written in.

A metrical system, or simply *meter,* singles out and then organizes, in a pattern of regular recurrence, a normative feature of language. The linguistic feature must be an obvious one; no meter can be based on features too faint or too indefinite for the ear to recognize easily. The two dominant English meters are based on the principle of recurring stress. The simplest and oldest English meter maintains a more or less regular number of stresses within the line; there is no fixed number of unstressed syllables. This is the *strong-stress meter* of Old English poetry—and of T. S. Eliot's *Four Quartets:*

> Hére is a pláce ‖ of dís af féc tion
> Tíme be fóre ‖ and tíme áf ter
> In a dím líght: ‖ néi ther dáy líght
> In vés ting fórm ‖ with lú cid stíll ness

Turn ing shad ow || into tran sient beau ty

With slow ro ta tion || sug gest ing per ma nence

Nor dark ness || to pu ri fy the soul

Emp ty ing the sen su al || with dep ri va tion

Cleans ing af fec tion || from the tem por al

Burnt Norton

The opening of Pound's *Canto 1* is also strong-stress meter. Pound maintains the alliterative pattern of Old English verse, which gives a characteristic archaism to the lines:

And then went down to the ship

Set keel to break ers, || forth on the god ly sea, and

We set up mast and sail || on that swart ship,

Bore sheep a board her, || and our bo dies also

Heavy with weep ing, || and winds from stern ward

Bore us out on ward || with bel ly ing canvas

Cir ce's this craft, || the trim-coifed god dess.

In scanning strong-stress meter we mark the main stresses and the position of the medial pause, or caesura. It is also useful to italicize the alliterated syllables. The norm of strong-stress meter is two stresses on either side of the caesura, but even in Old English verse we encounter lines of three or five stresses.

Modern poets revived strong-stress meter. Pound, Auden, the later Eliot, all made deliberate use of it. Occasionally what at first might seem free verse (or "cadenced prose") is the older meter:

Miss Hel en Slings by || was my maid en aunt,

And lived in a small house || near a fash ion a ble square

Cared for by ser vants || to the num ber of four.

T. S. Eliot, "Aunt Helen"

The appearance of the meter here is probably accidental; the rhythms of the conversational idiom fall into the recurrent patterns of strong-stress meter. Hopkins notes that sprung rhythm, his refinement on the native strong-stress meter, "is the rhythm of common speech and of written prose, when rhythm is perceived in them."[1] It is premature, however, to speak of sprung rhythm; Hopkins's theories and practices require detailed comment. Sprung rhythm, while deriving doubtless out of the native meter, exists also in syllable-stress meter; its analysis is a complicated, and needless to say, controversial matter.

Less controversial (one might think) is the scansion of syllable-stress meter. This is the traditional two-valued meter that established itself with Chaucer, was later ignored or misunderstood, and finally fixed as the norm for English poetry by Wyatt, Surrey, and Spenser. Its position as the basic metric for English verse was scarcely challenged until Whitman and Hopkins; and despite the revolution in prosody that accompanied modern poetry, syllable-stress meter carries a significantly large body of twentieth-century verse. The structure of syllable-stress meter is the subject of disagreement among recent theorists, incredible when we realize that poets have clearly understood the meter since Spenser and that historians like Jespersen described it with perfect structural accuracy as early as 1900.[2]

Our view on the scansion of syllable-stress meter is the traditional one. We use the conventional markings to indicate the stressed and unstressed syllables, the caesura, and the groupings into feet. Although we agree with the linguists that in English more than two levels of stress exist, a *metrical* foot consists of two values only: stressed and unstressed syllables. In the foot syllables are stressed and unstressed in relation to each other; our *metrical ear* hears only relative stress. In the line

> The Chair | she sat | in, like | a bur | nished throne

T. S. Eliot

the third foot is iambic even though "like" is rhetorically weak. If we mark only the speech stresses we have a four-beat line,

> The Chair she sat in, like a burnished throne.

But "like" is slightly more emphatic than "in"; this slight emphasis is enough to define the third foot as iambic. The pressure of meter tends to equalize discrepancies of stress; thus normally (that is, rhetorically) strong syllables become metrically weak when they occur between two other strong syllables:

> The páth | sick sòr | row toók, | the ma | ny páths . . .

Wallace Stevens, "Sunday Morning"

The second foot is iambic although it is made up of "sick" and "sor-," two rhetorically strong syllables. Similarly, a normally weak syllable gains in metrical strength when it occurs between two weak syllables:

> But drift | in still | ness, as | from Jór | dan's brow . . .

Hart Crane, "The River"

The third foot is iambic, "as" receiving slightly more stress than "-ness."

In our scansion notation spondees and pyrrhics are relatively rare. Spondees do occur, however:

> Dówn, dówn | —born pí | o neérs | in time's | de spíte.

Hart Crane, "The River"

The double foot of two unstressed and two stressed syllables also occurs in iambic verse. This is the syzygy of ancient prosody. These lines from Robert Lowell show examples of the double foot arranged in minor Ionics ($\smile\smile\prime\prime$):

> This is | the end | of the whale road | and the whale
> Who spewed | Nan tuck | et bones | on the thrashed swell
> And stirred | the troubl | ed wat | ers to whirl pools
> To send | the Pe | quod pack | ing off | to hell.

"Quaker Graveyard"

We must also recognize the monosyllabic foot. It can appear at the beginning of the line, as the stressed half of a headless iamb:

> Prin | cess Vol | u pine | ex tends

A meag | re, blue— | nailed, phthi | sic hand
To climb | the wa | ter stair. | Lights, lights,
She en | ter tains | Sir Fer | di nand
Klein. | Who clipped | the li | on's wings.

T. S. Eliot

The first feet of lines 1 and 5 are monosyllabic.

In all other positions but the first, the monosyllabic foot will "spring" or syncopate the line unless it immediately precedes or follows the caesura. In the first of the following lines, the monosyllabic foot precedes the medial pause; in the second, it follows:

The owls | trilled || with tongues | of night | in gale.

Robert Graves, "A Love Story"

In her | own hand, || signed | with her | own name . . .

Robert Graves, "The Straw"

This use of the monosyllabic foot does not seriously disturb the rhythmic stability of the line: it can smoothly substitute for iamb or trochee because the preceding or following pause is equivalent to the missing unstressed syllable. Lines are syncopated or sprung when the monosyllabic foot, appearing in an otherwise regular metrical context, cannot be counted as catalectic. "Springing" in syllable-stress metric is something other than what Hopkins calls sprung rhythm. It is related, of course; but as a feature of syllable-stress metric, it has its distinctive characteristics and occasions. As we note above, springing disturbs the rhythmic stability of the line; a number of consecutively sprung lines will destroy the sense of the dominant meter. Intrusive monosyllabic feet, the hammering of consecutive spondees,

Bones built | in me, flesh filled, | blood brimmed | the curse . . .

Hopkins, *I Wake and Feel*

can endanger the base metric so that we actually move toward stress and away from syllable-stress prosody. What Hopkins calls "counterpointing" can also shake the stability of syllable-stress metric. Any line in which a new rhythm bucks against the prevalent meter may be thought of as counterpointed. Counterpointing is a matter of degree. The reversal of the first foot, or of the foot after the caesura, is not likely to disturb the meter; these are the most usual kinds of substitutions in the pentameter line:

Dúnged with | the deád, || drénched by | the dý | ing's blóod . . .

David Gascoyne, "Spring MCMXL"

Although the first and third feet are trochees, this is clearly an iambic line—even out of iambic context.

The iambic balance can be disturbed, however, if certain sensitive feet in the line are reversed; or if too many trisyllabic feet (usually anapests) are substituted for iambs. John Crowe Ransom thus achieves the startling metrical effects of "Captain Carpenter":

Cáp tain | Cár pen | ter róse | úp in | his príme
Put ón | his pís | tols and | went rí | ding óut
But hád | got wéll | nigh nó | where át | that tíme
Till hé | fell ín | with lá | dies ín | a róut.

It wás | a prét | ty lá | dy_and áll | her tráin
That pláyed | with hím | so swéet | ly bút | be fóre
An hóur | she'd ták | en_a swórd | with áll | her máin
And twíned | him óf | his nóse | for é | ver móre.

Ransom plays metrical brinksmanship. He reverses the extremely sensitive second foot (line 1), and the fourth foot (line 1), and allows trisyllabic substitution (line 5, fourth foot; line 7, third foot). He also introduces lines that can, in scansion, be rationalized as syllable-stress metric, but which actually move in strong-stress rhythms:

And a bláde shóok || be tween rót ten teeth a láck.

The effect is like that in the popular ballads where intrusions of strong-stress metric, still viable in the fifteenth century, gave a characteristic archaic flavor:

> When shawes beene sheene, and shrads fyll fayre,
> And leeves both large and longe,
> Itt is merry, walking in the fayre fforest,
> To heare the small birds songe.

The third line must be wrenched into syllable-stress metric; if we scan,

$$\text{Itt ís} \mid \text{mer rý,} \mid \text{walk ing} \mid\mid \text{in the fáyre ffo rést,}$$

we are forced to distort normal speech stresses. But this is barbarous.
The line is a four-beat, strong-stress line:

$$\text{Itt is mér ry, walk ing} \mid\mid \text{in the fáyre ffó rest . . .}$$

In "Captain Carpenter" the archaism is calculated, not naive, creating
a prosodic irony to complement the pervading ironic tone. The sur-
face roughness conceals Ransom's skill; what on first reading seems
inept or baffling is, in fact, a prosodic tour de force.

Scansion is the basic technique of prosodic analysis. Its correct
application to syllable-stress metric involves the precise recognition of
the kinds of feet, and the ways these feet may be reversed or sub-
stituted. An objection to foot scansion is its apparent crudity. The
linguists recommend a subtler method of scansion, taking into ac-
count the four levels of English stress, juncture, and pitch. But our
belief is that meter *is* a simple, even crude, element in poetic structure.
An economy—not an abundance—of linguistic features generates
metrical patterns. Any scansion, of course, is a convenient fiction,
abstracting certain phonetic elements and ignoring others. But the
scansion must describe what is without doubt *really there*. It must in-
deed be descriptive and not interpretive. A prevalent mistake is to base
scansions on performance; and then analyze, either by means of musi-
cal notation or through acoustic recordings, the individual patterns a
reader imposes on the verse. Despite the pronouncements of contrary
camps such as the Projectivist and Language poets, Wellek and Warren
most cogently revealed the fallacies inherent in all such performative
scansions: they are either personal variations played on the metrical
pattern or worthless tautologies.[3]

Some may argue that in "Captain Carpenter" the first two feet in
this line are anapests:

If he rísk | to be woúnd | ed bý | my tóngue . . .

Some may suppress the fourth foot altogether and discover a three-beat line:

If he rísk | to be woúnd | ed by my tóngue . . .

However, if the foot structure of syllable-stress meter is understood, neither of these scansions is convincing. *Both scan speech stress, not metrical stress.* Our scansion,

Íf he | rísk to | be woúnd | ed bý | my tóngue,

shows the counterpointing (reversed second foot) that in this line is the significant tension between speech and metrical stress. The first foot, we agree, is probably controversial. Our scansion hears it inverted; it could also be a normal iambic. A similar ambiguity occurs earlier:

Tíll he | fell ín | with lá | dies ín | a roút.

But the structure of the initial foot in an iambic line is scarcely important; a quibble here merely confirms the notion that certain variations in syllable-stress metric are so frequent as to be normal.

❧ *II. Quantitative and Syllabic Meters*

Since the days of Gabriel Harvey prosodists and poets have dreamed of an English quantitative meter. The prosodists have tried to discover a quantitative base for English meter and to prove that our verse moves by the same laws that governed Homer and Virgil. Poets have tried to imitate in English the classical meters. Theorists and practitioners have had no remarkable success; indeed, the best of them have realized that a purely quantitative meter is impossible in English. Unlike Greek or Latin, English has neither fixed quantities, existing in nature or defined by rules of grammar, nor a metrical convention that, by artificial and traditional means, can create rhythms out of long and short syllables.

The scansion of Latin verse is highly artificial and sometimes arbitrary. No one doubts, however, that measured quantities provide the ground rhythm of Latin verse.

Twin be the gates o' the house of sleep: as fable opineth
One is of horn, and thence for a true dream outlet is easy:
Fair the other, shining perfected of ivory carven;
But false are the visions that thereby find passage upward.

"Ibant Obscuri"

According to Bridges's rules, these lines scan exactly as their Latin originals do. But our ears hear no metrical music; English quantity is too faint an element of linguistic structure, and too unstable—so often a matter of individual pronunciation—to set up a pattern of expectation. We must chant these lines, carefully following the Latin scansion and distorting normal syllabic length, to twist them into rhythmical shape. Bridges is not writing quantitative metric; he is setting lines of prose to Virgil's Latin music. It is not true in English that the *i* of *ivory* is exactly double the length of the other two syllables. Bridges is trying simultaneously to establish a convention and write in it. The experiment is noble but futile. We are reminded of those primitive flying machines that flapped and creaked but never got off the ground. They violated a basic law of physics: human beings cannot lift themselves by their own bootstraps.

Bridges himself doubted the success of his *Poems in Classical Prosody,* observing, "the difficulty of adapting our English syllables to the Greek rules is very great, and even deterrent."[4] He hoped, however, that his experiments might reveal new and expressive rhythms. Some modern poets have achieved successes in modified or what we call pseudo-quantitative meters. Pound's sapphics pay close attention to syllable length, meticulously reproducing the classic pattern:

Gōl dĕn | rōse thĕ | house, ĭn thĕ | pōr tăl | Ī saw

thēe, ă | mār vĕl, | cār vĕn ĭn | sūb tlĕ | stuff, ă

pōr tĕnt. | Life dīed | dōwn ĭn thĕ | lāmp ănd | flīck erĕd

cāught ăt thĕ | wōn dĕr.

"Apparuit"

But it is not quantity, as such, that forces our mind into a pattern of expectation. Pound is careful to make each "long" syllable also a stressed syllable; the meter we hear is made up of syllable-stress trochees and dactyls. The rhythms produced by this coincidence of stress and quantity have a limpid and elegiac quality; some may find these lines flaccid. The ear misses those delicate tensions and cross-rhythms produced by an occasional unstressed long syllable:

> She slowed | to sigh, | in that | long in | ter val . . .

> Theodore Roethke, "The Dream"

This effect is impossible in Pound's scheme, where stress and quantity are never in conflict. And this kind of conflict provides a ground of prosodic interest in English verse.

We find that those reworkings of classical meters that sound metrical to English ears always exhibit strong-stress or syllabic-stress structure. Vernon Watkins's beautiful "Ophelia" is also in the sapphic stanza. He keeps to the eleven-and-five syllabic structure; the meter is actually a strong-stress pattern:

> Stunned in the stone light, || laid among the lilies,
>
> Still in the green wave, || graven in the reed-bed,
>
> Lip-read by clouds || in the language of the shallows,
>
> Lie there, reflected.[5]

The best use of the classical meters has been in adapting them to the stress-based prosody of English, not in trying, as Bridges tried, to write an artificial language that could accommodate the meters. Eliot's absorption of Virgil's hexameter is apparent in these lines:

> I do not know much about gods; but I think that the river
> Is a strong brown god—sullen, untamed and intractable,
> Patient to some degree, at first recognized as a frontier;
> Useful, untrustworthy, as a conveyer of commerce;
> Then only a problem confronting the builder of bridges.
>
> "The Dry Salvages"

In modern poetry purely syllabic meters are more frequently encountered than quantitative meters. The principle of syllabic meter is

simplicity itself. The poet maintains the same number of syllables in
every line of the poem; Thom Gunn counts out seven syllables a line
for his "My Sad Captains":

> MY SAD CAPTAINS
> One by one they appear in
> the darkness: a few friends, and
> a few with historical
> names. How late they start to shine!
> but before they fade they stand
> perfectly embodied, all
>
> the past lapping them like a
> cloak of chaos. They were men
> who, I thought, lived only to
> renew the wasteful force they
> spent with each hot convulsion.
> They remind me, distant now.
>
> True, they are not at rest yet,
> but now that they are indeed
> apart, winnowed from failures,
> they withdraw to an orbit
> and turn with disinterested
> hard energy, like the stars.

Count of syllables will not, by itself, provide sufficient rhythmic inter-
est; in Gunn's poem a forceful syntax, a variable number of stresses
(from two to four), and the phrasing of the line endings overlay the
seven-syllable pattern.

Another syllabic technique, a slight variation on the classical Alcaic
stanza and favored by Auden and Marianne Moore, involves the con-
struction of a stanza in which analogous lines have an equal number of
syllables. Thus Auden devises for his "In Memory of Sigmund Freud" a
stanza of four lines in which the first two lines have eleven, the third
line nine, and the fourth line ten syllables. The pattern eleven, eleven,
nine, ten is kept throughout the poem:

> When there are so many we shall have to mourn,
> When grief has been made so public, and exposed

To the critique of a whole epoch
The frailty of our conscience and anguish,

Of whom shall we speak? For every day they die
Among us, those who were doing us some good,
And knew it was never enough but
Hoped to improve a little by living.

Strong-stress elements overlay the syllabic meter; Auden has four stresses in lines 1, 2, and 4; he changes to three stresses in the third line. The monotony of the old strong-stress meter is avoided by a number of cunning devices. The position of the caesura continually shifts; the third line has no caesura. The stresses do not occupy similar positions in each line but contract toward or expand away from each other. Iambic feeling is minimized by a prevailing rhythmic pattern of two and three consecutive unstressed syllables:

Those he had studied, the ner vous and the nights

And shades that still wai ted to en ter

The bright cir cle of his re cog ni tion . . .

The meticulous syllabism of Marianne Moore is another matter. Auden writes a hybrid metric, grafting strong-stress rhythms to a syllabic base. Moore counts syllables and shapes a stanza whose visual appearance suggests rhythmic function:

Pale sand edges England's Old
Dominion. The air is soft, warm, hot
above the cedar-dotted emerald shore
　　known to the red bird, the red-coated musketeer,
the trumpet-flower, the cavalier,
the parson, and the wild parishioner. A deer-
track in a church-floor
　　brick, and a fine pavement tomb with engraved top, remain.
The now tremendous vine-encompassed hackberry
　　　　starred with the ivy-flower,
　　　　shades the church tower;
And a great sinner lyeth here under the sycamore
　　　　　　　　　　　　　"Virginia Britannia"

The appeal to the eye is very great. The stanza emphasizes single words, separating them out of normal word groups: "Old / Dominion; a deer- / track in a church-floor / brick . . . " Words, and parts of words, are held up to the eye for special examination; the syllabic meter is analytic and visual. Moore's poetic lineage is through imagism. The doctrines of imagism are neither precise nor coherent; however, the effects of the views of Hulme, Pound, and others in modern poetry has led to a prosodical heresy: that visual devices can energize language with significant rhythm. Moore is only mildly heretical; she seldom neglects aural values in her verse. Rhyme, the sound qualities of words, quantity, are carefully balanced against syllabic count and stanzaic shape. But we must describe Moore as "a visualist of the imagination" in the specialty of her prosody.

❧ III. *Prosodic Analysis*

We name, as metrical, verse measured by the count of syllable-stress feet; verse measured by the count of strong stress; verse measured by the count of syllables; and, as far as it can be done in English, verse measured by the count of quantities. *Syllable-stress, strong-stress, syllabic,* and *quantitative:* these are the four metrical types basic to English verse. The historically established prosodic norm is, of course, syllable-stress meter; the greatest bulk of our poetry is composed in the familiar iambic, trochaic, or anapestic meters. Our ears, so accustomed to hearing the syllable-stress meters, often fail to recognize the other metrical forms. And occasionally we encounter verse that seems to fall between two metrical types. Scanning the opening lines of *The Waste Land* as syllable-stress meter, we get something like this:

> Áp ril | is the crúel lest | mónth, | bréed ing
> Lí lacs | oút of the | déad land, | míx ing
> Mém or y | and de síre, | stír ring
> Dúll | roóts with | spríng raín.

We can probably rationalize this as trochaic with many exceptions. However, the dominant falling rhythm, the crowding of stresses, and the curious mixture of metrical feet should tip us off. A better scansion reads the lines as strong-stress meter, four beats to the line:

April is the crúellest mónth, ‖ bréeding

Lílacs out of the déad lánd, ‖ míxing

Mémory and desíre, ‖ stírring

Dúll róots ‖ with spring ráin.

Prosodic analysis begins with recognizing the metrical type. In shorter poems we have little difficulty in determining whether we are dealing with one of the other, less frequently encountered, metrical types. The metrical architecture of the significant longer poems of our age requires special scrutiny. Twentieth-century poetry has developed no "carryall" metric comparable to Elizabethan blank verse or the eighteenth-century couplet; the prosody of *The Waste Land* and *Four Quartets,* of the *Cantos,* of *The Bridge,* of *Paterson,* and of *The Women at Point Sur* and *The Double Axe* is "organic," developed out of the subject and stance of the poem, and not an imposed or adapted style.

Once we have recognized and scanned the meter, we have completed the first step in prosodic analysis. But what of poetic rhythms: the interaction between meter and other elements of linguistic structure? Scansion does not take into account the *interplay* (Robert Bridges's apt term)[6] between meter and syllabic quantity, meter and syntax, meter and propositional sense. Two passages, which scan exactly alike, may be at opposite prosodic poles:

Nót as | a gód, | but ás | a gód | might bé,

Ná ked | a móng | them, líke | a sá | vage soúrce . . .

What are | the róots | that clútch, | what brán | ches grów

Oút of | this stó | ny rúb | bish? Són | of mán . . .

The only variations from the blank-verse norm are the inverted initial feet. We have a longer syntactical period before the caesura in the Eliot; the movement of the lines is heavier and slower than the lines from "Sunday Morning." Eliot's rhetoric derives from Ezekiel; we hear the deliberate and solemn thunder of the prophet's voice. The heavy rhythms, which the meter controls, are largely a matter of vowel quantity and consonant orchestration. We could devise a cumbersome notation for quantity and alliteration to supplement our scansion. But we feel it simpler to comment on these matters, pointing out the predominance of stressed *o* and *u* sounds; the consonant clusters *cl-*, *br-*, *gr-*; the final *-t* that lengthens the stressed vowel.

We cannot subject rhythm and rhythmic values to the kind of precise analysis that scansion accomplishes for meter. The notation of scansion defines with comfortable accuracy metrical structure; the rhythms of even the simplest poem are too complex to be ever completely analyzed. Every element in poetic structure contributes to rhythmic feeling. Sound effects, the spacing and repetition of images and ideas, diction and vocabulary, matters of texture—these are rhythmic matters, prosodic matters, too. We must talk about them if we wish to give some idea of a poet's prosody. We might occasionally use musical notation to represent quantitative patterns and other rhythmic motifs; we might occasionally resort to diagrams or mechanical aids.

The Riv | er spread | ing, flows || —and spends | your dream.

Hart Crane, "The River"

Actual measurement (with the oscillograph) shows that the intervals are far from equal. The third foot, with its "-ing" and "flows," is considerably longer in temporal value than the other feet. And what of the long pause at the caesura: how much *time* does it occupy? It depends, of course; it depends on how an individual reader performs the line. And we are back to the old performative fallacy. The meter remains what it has always been, revealed by the traditional method of scanning the stressed and unstressed syllables.

Meter releases rhythmic potential; it creates an illusion of time, not a chronometric interval. If we measure the feet in the example from Hart Crane, we can show significant differences in actual length. But we have the illusion that the feet occupy units of equal time because the total effect of metrical organization seemingly eliminates temporal discrepancies. Meter is analogous to perspective. If we measure with a ruler the distance between Mona Lisa's nose and her fingertips, and between her nose and one of the rocks she sits among, we may conclude that it is no farther from her nose to her hand than it is from her nose to an imagined point two or three hundred yards distant. What we measure with our ruler is literal space on the canvas, not the illusion of space created by perspective. Perspective creates illusory space; meter creates illusory time. That meter also occupies literal time—the minutes elapsing as we read a poem—is irrelevant just as the measurable dimensions of a painting in perspective are irrelevant.

We must realize that rhythmic analysis is subjective and interpretive; it is not scansion but ancillary to it. Scansion, although not devoid of subjective elements, is more objective. Scansion shows the give and take between language and meter; the variations possible within the imposed pattern; the limits between which language may move and still be counted as metrical. Scansion does not, however, tell us everything we need to know about a poem's prosody. We may need metaphoric language, phonetic symbols, and musical notation to supplement metrical analysis. We need the basic approaches and techniques of literary criticism to place prosodic analysis in the larger context of humanistic scholarship. Finally, we must understand that while prosody is largely a matter of metrics, it is also the totality of structures controlling the significant movement of a poem's language.

III

Modern Poetry in the
Metrical Tradition

Our inquiry begins with those poets who remained largely unaffected by the prosodical revolution of the teens and the twenties, and who composed the bulk of their work in syllable-stress metric. This does not mean that the poets of this chapter are unhappy holdovers from Victorianism, or representatives of an archaizing poetic spirit. They deal with the problems of our age; they write in an idiom derived from contemporary speech. But they catch and hold the rhythms of speech in metrical nets. Thomas Hardy is Victorian in origin and not a full-fledged "modern poet." He does not exhibit that neurotic sensitivity to the Zeitgeist characteristic of a poet like Auden. But Hardy's work reaches down into our time, surprising us again and again with its sudden aptness and vivid understanding. After reading Hardy's war poems, who can say he was not a man of the twentieth century?

Passages from these poets—they range from Hardy, Bridges, and Yeats to Frost, Robinson, Edwin Muir, and John Crowe Ransom—provide examples of traditional style in modern prosody. With no attempt to treat in depth the prosodic development of each poet or to make a detailed genetic study of origins and influences, the passages are offered as specimens for analysis so that we can see the richness, the variety, and the individuality possible within the traditional metrical system.

⪧ 1. Thomas Hardy

Hardy's prosody sometimes fails as an expressive form. In some of his poems the versification is clumsy, neither subtle nor emphatic. Words are forced into the metrical patterns; the meters themselves are frequently inappropriate to the subject.

THE NEWCOMER'S WIFE

He paused on the sill of a door a-jar
That screened a lively liquor-bar,
For the name had reached him through the door
Of her he had married the week before.

"We called her the Hack of the Parade;
But she was discreet in the games she played;
If slightly worn, she's pretty yet,
And gossips, after all, forget."

The uncertain mixture of trisyllabic and iambic feet makes it difficult to hear the metrical direction; the fifth line above confirms us in the feeling that we are reading badly versified prose, as if Hardy were ghostwriting the amazing verses of Muhammad Ali in his prime. It is difficult to read the line without placing an inappropriate stress on the second "the":

We called | her the Hack | of the | Pa rade.

Hardy's best poems move to a different music. In that little comic masterpiece, "The Ruined Maid," the anapestic base meter is exactly right to catch the querulous, jealous whine of the girl who stayed home, and the newly acquired insolence, and as yet tentative affectation of the girl who is "ruined." Here are the last three stanzas:

—"Your hands were like paws then, your face blue and bleak
But now I'm bewitched by your delicate cheek,
And your little gloves fit as on any la-dy!"—
"We never do work when we're ruined," said she.

—"You used to call home-life a hag-ridden dream,
And you'd sigh, and you'd sock; but at present you seem
To know not of megrims or melancho-ly!"—
"True. One's pretty lively when ruined" said she.

—"I wish I had feathers, a fine sweeping gown,
And a delicate face, and could strut about Town!"—
"My dear—a raw country girl, such as you be,
Cannot quite expect that. You ain't ruined," said she.

The appropriateness of the meter is no better illustrated than in the slight wrenching at the ends of the line:

And your lít | tle gloves fít | as on á | ny la-dý . . .

To knów | not of mé | grims or mél | an cho-lý . . .

Metrical stress forces a rise in pitch (la-dy . . . melancho-ly), mimicking the country girl's peevish complaint, and suggesting that her pronunciation of certain words is affected by the prevailing dialect. The meter also makes subtle what could never be fully expressed by the words alone; that the ruined girl's pride in her new clothes and recently acquired social status is qualified by certain misgivings. Her attitude is not quite jeering; she is really friendly—a little proud, but also a little ashamed. The meter supports a complexity of tone, providing, as in "Captain Carpenter," a prosodic irony to complement the ironies of character and circumstance.

The first stanza of "An August Midnight" mixes trisyllabic and disyllabic feet:

A shaded lamp and a waving blind,
And the beat of a clock from a distant floor:
On this scene enter—winged, horned, and spined—
A longlegs, a moth, and a dumbledore;
While 'mid my page there idly stands
A sleepy fly, that rubs its hands.

The measure is iambic tetrameter, though one line is mainly anapestic,

And the beát | of a clóck | from a dís | tant flóor

and one contains a monosyllabic foot,

On thís | scene én | ter—wínged, | hórned, | and spíned . . .

These rhythmic changes follow the poet's shifting perceptions. The clock beats trisyllabically; the "winged, horned, and spined" creatures enter in bumpy confusion. In the last line the recurrent labials (A slee(p)y (f)ly, that ru(b)s its hands) underscore the controlling tetrameter meter and the smooth, graceful movement of the fly.

Some stanzas from "In a Wood" show Hardy working in variations on a two-stress dactylic, a meter uncommon in English,[1] but suited to pathos and elegy:

> Touches from as, O wych,
>   Sting you like scorn!
> You, too, brave hollies, twitch
>   Sidelong from thorn.
> Even the rank poplars bear
> Lothly a rival's air,
> Cankering in black despair
>   If overborne.
>
> Since, then, no grace I find
>   Taught me of trees,
> Turn I back to my kind,
>   Worthy as these.
> There at least smiles abound,
> There discourse trills around,
> There, now and then, are found
>   Life-loyalties.

Alternate lines are catalectic; the final foot lacks the two unstressed syllables:

> Tóuch es from | ásh, O wỳch,
>   Stíng you like | scórn!
> Yóu, too, bràve | hól lies twìtch
>   Síde long from | thórn.

A feature of the odd lines is the heavy final stress, although in authentic dactyls falling rhythm would persist through the last foot. We have, in effect, a cross-rhythm; if we scan the lines as disyllabic, we get trochees and iambs:

Touch es | from ash, | O wych,

Sting you | like scorn!

Three against two. The final stressed syllable obviates the awkward and sometimes poetically embarrassing unstressed rhyme. The fifth line of each stanza consists of two accentual amphimacs (or cretics):

Even the rank | pop lars bear . . .

There at least | smiles a bound . . .

and from the first stanza (not quoted)

When the rains | skim and skip . . .

Whether or not we recognize the amphimac in syllable-stress prosody (it can always be rationalized into iambs and trochees, which may prove more helpful to the modern reader), we recognize Hardy's awareness of metrical possibilities—an awareness sharpened by classical reading and musical training.

Hardy's music is not an accidental virtue, nor is it the mellifluous sound of vowels and consonants in regular sequences. Hardy's best poems show the advantages meter can afford the poet. In his poems that affect us like music, the music moves where feeling and order interact: at that level of metrical intensity and delicacy which allows language to shape itself into significant rhythmic forms. Hardy's theme in these stanzas is the oldest in the history of poetry—the pathos of mutability:

DURING WIND AND RAIN

They sing their dearest songs—
He, she, all of them—yea,
Treble and tenor and bass,
   And one to play;
With the candles mooning each face . . .
   Ah, no; the years O!
How the sick leaves reel down in throngs!

They clear the creeping moss—
Elders and juniors—aye,

Making the pathways neat
  And the garden gay;
And they build a shady seat . . .
  Ah, no; the years, the years;
See, the white storm-birds wing across!

They are blithely breakfasting all—
Men and maidens—yea,
Under the summer tree,
  With a glimpse of the bay,
While pet fowl come to the knee . . .
  Ah, no; the years O!
And the rotten rose is ript from the wall.

They change to a high new house,
He, she, all of them—aye,
Clocks and carpets and chairs
  On the lawn all day,
And brightest things that are theirs . . .
  Ah, no; the years, the years;
Down their carved names the rain-drop ploughs.

We scan only the last lines of each stanza; even in this brief analysis, we see the amazing rhythmical variety within a basic iambic pattern:

How the | sick leaves | reel down | in throngs!

See, the | white storm- | birds wing | across!

And the rot | ten rose | is ript | from the wall.

Down their | carved names | the rain- | drop ploughs.

Hardy strains the meter with every possible variation: inverted, mono-syllabic, and trisyllabic feet; heavy pauses and heavy rhetorical stresses. The family, depicted in all its activity, works and plays to the sometime hesitating, sometime headlong rhythms. Hardy gives a direct revela-tion of the curve of life, from birth and growth to decay and death. It is a revelation tormented by time; work, pleasure, the good fortune yield to the years. The prosody, with its nervous and passionate tension between meter and rhetorical stress, moves us along in time: the psy-chological time in which we experience the life of feeling.

❧ *II. William Butler Yeats*

It is a critical commonplace that Yeats started out as a Victorian and ended up as the highest of the moderns. His earliest poems show Swinburnian fluency, especially in the use of triple meter:

> I would that we were, my beloved, white birds on the foam
>   of the sea!
> We tire of the flame of the meteor, before it can fade and flee;
> And the flame of the blue star of twilight, hung low on the
>   rim of the sky,
> Has awaked in our hearts, my beloved, a sadness that may
>   not die.
>
> "The White Birds," 1893

But Yeats was dissatisfied with the current fashions of versification of the 1880s: the long dactylic and anapestic lines; the elegant and over-ripe Alexandrine, popularized by Ernest Dowson and Lionel Johnson. Yeats remarks, in "The Symbolism of Poetry" (1900):

> we would cast out of serious poetry those energetic rhythms, as of a man running, which are the invention of the will with its eyes always on something to be done or undone; and we would seek out those wavering, meditative, organic rhythms, which are the embodiment of the imagination.[2]

The casting out of the energetic and obvious rhythms is complete by the time Yeats published *Responsibilities* (1914). We find none of the inordinate prepositional stuffing of

> And the fláme | *of* the blúe | stàr *of* twí | light, hung lów | *on*
>   the rím | *of* the ský

to fill out the hexameter line. We do find sureness, subtlety, a controlled sensuousness, in the metric of "The Magi," perhaps the most remarkable of Yeats's pre–World War I poems. We scan the last four lines:

> And áll | their hélms | of síl | ver hóv | er‿ing síde | by síde,
> And áll | their éyes | still fíxed, | hóp ing | to fínd | once móre,

Be ing | by Cal | va_ry's túr | bu lénce | un sa | tis fíed,

The un | con trol | la_ble mys | te_ry on | the bés | ti_al floor.

Yeats, like Milton, follows a principle of elision: *syllables, ordinarily spoken in performance, do not count in scansion. Hovering, Calvary, mystery,* and *bestial* are disyllabic. Whether Yeats himself said, in rich Irish brogue, "hov'ring" and "myst'ry," does not matter; the metrical paradigm calls for six iambic feet in the line.

This is not, however, the hexameter of

> But when the storm is highest, and the thunders blare,
> And sea and sky are riven, O moon of all my night!
> Ernest Dowson, "Seraphita"

Yeats's rhetorical energy submerges all sense of metronomic metrical pulse; the astonishing last line has only four speech stresses:

> The uncontrollable mystery on the bestial floor . . .

The Magi seek another incarnation, not a repetition of Virgin and Dove, but as Yeats later conceived it in "Leda and the Swan," a bestial coupling of god and woman. The rhythmic change in this last line isolates it from the rest of the poem, holding it before our minds for special contemplation, frightening us into thought.

The opening lines of "The Second Coming" are strongly cross-rhythmical. Overlaying blank verse is a falling rhythm of dactyls and paeons. Double lines mark the rhythmical periods; single lines mark metrical feet:

> Túrn ing | and || turn | ing ín | the || wí | den_ing || gýre

> Túrn ing and || turn ing in the || wi den ing || gýre

The interplay of meter and rhythm produces a prosodic texture of opposing movement and feeling. The rhetorical "tune" of falling feet reappears in the last line:

> Slóu | ches tówards | Béth le | hém to | be bórn. (meter)

> Slóu ches towárds || Béth le hém || tó be bórn. (rhythm)

Since the penultimate line is regular,

And what | rough beast, | its hour | come round | at last . . .

the last lines of the poem show symmetry and asymmetry in sharp rhythmical contrast. There can be no comfortable scansion of the last line; we might read its meter this way:

Slou ches | towards Beth | le hem | to be born.

However conceived in scansion, the line is rhythmically unresolved. The poem ends taut with expectancy; prosodic energy does not diminish but reaches out into the surrounding darkness.

An earlier question returns: what is the relationship between meaning and prosody? Are the cross-rhythms of "The Second Coming" onomatopoeic; does Yeats's prosody *look like* the spiraling ascent of the falcon and *sound like* the shambling, mindless tread of the great stone beast? Do these rhythms represent the movements of falcon and beast? Rhythms are structures symbolic of feelings that evoke representations of things or actions. What we experience when we read "The Second Coming" is not kinesthesia, "but how feelings go." Yeats's images, the observed falcon and imagined beast, are suffused with emotions of horror and awe. The function of the smoothly falling rhythm of the opening line, or the curiously broken rhythm of the last line is "not communication but insight."[3] Still, though one can hardly proffer insight without communicating, if we do not make this distinction, we could say the pattern,

sounds like the motion of a falcon in flight, and that prosody could *communicate* detonational sense. This is absurd when we realize that such a pattern can be found in poems ranging over a whole alphabet of feelings: from anger to xenophobia. Rather, the rhythmic pattern is contextually appropriate to the subject and forms an emotional resemblance consonant with meaning. The rhythmic luck of "Slouches towards Bethlehem to be born" gives a penetrating vision of indifferent, relentless, and uncontrollable movement; a sudden insight into the horrified and helpless feelings we might have when, at the next turn of history, the world erupts in apocalyptic violence.

Rhythmical structure is a contextually appropriate aural symbolism. I. A. Richards complains, with some justice, that prosodists neglect to show the important interaction of rhythmic form and propositional sense in the poem.[4] In "The Second Coming" we see how rhetorical stress, the rhythm of semantic emphasis, contradicts the expectations set up by the abstract meter. This new rhythm has a content of feeling generated by the meanings of words but, at the same time, has formal movement of its own: structure not denotative of feelings, but articulating and reenforcing them.

Among the triumphs of Yeats's versification are his poems in short lines. "Easter 1916" is written in three-stress lines, built with exquisite rhythmical variety and balance. There is no regular foot, but each line modulates metrical periods; we quote and scan various sections from the poem:

> I have met | them at close | of day
>
> Com ing | with vi | vid fa | ces
>
> From coun ter or desk | a mong grey
>
> Eigh | teenth-cent | ury hou | ses.
>
> Being cer | tain that they | and I
>
> But lived | where mot | ley is worn:
>
> All changed, | changed ut | ter ly:
>
> A ter | ri ble beau | ty is born.
>
> A horse | hoof slides | on the brim,
>
> And a horse | plash es | with in | it;
>
> The long- | leg ged moor- | hens dive,
>
> And hens | to moor- | cocks call;
>
> Min ute | by min | ute they live:
>
> The stone's | in the midst | of all.

We have great intricacy, born of a great ear, in apparent simplicity. Disyllabic and trisyllabic feet are interchanged freely; unaccented syllables provide either emphatic upbeats or delicate end assonance;

lines are counterpointed by monosyllabic or inverted feet. Syntax tersely controls the argument, sometimes stopping at the end of the line, sometimes flowing over:

> We know their dream; enough
> To know they dreamed and are dead;
> And what if excess of love
> Bewildered them till they died?

Because Yeats arranges the poem into four alternating sections of sixteen and twenty-four lines and not into short stanzas, he must take special care to avoid the flaccid long sentence or the monotonous short one. The balance is nearly perfect; a short question is answered by the murmuring simile of mother and child, then followed by another question:

> O when may it suffice?
> That is Heaven's part, our part
> To murmur name upon name,
> As a mother names her child
> When sleep at last has come
> On limbs that had run wild.
> What is it but nightfall?

In Yeats's poetry syntactical control deserves special notice. Although Yeats came under strong symbolist influence, especially in the quality of his images, he rarely fails to supply the hard skeleton of logical thought that close syntactical form affords. The opening "Song" from *The Resurrection* is a good example of relating images, not by free grammatical apposition, but through a linking network of active verbs:

> I saw a staring virgin stand
> Where holy Dionysus died,
> And tear the heart out of his side,
> And lay the heart upon her hand
> And bear that beating heart away;
> And then did all the Muses sing
> Of Magnus Annus at the spring,
> As though God's death were but a play.

Yeats's images have, as they generally have in symbolist poetry, meanings peculiar and private; and they must be understood in the context of his mythological philosophy of history. But no mystery attaches itself to the plot of the poem. "Stand," "tear," "lay," "bear" fully explain the activities of the savage virgin. The Muses "sing" as if they were the accompanying chorus in a festival tragedy performed at the great Athenian Dionysia.

A meter of absolute iambic regularity enforces the rigid syntax. The song is a hieratic chant and serves to introduce a play on the meaning of the Resurrection to the culture and stability of the Hellenic world. Christianity for Yeats was an irruption of the irrational in history, a force that would destroy the humane civilizations of Athens and Rome. The subject of the song is the violence of this new historical energy: a violence paradoxically rendered in regular metric and closely ordered syntax.

We find in Yeats's later verse a characteristic use of the monosyllabic and counterpointed foot, which is a signature, a way of saying in rhythm, "This line is written by Yeats":

> I know, | although | when looks | meet
> I trem | ble to | the bone.
>
> > "Crazy Jane and Jack the Journeyman"

> Speech af | ter long | si | lence; it | is right.
>
> Wrap | ping that | foul bo | dy up . . .
> On Crua | chan's plain | slept he
> That must | sing in | a rhyme.
>
> O | but heart's | wine shall | run pure,
> Mind's bread | grow sweet.

The last example is spectacular and sounds very much like Hopkins; the consecutive heavy stresses produce the typical movement of sprung rhythm. Much of the late verse pays little attention to syllabic count; Yeats clearly moves away from syllable-stress to strong-stress metric.

It is the strong-stress principle that dominates the lean textured verse of Yeats's penultimate play, *Purgatory* (1939). Its verse is Yeats's most successful fusion of colloquial naturalness and poetic intensity.

Boy.   Half-door, hall door,
           Hither and thither day and night,
           Hill or hollow, shouldering this pack,
           Hearing you talk.

Old Man.   Study that house . . .

           Great people lived and died in this house;
           Magistrates, colonels, members of Parliament,
           Captains and Governors, and long ago
           Men that had fought at Aughrim and the Boyne . . .

                                   Study that tree.
           It stands there like a purified soul,
           All cold, sweet, glistening light.
           Dear mother, the window is dark again,
           But you are in the light because
           I finished all that consequence.

We have a norm of four stresses in the line. Yeats carefully spaces his stresses; at moments of poetic excitement, the stressed syllables crowd together in an effect of emotional acceleration:

Half-door, ǁ hall door,

Hith er and thi ther ǁ day and night,

Hill or hollow, ǁ shoul der ing this pack . . .

All cold, sweet, ǁ glis ten ing light . . .

When emotion slackens, the lines slow down; the freer use of the unstressed syllables results in a more leisurely, conversational idiom:

           Great people lived and died in this house;
           Magistrates, colonels, members of Parliament,
           Captains and Governors, and long ago
           Men that had fought at Aughrim and the Boyne.

ঌ *III. Robert Bridges*

Bridges experimented ceaselessly to extend and widen the prosodic possibilities of English poetry. Devising, or adapting, rules and theories for quantitative, accentual, and syllabic verse, he then sought to apply them to his poetry. With what success, we assess below. First, we must note that Bridges is the only conscious and deliberate scholar-prosodist among the poets of the late Victorian and early modern period. He was aware of the free-verse experimentation of the teens and twenties but rejected nonmetrical techniques. He theorized that free verse encouraged monotony in poetic structure: it had little sustaining power; it required the poet to seek out an "absolute rhythm" for every thought and phrase; it identified line length with syntactical unit and consequently precluded the interplay between grammatical structure and prosodic stress.

Bridges attempted, by either reviving old or devising new meters, to escape the tyranny of syllable-stress metric.

> No art can flourish that is not alive and growing, and it can only grow by invention of new methods or by discovery of new material. In the art of English verse my own work has led me to think that there is a wide field for exploration in the metrical prosody, and that in carrying on Milton's inventions in the syllabic verse there is better hope of successful progress than in the technique of free verse as I understand it.[5]

A full account of Bridges's work in theoretical prosody and practical metrical invention goes beyond the scope of our study. Indeed, as Albert Guérard says, "A full account of Bridges' prosody would require a volume at least as large as the poet's own *Milton's Prosody.*[6] We refer the reader to Guérard's discriminating critique of Bridges's meters for more detailed technical information than we offer here.[7] Our effort is more pragmatically critical: is Bridges's poetry, in his new meters, vigorous and relevant; how much of this poetry is written for the metric, to test and illustrate a theory; how useful have Bridges's experiments been to the rhythmic life of twentieth-century verse?

Bridges wrote in the three meters possible, and in one impossible, to the English language. His poems in syllable-stress meter reveal a musician's ear for quantity; as conscious a prosodist as Tennyson,

Bridges pays close attention to vowel length and to placing of unstressed long syllables. An early sonnet in traditional meter shows consummate technical skill:

> Spring hath her own bright days of calm and peace;
> Her melting air, at every breath we draw,
> Floods heart with love to praise God's gracious law:
> But suddenly—so short is pleasure's lease—
> The cold returns, the buds from growing cease,
> And nature's conquer'd face is full of awe;
> As now the trait'rous north with icy flaw
> Freezes the dew upon the sick lamb's fleece,
>
>   And 'neath the mock sun searching everywhere
> Rattles the crisped leaves with shivering din:
> So that the birds are silent with despair
> Within the thickets; nor their armour thin
> Will gaudy flies adventure in the air,
> Nor any lizard sun his spotted skin.
>
> *The Growth of Love*

Bridges has absorbed his influences well: Wordsworth, Keats, and Shakespeare are discernible but not obtrusive. One line moves with extraordinary rhythmic power and grace:

> *Floods* heart | with love | to praise | *God's* gra | cious law.

"Floods" and "God's" do not fall under the metrical ictus, but their position as rhetorically stressed long syllables singles them out for rhythmic emphasis. Since the metrical base is scarcely disturbed, we cannot consider the line sprung.

The apparent influence of Gerard Manley Hopkins appears in a prosodically transitional poem, "The Downs" (1879). The poem is transitional because it hovers between traditional syllable-stress and strong-stress meter.

> O bold majestic downs, smooth, fair and lonely;
> O still solitude, only matched in the skies:
>   Perilous in steep places,
>   Soft in the level races,

Where sweeping in phantom silence the cloudland flies;
With lovely undulation of fall and rise;
   Entrenched with thickets thorned,
By delicate miniature dainty flowers adorned!

––––––––

The accumulated murmur of soft plashing,
Of waves on rocks dashing and searching the sands,
   Takes my ear, in the veering
   Baffled wind, as rearing
Upright at the cliff, to gullies and rifts he stands;
And his conquering surges scour out over the lands.

We can scan it in traditional feet, but in some lines the strong stresses
crowd together, in a characteristic Hopkins-like effect:

O bold majestic downs, smooth, fair and lonely . . .

Of waves on rocks dashing and searching the sands . . .

And his conquering surges scour out over the lands.

Compared to "The Wreck of the Deutschland" this is prosodically
tame; Bridges was not the man to have closely followed his younger,
more exuberant friend. Yet in developing the principles of his own
strong-stress prosody (Bridges terms it *accentual verse*), he is close to
Hopkins's strictures for the measurement of sprung rhythm. Indeed,
Bridges and Hopkins make the same mistake about the nature of
strong-stress meter; in their theoretic passion for reducing their metri-
cal discoveries to rules, they apply a foot scansion to what is essentially,
and by nature, not a foot-measured meter.

   Guérard tries gamely to scan Bridges's accentual verse according to
the rules Bridges outlines in part 4 of *Milton's Prosody*.[8] His reading of
the first stanza of "Nightingales" is

Beautiful | must be | the mountains | whence | ye come

And bright | in the fruitful | valleys | the streams, | wherefrom

   Ye learn | your song:

Where are | those starry | woods? | O might | I wander | there,

Ā́mŏng | thĕ flŏẃĕrs, | whĭch ĭn thát | héavĕnlȳ | aĭr

Blŏóm thĕ | yĕār long!⁹

Guérard concedes the poem may also be scanned on syllable-stress principles. All we need to recognize is the traditional substitution of trisyllabic for disyllabic feet, and we have a stanza of irregular line length in iambic meter:

Bĕaútĭfŭl | mŭst bĕ́ | thĕ mŏún | tăins whĕ́nce | yĕ cŏ́me,

Ănd bríght | ĭn thĕ frŭít | fŭl vắl | lĕys thĕ strĕáms, | whĕrefrŏ́m

Yĕ lĕárn | yŏur sŏ́ng, etc.

This scansion is not in accord with Bridges's metrical intention; but we cannot hear this as accentual or stress verse: we hear the limpid meters of romantic prosody, the facility of Shelley or the vowel music of Tennyson.

Bridges's later poems in accentual meters have greater vigor: probably because he breaks his own rules and follows the native strong-stress line:

> Fool that I was: my heart was sore,
> Yea sick for the myriad wounded men,
> The maim'd in the war: I had grief for each one:
> And I came in the gay September sun
> To the open smile of Trafalgar Square;
> Where many a lad with a limb fordone
> Loll'd by the lion-guarded column
> That holdeth Nelson statued thereon
> Upright in the air.
>
> "Trafalgar Square," 1917

Two defects weaken the metrical effect: the use of rhyme and the anapestic gallop:

The maim'd | in the war: | I had grief | for each one:

And I came | in the gay | Sep tem | ber sun.

Pound better exploits the rich possibilities of stress meter and uses it with greater power in his "The Seafarer":

> There come now no kings or Caesars
> Nor gold-giving lords like those gone.
> Howe'er in mirth most magnified,
> Whoe'er lived in life most lordliest,
> Drear all this excellence, delights undurable!

This may be an unfair comparison, but it shows what Bridges lacks in rhythmic distinction. One line of Bridges has strong movement,

> Loll'd by the lion-guarded column . . .

but the next is doggerel,

> That holdeth Nelson statued thereon.

Unlike Pound, Bridges cannot keep prosodical energy alive throughout the whole poem.

Bridges's other important metrical innovations were in syllabic meters. Unfortunately he confuses his terminology, calling syllable-stress meter "syllabic." In his "Letter to a Musician on English Prosody," he tells us that English blank verse, as practiced by Milton and Shakespeare, is "syllabic":

> I would not wish to seem to underestimate the extreme beauty to which verse has attained under the syllabic system. Shakespeare and Milton have passages of blank verse as fine as poetry can be. . . . On the simplest syllabic scheme it is impossible in English to write two verses exactly alike and equivalent, because of the infinite variety of the syllabic unit and its combinations.[10]

We must, of course, sympathize; most prosodists come away torn and bleeding after an encounter with the Terminological Menace. Bridges's early syllabic poems were written in short "sixes"; extrametrical syllables are elided "the same as in Milton, and as with him optional; only it is less optional, since it is ruled by speech-practice and not by metrical demands."[11]

Since the line is regulated neither by fixed numbers of feet nor by speech stresses, it can accommodate a great variety of rhythmic movement. "It was plainly the freest of free-verse, there being no speech rhythm which it would not admit."[12] Bridges developed his twelve-syllable line as a carryall metric, using it in his most ambitious poetic undertaking, *The Testament of Beauty.* Unfortunately, we find Bridges's masterwork unreadable. His "loose alexandrines" (book 2, 841) lull rather than excite; his philosophic meanderings are priggish daydreams. Perhaps the unhappiest feature of the poem is Bridges's Jovian detachment. He makes occasional reference to ordinary humanity and their all too human activities (the ways of the rich; crowds at football games, etc.); but *The Testament of Beauty* does not engage the world of common experience: it has no people in it, and consequently no human smell about it.

Finally, we must mention Bridges's work in quantitative metric. Our general remarks on adapting classical prosody to English need not be repeated here. We refer the reader back to chapter 2. However, the reader might like to play a little game to see if his or her ear can tell which of the following passages is composed in Bridges's "free" syllabic meter, which in his "English hexameters":

> Not knowing the high goal of our great endeavour
> Is spiritual attainment, Individual worth,
> At all cost to be sought and at all cost pursued,
> To be won at all cost and at all cost assured;
> Not such material ease as might be attain'd for all
> By cheap production and distribution of common needs,
> Were all life level'd down to where the lowest can reach.[13]

> Turn our thought for awhile to the symphonies of Beethoven,
> Or the rever'd preludes of mighty Sebastian; is there
> One work of Nature's contrivance beautiful as these?
> Judg'd by beauty alone man wins, as sensuous artist . . .[14]

"Cadenced prose" would be the judgment of most readers. The second selection, from "Wintry Delights," was written to test the theories of Bridges's friend, William Johnson Stone.[15] Stone formulates a system of rules for quantitative verse: like all such systems it is based on very personal and very odd ways of pronouncing English vowels. Stone's "quantities" must be accepted on religious faith; they are quite undemonstrable. "Wintry Delights" begins auspiciously; its rhythmic swing, however, derives more from *Piers Plowman* than from the *Aeneid:*

> Now in wintry delights, and long fireside meditation,
> 'Twixt studies and routine paying due court to the Muses,
> My solace in solitude, when broken roads barricade me
> Mudbound, unvisited for months with my merry children . . .

The distribution of heavy speech stresses and repetition of initial consonants suggest Middle English alliterative verse:

> My sol ace in so li tude, ‖ when bro ken roads bar ri cade me
> Mud bound, un vi si ted ‖ for months with my mer ry chil dren . . .

Again, this is not Bridges's prosodic intent. If we hum some hexameter music to ourselves *(Arma virumque cano,* or *This is the forest primeval),* we might be able to hear and scan

> Now in win | try de | lights, and | long fire | side me di | ta tion . . .

The two syllables "me-di-" are actually more than half as short as "side"; and we have, as C. S. Lewis points out, for the last two feet not the music of the slow movement of Beethoven's Seventh Symphony, but the "Ride of the Valkyries."

One poem in the *Poems in Classical Prosody* stands out as a work of considerable rhythmic power, "Johannes Milton, Senex":

> Since I believe in God the Father Almighty,
> Man's Maker and Judge, Overruler of Fortune,
> 'Twere strange should I praise anything and refuse Him praise,
> Should love the creature forgetting the Creator,
> Nor unto Him in suff'ring and sorrow turn me:
> Nay how could I withdraw me from His embracing?

Unlike the other quantitative poems these lines neither "limp nor twitch" but move with Miltonic sonority and smoothness. The classical

meter imitated here is the scazon or choliambic: a six-footed iambic
line with the final foot reversed:

Since Ī | be lieve | in God | the Fa | ther Al | migh ty . . .

The poem's rhythmic success depends on a normative coincidence of
vowel length with syllabic stress: we hear syllable-stress iambics under-
lying, and occasionally combating, the quantitative measure.

Our estimation of Bridges as prosodist and poet cannot be based on
the effort and variety of his technical experimentation; his "new" me-
ters have proved more interesting than useful. No great metric—like
that of Eliot's "Gerontion"—evolved out of either his accentual or
syllabic verse. His achievement as a poet rests on his lyrics in tradi-
tional meter. Even in these, exquisite as they are, we find none of the
force or penetration of Hardy's metrically less sophisticated but rhyth-
mically more impressive lyrics. If this seems a paradox, it is only saying
that craftsmanship alone cannot produce great poetry—or great pros-
ody. A platitude is thought without style; rhythmic platitude is move-
ment without grace or direction. An impressive rhythm grows like a
living thing out of the poem's feeling, which springs from the life
intensely and honestly lived; the feeling is matured and shaped by that
rhythm:

> O body swayed to music, O brightening glance,
> How can we know the dancer from the dance?

⁊ IV. *Edwin Arlington Robinson*

In selected examples of Robinson's loosened blank verse, metrical
analysis shows how the lilt of New England speech gets into the ver-
sification. Here are some passages from *Isaac and Archibald:*

> Isaac and Archibald were two old men.
> I knew them, and I may have laughed at them
> A little; but I must have honored them
> For they were old, and they were good to me.
>
> But somewhere at the end of the first mile . . .

I told him that I could not think of them.

And that pleased me—for I was twelve years old . . .

Characteristic is Robinson's use of the inverted second foot:

I knéw | them, and | I máy | have laughed | at thém.

But some | where at | the end | of the | first mile . . .

And that | pleased me | —for I | was twelve | years old.

Inverting the second foot in lines 1 and 3 loosens metrical rigidity and brings the line close to the music of ordinary speech.

Warner Berthoff aptly described Robinson's as a poetry of "phrase rather than image," phrases consisting of "the most flexible working vocabulary in modern American poetry." Reflecting a lifelong devotion to music and drama, Robinson's blank verse proved capable of carrying meditative narratives of middle and greater length, and book-length poems. The poet was also successful in scaling down to shorter forms, becoming *the* American master of the sonnet:

THE PITY OF THE LEAVES
Vengeful across the cold November moors,
Loud with ancestral shame there came the bleak
Sad wind that shrieked, and answered with a shriek
Reverberant through lonely corridors.
The old man heard it; and he heard, perforce,
Words out of lips that were no more to speak—
Words of the past that shook the old man's cheek
Like dead, remembered footsteps on old floors.

And then there were the leaves that plagued him so!
The brown, thin leaves that on the stones outside
Skipped with a freezing whisper. Now and then
They stopped, and stayed there—just to let him know
How dead they were, but if the old man cried,
They fluttered off like withered souls of men.

This Italian sonnet illustrates several characteristics of Robinson's verse. The trochaic launch of certain lines creates momentum, catapulting us into the poem—

Venge ful | a cross | the cold | No vem | ber moors,
Loud with | an ces | tral shame | there came | the bleak . . .

The effect is akin to the thrill of rafting through rapids, then suddenly finding one's boat settled again in a calm current. The sestet also alters momentum, building to an abrupt, memorable turn:

And then | there were | the leaves | that plagued | him so!

The brown, | thin leaves | that on | the stone | out side

Skipped with | a freez | ing whis | per. Now | and then . . .

In the third echoic line above, note also Robinson's daring positioning of the caesura in the middle of the fourth foot. That and the enforced pause so early in the first line above suggest an often overlooked playfulness in Robinson's verse, a supple variety that is everywhere apparent, as in the alcaics of "Late Summer":

Confused he found her lavishing feminine
Gold upon clay, and found her inscrutable;
And yet she smiled. Why, then, should horrors
Be as they were, without end, her play things?

Robinson flawlessly executes this traditional stanza's most common scheme, though he stamps his own signature on it by reversing the stress at the beginning of the second line. In the monologue, "Ben Jonson Entertains a Man from Stratford," humor dances out of the blank verse as Jonson speaks of Shakespeare, and Shakespeare's dog:

and the dog
Most likely was the only man who knew him . . .
A dog of orders, an emeritus,
To wag his tail at him when he comes home,
And then to put his paw up on his knees
And say, "For God's sake, what's it all about?"

This is the poetry of talk, and it is the poetry at which Robinson excelled. His long apprenticeship translating Cicero and Virgil, his close reading of Shakespeare, Milton, the New Testament, George

Crabbe, and William Cowper instilled in his conception and execution of the poetic line a magnificent flexibility. Those who do not like his verse may mutter about low words creeping in dull lines; others will declare that the monosyllabic word has been a traditional source of power in English blank verse. We are inclined to side with the latter, and in closing we offer in support two longer passages, the first from the final section of the book-length *Lancelot*, the second from *Isaac and Archibald:*

> when he rose again
> The reapers had gone home. Over the land
> Around him in the twilight there was rest.
> There was rest everywhere; and there was none
> That found his heart. "Why should I look for peace
> When I have made the world a ruin of war?"
> He muttered; and a Voice within him said:
> "Where the light falls, death falls; a world has died
> For you, that a world may live. There is no peace.
> Be glad no man or woman bears for ever
> The burden of first days. There is no peace."

> Down we went,
> Out of the fiery sunshine to the gloom,
> Grateful and half sepulchral, where we found
> The barrels, like eight potent sentinels,
> Close ranged along the wall. From one of them
> A bright pine spile stuck out alluringly,
> And on the black flat stone, just under it,
> Glimmered a late-spilled proof that Archibald
> Had spoken from unfeigned experience.
> There was a fluted antique water-glass
> Close by, and in it, prisoned, or at rest,
> There was a cricket, of the soft brown sort
> That feeds on darkness. Isaac turned him out,
> And touched him with his thumb to make him jump.

The syntax is close; smooth enjambment and grammatical precision urge along a steady narrative movement. The meter, too, is as close as the syntax:

The reap | ers had | gone home. | O ver | the land
A round | him in | the twi | light there | was rest.

There was | a cri | cket, of | the soft | brown sort
That feeds | on dark | ness. I | saac turned | him out,
And touched | him with | his thumb | to make | him jump.

The supple simplicity of these lines (and of Robinson's poetry in general) accomplishes what most prose cannot—the distilled accuracy, compression, and dramatic sweep of natural speech in service to story.

❧ *v. Edwin Muir*

Unjustly neglected, the poems of Edwin Muir are finally appearing in some of the standard anthologies, and his influence can be seen in some of the later work of an important contemporary poet like John Haines. Muir shares certain qualities with Yeats; his poems in short lines have similar subtleties of rhythm, but their themes and images are less spectacular. Muir is haunted but not obsessed. The most powerful thematic influence on his work comes from modern German literature. Such allegorical pieces as "The Interrogation" or "The West" suggest Kafka's world, where the ordinary and the fabulous mingle in mysterious relationships. "The Animals," "The Toy Horse," and "Orpheus' Dream" have affinities with Rilke; they are gnomic, abrupt in beginnings, concerned with the ineffable pathos of creatures and *things.*

Those of his poems that derive from classical mythological sources possess singular power; however, unlike many modern poets who adapt Greek myths, Muir tells of Ulysses and Penelope, Theseus and Orpheus with utter lack of literary affectation. "The Labyrinth" is about reality and illusion. Theseus, free of the labyrinth but dazed by memories, struggles on middle earth to shake himself free of his past:

> Since I emerged that day from the labyrinth,
> Dazed with the tall and echoing passages,
> The swift recoils, so many I almost feared
> I'd meet myself returning at some smooth corner,
> Myself or my ghost, for all there was unreal

After the straw ceased rustling and the bull
Lay dead upon the straw and I remained,
Blood-splashed, if dead or alive I could not tell
In the twilight nothingness (I might have been
A spirit seeking his body through the roads
Of intricate Hades)—ever since I came out
To the world, the still fields swift with flowers, the trees
All bright with blossom, the little green hills, the sea,
The sky and all in movement under it,
Shepherds and flocks and birds and the young and old,
(I stared in wonder at the young and the old,
For in the maze time had not been with me;
I had strayed, it seemed, past sun and season and change,
Past rest and motion, for I could not tell
At last if I moved or stayed; the maze itself
Revolved around me on its hidden axis
And swept me smoothly to its enemy,
The lovely world)—since I came out that day . . .

The poem continues for twelve more lines before coming to its first full stop. Its remarkable, sustained syntax winds and turns upon itself, pausing in parenthesis, then moving on to complete its full statement only after thirty-five lines. The syntax *acts out* the journey of Theseus; when we emerge from the twisting, mazelike opening sentence, we issue on to the straight roads of the outer world. Once in the clear outside, the syntax is rapid and concise:

> But taking thought
> I'd tell myself, "You need not hurry. This
> Is the firm good earth. All roads lie free before you."
> But my bad spirit would sneer, "No, do not hurry."

The syntax offers us the sensation of wandering in the maze, then moves us along a straight road. The "silent rhythm of thought" powerfully directs our feelings to the experience behind words and meanings.

The strong syntax so dominates the prosody that the meter may seem to have little or no function. Indeed, J. C. Hall makes the astonishing claim that the poem is without meter: "In his poem "The Labyrinth" Muir sustains the first sentence for 35 lines without metrical support and without forfeiting our attention—surely a remarkable achievement!"[16] We agree the poem's syntax undergirds its structure; but if we scan a few lines, it is clear that the poem has a blank-verse base:

> Since Í | e mérged | that dáy | from the lá | by rínth,
>
> Dázed with | the táll | and éch | o_ing pás | sa gés,
>
> The swíft | re cóils, | so má | ny_I ál | most féared
>
> I'd méet | my sélf | re túrn | ing at sóme | smooth cór | ner.

Like much modern loosened blank verse, trisyllabic substitution allows Muir considerable rhythmic freedom. Many lines are phrased as prose and are absorbed into the metrical scheme without distortion or rhythmic upheaval. Muir carefully paces rhythmic movement; the lines proceed from regularity to freedom, and back to regularity.

> But they, the gods, as large and bright as clouds,
> Conversed across the sounds in tranquil voices
> High in the sky above the untroubled sea;
> And their eternal dialogue was peace
> Where all these things were woven; and this our life
> Was as a chord deep in that dialogue,
> An easy utterance of harmonious words,
> Spontaneous syllables bodying forth a world.

The first line above is normal iambic; the last two are packed with substitution. When the poem concludes, the prosody firmly returns to regular blank verse:

> Oh these deceits are strong almost as life.
> Last night I dreamt I was in the labyrinth,
> And woke far on. I did not know the place.

Among the many superb poems in short lines, we offer "The Fathers" and "The Animals" for prosodic scrutiny. They show how much variety is possible in the three-beat line; how the shifting of the strong stresses and an occasional trisyllabic foot control a realm of rhythmic possibility. The second stanza of "The Fathers" recalls, on first reading, Yeats:

> Archaic fevers shake
> Our healthy flesh and blood
> Plumped in the passing day
> And fed with pleasant food.
> The fathers' anger and ache
> Will not, will not away
> And leave the living alone,
> But on our careless brows
> Faintly their furrows engrave
> Like veinings in a stone,
> Breathe in the sunny house
> Nightmare of blackened bone,
> Cellar and choking cave.

A good poet may be measured by what he or she can, in matters of technique, get away with. Muir handles a line of three alliterated metrically stressed syllables

> And *l*eave the *l*iving a*l*one.

by deftly modulating vowel length and quality. What might be an uncomfortable mouthful of consonants becomes song; the pattern of syllables, like a phrase of melody, carries a measured burden of feeling.

"The Animals" is Rilkesque. We give the first and last stanzas:

> They do not live in the world,
> Are not in time and space.
> From birth to death hurled
> No word do they have, not one
> To plant a foot upon,
> Were never in any place.
> . . . .
> But these have never trod
> Twice the familiar track,
> Never never turned back
> Into the memoried day.

> All is new and near
> In the unchanging Here
> On the fifth great day of God,
> That shall remain the same,
> Never shall pass away.
>
> On the sixth day we came.

Muir avoids every obvious poeticism. We have few adjectives, a simple diction, terse and correct syntax. The meter is compressed; a sense of powerful feeling, held in check, is conveyed by the use of the monosyllabic foot. Muir varies its position:

> From bírth | to deáth húrled . . .
>
> Áll | is néw | and neár . . .
>
> On the síxth | dáy | we cáme . . .

A good example of "imitative meter" is the line

> Né ver | ne ver | turnèd báck

where the meter twice *turns back* in consecutive trochees and then comes to rights with a final heavy foot.

The last line is separated from the rest of the poem by a visual pause: a heavy silence indicated by the double line spacing. This device of fixing the poem's emotional climax in significant isolation is a frequent mannerism of Rilke's. Muir isolates his last line in a few other poems ("The Usurpers," "The Good Town," "Head and Heart"). These final lines are not portentous: not "clinching" afterthoughts or obvious précis. In "The Good Town" the last line makes a quiet observation, disturbed by a significant variation in the metrical pattern—an inverted third foot that belies the narrator's surface equanimity:

> "We have seen
> Good men made evil wrangling with the evil,
> Straight minds grown crooked fighting crooked minds.
> Our peace betrayed us; we betrayed our peace.
> Look at it well. This was the good town once."
>
> These thoughts we have, walking among our ruins.

❧ *vi. Langston Hughes*

The agitation of Langston Hughes's early life is apparent in much of his poetry. Countee Cullen, Hughes's counterpart and African-American contemporary, wrote poems rooted in the English tradition by way of Keats; Hughes turned for models to the poems of Carl Sandburg, the music of jazz, and the sonorous phrasing of spirituals. It is a charming historical tale, the story of the young busboy Hughes, nervously placing a sheaf of poems on the table where the well-known poet, Vachel Lindsay, dined one night in Washington. Lindsay's enthusiastic support set the course of Hughes's life, who went on to produce a celebrated body of work. By the time of his death in 1967, Hughes's reputation had declined as more militant voices from the African-American community came into vogue. But in poetry popularity and endurance have nothing to do with each other except, perhaps, in this way: deprived of the former, a true poet is reminded to keep one's mind set on achieving the latter. So it is little wonder that as many of the louder voices of the 1960s and 1970s have faded, Hughes's work remains an essential, living model. "Aunt Sue's Stories" is but one of many poems showing us why:

> Aunt Sue has a head full of stories.
> Aunt Sue has a whole heart full of stories.
> Summer nights on the front porch
> Aunt Sue cuddles a brown-faced child to her bosom
> And tells him stories.
>
> Black slaves
> Working in the hot sun,
> And black slaves
> Walking in the dewy night,
> And black slaves
> Singing sorrow songs on the banks of a mighty river
> Mingle themselves softly
> In the flow of old Aunt Sue's voice,
> Mingle themselves softly
> In the dark shadows that cross and recross
> Aunt Sue's stories.
>
> And the dark-faced child, listening,

> Knows that Aunt Sue's stories are real stories.
> He knows that Aunt Sue never got her stories
> Out of any book at all,
> But that they came
> Right out of her own life.
>
> The dark-faced child is quiet
> Of a summer night
> Listening to Aunt Sue's stories.

The strength of the prosody lies in its deft combination of alternate phrasing. As in jazz and the blues, clusters of phrases make up units of repetition, expanding on the springboard repetition of certain words ("Aunt Sue," "stories," "And"). This phrasing, by way of the Psalms of Hebrew prosody, is the ordering of experience itself. As we read the poem's last line, we return to the poem's beginning in quiet celebration of the circular *rightness* of life's patterns. Along the way, we are reminded of the central importance of storytelling to the recognition and continuation of such patterns.

➨ *VII. John Crowe Ransom*

John Crowe Ransom and Yvor Winters, alone among the New Critics, devoted meticulous attention to prosodical matters. We shall enlarge our previous, brief comments on Ransom's theories of metrical function and make a distinction between Ransom's views expressed in the late 1930s and 1940s and those he came to hold in later years. His most fully developed theory limits meter to providing aesthetic surface, or what he names "local texture" for the poem. In an article published in 1956, Ransom considers the matter of rhythm, apostrophizing it as "the marriage of the meter and the language."[17] More of this blissful metaphor later. We must first note that Ransom's (from our point of view) cramped theorizing does not interfere with his sensitivity to metrical matters and with the soundness of his practical prosodical criticism. He could correctly scan a line of metered verse; he understood the foot structure of traditional meter; he could hear what the immediacies of metrical structure contribute to a line and to the whole poem.

Ontology and *ontological* are Ransom's favorite critical words; the mode of existence of the poem "is a logical structure having a local texture." Ransom proceeds with an elaborate architectural conceit ("a negotiable trope"): the poem is a room whose beams, boards, and plaster are its structure; "and perhaps it has been hung with tapestry, or with paintings, for 'decoration.' The paint, the paper, the tapestry are texture. It is logically unrelated to structure."[18] The structure-texture dichotomy is particularized for meter:

> The meter on the whole is out of relation to the meaning of the poem, or to anything else specifically; it is a musical material of low grade, but plastic and only slightly resistant material, and its presence in every poem is that of an abstractionist element that belongs to the art.[19]

Ransom rejects, of course, all "expressive" heresies. "It is not the business of the meters to be expressive of the meaning."[20] The meters enter into no logically accountable relationship with the propositional sense; nor do they, in their rhythmic varieties, suggest any qualities of feeling. Indeed, Ransom's poetics scarcely allow that poetry can have emotive meanings. Poets and readers may have gross and disorderly emotions at the moments of composition and reading; the poem, in its severe ontological purity, has only structure and texture. "Art is more cool than hot."[21] Reading Ransom we are often seized with the infuriating notion that poems are neither written nor read; they exist, like the unborn and unconceived children of Kipling's "They," in their mysterious ontological heaven.

Ransom's views seem to us unnecessarily fastidious. They allow little of "the reek of the human" into the poem. We suspect Ransom's battle against "science" (his beckoning windmill) led him to theoretical excess; he wanted poetic discourse to be as tidy and rational as the universe of the scientists. We must also remember the historical situation. Ransom had been much impressed (as had every other New Critic) with the work of I. A. Richards in initiating a criticism ostensibly free of messy subjectivity. Neither Ransom's "ontology" nor Richards's neurology established a science of criticism; Ransom elegantly restates neoclassic poetics. The poem is a logical or prose discourse draped in poetic robes. What is Ransom's "texture" but neoclassic "ornament"? Meter enters into no intrinsic relationship with the meaning; its function is ornamental: paper and plaster for the poem. Ransom combats all Coleridgean attempts to view the poem as an organism, preferring to consider "the essential dualism of a poem" and poetry as "an inorganic activity."[22]

Long ago Eliot observed that poets devise theories to defend the kind of poetry they write—or think they write. Ransom wrote, in an age of "free verse" and blank prose, richly textured and intricately metered poems. He strikes archaic attitudes, and he is fond of old words; we run to our dictionaries to discover the meaning of transmogrifying, pernoctated, diurnity, stuprate. His theories, read together with his poetry, call us to his poetic devices and his craftsmanship. Everything that art can accomplish for poetry is lovingly bestowed on Ransom's verse. But like all theorizing poets, his poetry goes beyond anything his theory can account for; it is often a poetry which the theory would not recognize, or better, it is poetry superior to the theory.

We return to "Captain Carpenter" to see how it sanctions Ransom's views. The metrical peculiarities of the poem certainly furnish a texture distracting enough to the unwary reader. It draws, on first reading, sufficient attention to itself so that we might wonder what relationship exists between the meter and the meaning. We know Ransom roughens his lines to achieve an intended effect; if anyone thinks the versification of "Captain Carpenter" is inept or accidental, we have this self-conscious testimony:

> It is no very late stage of a poet's advancement that his taste rejects a sustained phonetic regularity as something restricted and barren, perhaps ontologically defective. Accordingly he is capable of writing smooth meters and then roughening them on purpose.[23]

We have examined the metrical features of the poem in chapter 2. Ransom inverts the sensitive second and fourth feet; he also wrenches the accents:

The bitch bit off his arms at *the* el *bows*.

This handling of meter, far from proving distracting and irrelevant, supplies a prosodic tone that qualifies meaning. The wrenched accents allude to the metrical mannerisms of the popular ballads; the conflicts between meter and speech stress produce a rhythm that is itself "meaning."

If texture were ornamental, Ransom could have written

Captain Decatur rose up in his prime

and would have achieved, if we can buy Ransom's theory, only another kind of irrelevancy. The meaning the meter complements, and inter-acts with, is the poem's complex irony: the calculated discrepancy between Ransom's fable and the way he feels about it. The meter tips us off about the feeling. By itself the meter could not carry Ransom's many ironies; the archaic diction and syntax and the macabre humor of Captain Carpenter's gradual dismemberment place the poem at its proper aesthetic distance. Captain Carpenter's quest is simple and commendable; single-handedly, he sets out to rid the world of evil. Ransom judges the quest and finds it, all at once, quixotic, horrible, comic, and deeply touching. The ironies do not blunt Ransom's total judgment: Captain Carpenter deserves our admiration and pity. Irony allows compassion without mawkishness. Ransom's sophisticated met-rical manipulation—the "affective" contortions of the iambic line—infuses structure with texture and fits rhythm to feeling.

As deliberately metered as "Captain Carpenter," but without its textural eccentricities, is "The Equilibrists." Ransom counterpoints the meter in this poem but adheres to the metrical code of traditional syllable-stress meter. He uses every "allowable" metrical variation: the substitution of trochee for iamb; the double or Ionic foot; the hyper-metrical or "feminine" ending; the elision of two unstressed syllables to make up one metrical syllable.[24] Three selected stanzas exemplify all the possible departures:

Eyes talking: Never mind the cruel words,
Embrace my flowers, but not embrace the swords.
But what they said, the doves came straightway flying
And unsaid: Honor, Honor, they came crying.
But still I watched them spinning, orbited nice.
Their flames were not more radiant than their ice.
I dug in the quiet earth and wrought the tomb
And made these lines to memorize their doom:—

Epitaph

Equilibrists lie here; stranger, tread light;
Close, but untouching in each other's sight;
Mouldered the lips and ashy the tall skull,
Let them lie perilous and beautiful.

Lines 3 and 4 illustrate the feminine ending:

But whát | they sáid, | the dóves | came stráight | way flý | ing
And un | said: Hó | nor, Hó | nor, théy | came crý ing.

Lines 6 and 7 show trisyllabic feet that are theoretically elided in scansion:

Their flámes | were nót | more ra | di‿ant thán | their íce.
I dúg | in‿the quí | et eárth | and wróught | the tómb.

Lines 9 and 10 show inverted feet. The inversions, however, occur in the least sensitive positions—the first foot, and the foot after the caesura:

É qui | li brísts | lie hére; | strán ger, | tread líght;
Clóse, but | un tóuch | ing ín | each óth | er's síght.

The final couplet brings together initial inverted feet, the rising Ionic (fourth foot, line 11), and the rarer falling Ionic (second foot, line 12).

Móul dered | the líps | and á | shy the táll skúll,
Lét them | líe pe ri lous | and béau | ti fúl.

The last foot must be wrenched in scansion; in *reading* the line we would emphasize the prevailing falling rhythm.

Donne, "a great master of meters,"[25] is Ransom's master in this poem. Metrical technique echoes the poem's metaphysical dissonances: honor against desire, Heaven against Hell, fire against ice, love against death. Metrical variation opens a world of feelings, balanced and opposed. There is no violent strain between meter and meaning; but rather, we have lines where the meter releases rhythms as unsettling as Ransom's alternation of feelings: anger and frustration, pity and admiration, and finally, wonder and religious awe. Ransom protests that meter cannot imply meaning, but what do the "procession of strong monosyllables"[26] and the curious falling Ionic do in this line:

Till cold I words came I down spi ral from I the head

but provide a rhythm contextually appropriate to sense and feeling? Do not the five contiguous speech stresses "[open] up the possibilities of ambiguous meaning . . . and let [the reader] construe a meaning out of them, or a multiplicity of meanings?"[27]

Our last three citations come from Ransom's statement in the *Kenyon Review*'s symposium, "English Verse and What It Sounds Like" (summer 1956). He considerably modifies his earlier views. He abandons the structure-texture dichotomy and clearly sees meter as a crucial means of semantic emphasis: "But it is surprising how often the stress at a new place puts a new light on a given situation; or rather, looks at the situation from a new but quite possible perspective."[28] He no longer seems concerned that the poem's existence be fixed in hygienic isolation. He talks about rhythm, feeling, and emotion; about the poem's "human materials," and its "deliverance of an emotional burden." Rhythm is the marriage of the meter and the language.

At the close of our discussion of Ransom we grant him these last significant words. He is commenting on Arnold Stein's sensitive and brilliant readings of Milton's metric.[29] We are greatly mistaken if Ransom is not expounding, most eloquently and persuasively, the idea that prosody controls, modifies, and *signifies* emotive qualities in poetry:

[Arnold Stein] . . . takes three short passages from Milton, and within them he goes from line to line to show what the meter is trying to do with the human materials, always against resistance but eventually with success, till we have to say that it has had its way with them and transformed them. The action focuses technically upon the conflict between the natural prose stresses and the ideal metrical ones, but in every one of the picked passages a resolution or harmony is finally accomplished between the two orders. It is not a technical conflict only, as it might be if the game were being played just for sport. The prose stresses define the deliverance of an emotional burden, but the passion would be undelivered if the meter prevailed too easily over them. It wins gradually, so that in the end the passion is spent, the troubled spirit is serene; and is there an inclination to say that the human spirit has attained to a heavenly peace?[30]

IV

Nineteenth-Century Precursors

The nineteenth century has been described as an age of many stylizations but no definite style: an age in which artists experimented, "and the experimenters all had one purpose in mind: to find a style instead of trying to get along with parodies of style."[1] Nineteenth-century prosodic style departs from the strict iambic discipline of the neo-classic closed couplet and end-stopped blank verse. We find, as early as Blake, free use of trisyllabic and inverted feet; we also find in Blake's prophetic books a long line of varying syllabic length that moves away from syllable-stress metric toward newer freedoms.

The general prosody of Romantic and Victorian poetry strains but does not abrogate the syllable-stress tradition. Eclecticism flourishes; Tennyson and Browning, the Victorian Establishment, are linked together in academic contexts, but their prosodies are miles apart. If a prevailing nineteenth-century prosodic style exists, Saintsbury confesses it has eluded him:

> I have not attempted to sum up the general prosodic character of Mr. Swinburne and Mr. Morris, of Tennyson and Browning, even perhaps of Shelley and Keats. . . . I doubt whether the person is yet born—he is certainly not long out of his cradle—who can do this, or for many years will be able to do it. The perspective of the past is not yet firm enough for that.[2]

The nineteenth-century picture has become sharper, and for the viewer eighty years after Saintsbury, the perspective shows different relationships. The prosodies of Shelley, Tennyson, and Swinburne move toward a distant horizon; Blake, Whitman, Hopkins, and Browning are now in the foreground, recognized as crucial influences and important points of prosodic departure. The nineteenth century swung gradually away from the dominance of syllable-stress metric toward open rhythms. In our own prosodic age—post-Saintsbury—a spate of experimental prosodies has obscured the main streams of prosodical practice, but this seems clear: the nineteenth-century movement toward greater prosodical flexibility culminated in the "free verse" movements of the teens and twenties; with Auden in the early 1930s, and again through the work of several poets sometimes referred to as New Formalists in the 1980s, prosody once more stabilized itself in traditional metric.

Before we assay the prosodies of our contemporaries, we turn to Browning, Whitman, Dickinson, and Hopkins: poets who struggled against the English prosodic norm and who foreshadowed the revolt of the early twentieth century—the temporary dislodgment of the syllable-stress foot. Each of these poets arrived at a new prosody in ways important to later poets; each, though vaguely aware of the others' activities, found individual solutions. Browning, Whitman, Dickinson, and Hopkins are the ancestors whose progeny have increased and multiplied; the prosodical innovations of our age have their origins in their practice or influence.

❧ 1. Robert Browning

The "irregularities" in Browning's prosody dismayed his Victorian contemporaries, who were nurtured on Shelleyan and Tennysonian suavities. Yet Browning's verse scans according to the letter of metrical law. More objectionable than the supposed roughness of his metrical practice are the irritating rhythms that establish themselves in lines like these:

> At the midnight in the silence of the sleep-time,
>   When you set your fancies free . . .
>
> No, at noonday in the bustle of man's work-time
>   Greet the unseen with a cheer!
>
> *Asolando*

Such rhythmical tunes persist in memory long after critical discrimination rejects Browning's noisy and automatic optimism. These lines—

as many of Browning's do, when he is seized with the affirmative mood—*march* to a procession of strong equal stresses. That they march with equal boisterousness *in the silence of the sleep-time* and at noonday is a mark of Browning's prosodical insensitivity.

It is not, however, Browning's prosodical mannerisms but his handling of traditional blank verse that becomes important for modern poetry. In the famous dramatic monologues he took blank-verse measure and trimmed and stretched it to fit the rhythms of colloquial speech. The garrulous apology of "Mr. Sludge, the Medium" illustrates Browning's mature practice and the general tone of the later monologues. Mr. Sludge, a fraudulent spiritualist, has been nearly strangled by one of his victims:

> Well, if the marks seem gone,
> 'T is because stiffish cock-tail, taken in time,
> Is better for a bruise than arnica.
> There, sir! I bear no malice: 't is n't in me.
> I know I acted wrongly: still, I've tried
> What I could say in my excuse,—to show
> The devil's not all devil . . . I don't pretend,
> He's angel, much less such a gentleman
> As you, sir! And I've lost you, lost myself,
> Lost all-l-l-.

Browning intends American speech: the original "Sludge" was D. D. Home, a notorious American medium who had duped the credulous Mrs. Browning. After her death Browning published "Sludge." It is a savage attack—doubtlessly a release of Browning's suppressed rage and chagrin.

The lines show a wealth of strong rhetorical stresses and some anomalous feet:

> 'T is be | cause stif | fish cock- | tail, ta | ken in time . . .
>
> There, sir! | I bear | no ma | lice: 't is | n't in me.
>
> As you, | sir! And | I've lost | you, lost | my self.

The main departures from normal metrical procedure are the spondee (line 2, first foot) and the inverted second foot (line 3). But the rhythmical freedom of these lines does not issue from gross viola-

tion of metrical law; their suppleness is a matter of syntactical phras-
ing. Syntax tumbles and rushes along, combating the meter at
caesuras and the ends of lines:

> Well,
> if the marks seem gone,
> 'T is because stiffish cock-tail,
> taken in time,
> Is better for a bruise
> than arnica.
> There, sir!
> I bear no malice:
> 't is n't in me.
> I know I acted wrongly:
> still, I've tried
> What I could say in my excuse.

Browning breaks up the line into short speech periods; the effect, in
working against the persistent meter, is taut and hesitant.

The practice of multiplying the number of caesuras in the blank-
verse line—actually, a process of rhetorical fragmentation—increases
in Browning's later work. In *The Ring and the Book* (1868–69) we find
lines broken by as many as four heavy pauses:

> To stop song, loosen flower, and leave path.
>   Law . . .
>
> You were wrong, you see: that's well to see,
>   though late . . .
>
> There, I was born, have lived, shall die, a fool!

Caponsacchi

A complete passage from *The Ring and the Book* reveals a metric that is
prophetic; we find here the early Pound and Eliot:

> Oh, though first comer, though as strange at the work
> As fribble must be, coxcomb, fool that's near
> To knave as, say, a priest who fears the world—
> Was he bound brave the peril, save the doomed,

Or go on, sing his snatch and pluck his flower,
Keep the straight path and let the victim die?
I held so; you decided otherwise,
Saw no such peril, therefore no such need
To stop song, loosen flower, and leave path. Law,
Law was aware and watching, would suffice,
Wanted no priest's intrusion, palpably
Pretence, too manifest a subterfuge!

Caponsacchi

The meter is frequently counterpointed; some heavily stressed lines bear a superficial resemblance to Hopkins:

Wás he | boúnd bráve | the pér | il, sáve | the doómed . . .
To stóp | sóng, loós | en flówer, | and leáve | páth. Láw . . .

We have Hopkins-like distortion of grammar ("bound brave the peril"), and much spondaic springing. The lines are metrically precarious, but Browning always recovers the meter at the point when it seems ready to dissolve in the uncontrolled excitement of passionate speech.

Eliot protests—too loudly we think—that Pound's verse and his own owe nothing to Whitman.[3] Possum-like, he is less explicit about Browning's influence on their prosodies. On superficial examination these lines appear as "free" as the *Song of Myself*:

"My nerves are bad to-night. Yes, bad. Stay with me.
"Speak to me. Why do you never speak. Speak.
"What are you thinking of? What thinking? What?
"I never know what you are thinking. Think."

The Waste Land

But scansion shows their metrical structure: a jazzing of the normal blank-verse line:

"Spéak to | me. Whý | do you né | ver spéak. | Spéak.
"Whát are | you thínk | ing óf? | What thínk | ing? Whát?

Rhythmic character here is determined by the same nervous hesitancies, the expressive pauses within the line, that we found in Browning.

ᴥ *II. Walt Whitman*

Whitman's prosody shows no development from traditional syllable-stress metric. It is our first great *nonmetrical* prosody in English, relying on the various techniques of enumeration, syntactical parallelism, and (Hopkins's term) "figures of grammar" to shape words to rhythm. Eliot tells us that Whitman is a great prose writer. Eliot is mistaken; the formal bases of Whitman's prosody are as open to analysis as those traditional meters. We must remember, however, that the scansion of stressed and unstressed syllables has no relevance to Whitman's prosody (as traditional scansion has no relevance to the later poems in sprung rhythm by Hopkins). Occasionally Whitman's lines fall into scannable hexameters, but their rhythmic base is not provided by a pattern of metrical feet. The proof of this is the total absence of counterpointing, or syncopation, in Whitman's verse. Nowhere in Whitman do we find the jazzing that we have shown in the lines from Eliot. Jazzing is possible only against a distinctly felt pattern of metrical expectancy—as in the syncopations of jazz that contradict with predictable irregularity a steady pulse in double or common time.

It may seem that we belabor the obvious in insisting that Pound and Eliot are not heirs to Whitman's prosody. Or to be more accurate: they did not find, as young poets, Whitman's rhythms appropriate to their tone and subject. The monotony of Prufrock's life could not be imaged in the long, open cadences of *Out of the Cradle;* his boredom and triviality are all of a more contemporary piece, neatly rendered in a tetrameter couplet:

> In the room the women come and go
> Talking of Michelangelo.

Whitman's prosody is formal and ceremonious. Despite his occasional and misguided attempts to use what he thought was common speech, Whitman's diction is part of a self-conscious literary dialect born of the great rhetorical orators of the nineteenth century. His proper mode is not speech but invocation; not conversation, but chant and ceremony. Significantly enough, we catch echoes of the Whitmanian hexameter in Eliot's later liturgical music:

> I do not know much about gods; but I think that the river
> Is a strong brown god—sullen, untamed and intractable.

Robert Graves gleefully believes that Eliot is here "true to a boyhood's admiration for Longfellow's *Evangeline*."[4] Our impulse is more accurate: the music of *Four Quartets* is closer to Whitman than Longfellow.

Whitman's revolution in prosody was so simple and complete that it has never been properly assessed. Whitman did not fuss about his innovations in technique, as did Hopkins who agonized over every stress and syllable; consequently the theorists have left Whitman's prosody untouched.[5] Whitman's basic contribution was the substitution of syntax for meter as the controlling prosodic element in his poetry. The syllable-stress foot has no primary function in Whitman's verse, although these feet occur frequently enough as decorative but never as integral parts of rhythmic structure. The primary rhythms of Whitman's verse are all the various functions of syntax.

This leaves us with Donald Davie's contention that Whitman may belong with those poets who exploit "syntax like music."[6] Davie points out that certain modern poets, especially those who came under the influence of Symbolism, abandoned the logical forms of grammar and attempted to articulate the *feelings of an experience* without clearly defining the experience. A celebrated example of "syntax like music" occurs in Eliot's "Gerontion":

> In the juvescence of the year
> Came Christ the tiger

> In depraved May, dogwood and chestnut, flowering judas,
> To be eaten, to be divided, to be drunk
> Among whispers; by Mr. Silvero . . .

> By Hakagawa, bowing among the Titians;
> By Madame de Tornquist, in the dark room
> Shifting the candles; Fraulein von Kulp
> Who turned in the hall, one hand on the door.

If we scrutinize the grammar of these lines with any care, we see there are numerous ambiguities of reference, modification, and sentence structure. Do the eating and drinking of Christ (or is it the flowering judas that is consumed?) refer to actual communion or to mere symbolic participation in a meaningless act? Who are the characters in this drama? Where did they come from; why are they doing the things they are doing? Did Fraulein von Kulp invite Mr. Silvero into her room; or is it only a passing thought that made her hesitate before she closed her door? Only feeling, given its form by the movement of syntax, is clearly articulated in these lines; the experience that generated the feeling is left vague and undefined. We sense mystery, fraud, a general unwholesome quality—without ever knowing exactly what Madame de Tornquist was doing in the darkened room, or why Hakagawa was bowing among the Titians rather than among the El Grecos.

Like music these lines affect the reader by movement of sound; they offer the structure of feeling without denoting the human problems that gave rise to the feelings. John Ashbery and his legion of imitators are the obvious contemporary inheritors of this practice, though none has ever achieved the density and urgency of emotion packed into the lines above. They fail because they assume (with more than a little late-century arrogance?) that the pattern is all-inclusive, allowing in and accommodating any thought that comes to the writer's mind. The result is prosodic overkill, windy passages consumed by inane asides, boring prose. Music, however, is the art that deals with emotion in the abstract; the joy or agony we feel when we listen to music is never an explicit joy or agony. By suppressing the logical forms of grammar and blurring the edges of experience, Eliot achieves a quasi-musical effect. Syntax, the very form of thought, becomes a means for conveying feeling. Rhythm tends to become autonomous and separate itself from the rational structure of the poem.

Musical syntax is an important element in the newer prosodies. Whitman first discovered its resources and showed how much could be done to communicate feeling by manipulating the order of words. Violence must be committed on grammar to produce syntactic rhythm and its attendant music, but like the "organized violence" of meter, it is often salutary mayhem. The most important single device in Whitman's prosody is syntactical parallelism; each line comprises a rhythmical unit whose grammar is precisely echoed in subsequent lines (the following examples are all taken from "When Lilacs Last in the Dooryard Bloom'd"):

As I stood on the rising ground in the breeze in the cool
    transparent night,
As I watch'd where you pass'd and was lost in the netherward
    black of the night,
As my soul in its trouble dissatisfied sank, as where you sad orb,
Concluded, dropt in the night, and was gone.

The order of words is formal, spun from the pulpit or podium; rhythm rises to the last line and then quietly falls with the western star. Whitman uses various and intricate forms of parallel techniques. We find numerous passages in anaphora:

Coffin that passes through lanes and streets,
Through day and night with the great cloud darkening
    the land,
With the pomp of the inloop'd flags with the cities draped
    in black,
With the show of the States themselves as of crape-veil'd
    women standing,
With processions long and winding and the flambeaus
    of the night,
With the countless torches lit, with the silent sea of faces and
    the unbared heads . . .

The passage in which these lines are set is grammatically elliptical: a sentence is begun, continued with great rhetorical sonority, but never completed. Each line is a solemn rhythm, and the syntax controls the prosody without relating one line to the next. The structure that holds the lines together is a logic of feeling, not the "authentic syntax"[7] that can follow the silent rhythm of human thought itself. Whitman's syntax exerts no intellectual control; it functions nearly exclusively as prosody, creating and organizing rhythmic structure. Whitman chose to showcase little narrative talent: to tell a story usually requires the traditional close syntax and some conscious ordering of human experience into intelligible relationships.

    We shall note two other features of Whitman's prosodical method. First, the technique of enumeration. Again the passage shows ellipsis; Whitman makes music with the order of words:

Lo, the most excellent sun so calm and haughty,
The violet and purple morn with just-felt breezes,
The gentle soft-born measureless light,
The miracle spreading bathing all, the fulfill'd noon,
The coming eve delicious, the welcome night and the stars,
Over my cities shining all, enveloping man and land.

We have no comfortable syntax at all, nor is any necessary to render Whitman's impression of the growing and then fading day. Feeling is all. Our last example of syntactical rhythm shows Whitman gradually expanding, then contracting the line:

And I saw askant the armies,
I saw as in noiseless dreams hundreds of battle-flags,
Borne through the smoke of the battles and pierc'd with
    missiles I saw them,
And carried hither and yon through the smoke, and torn
    and bloody,
And at last but a few shreds left on the staffs, (and all
    in silence,)
And the staffs all splinter'd and broken.

The danger of Whitman's method is that it persuades many who command rhetoric into believing that they command a prosody. We may think of Sandburg, or of contemporary examples such as the middle and late work of Allen Ginsberg, the writing of Gerald Stern, and a host of less visible (but no less present) magazine scribes. Rhetoric and the music of syntax can simulate prosody, giving us the illusion of feeling when the poet is only pretending emotion. Our objection to Poe's "The Raven" centers on its meaningless metric with its appalling double meters and insistent repetitions. The result is a simulacrum of feeling, aimless gesture, howl. Whitman's nonmetrical prosody is as capable of doggerel as Poe's metronome. Neither the restraint of a rigidly imposed metrical form nor the freedom of syntactical cadence can guarantee a prosody that quickens language with rhythmic purpose.

ᵅ III. *Emily Dickinson*

If the irregularities in Browning's prosody dismayed his contemporaries, the eccentricities in Dickinson's mystified hers. Reclusive, ironic, coy, mysterious—all describe this poet who published only seven poems (and those anonymously) in her lifetime. And yet, with Whitman she stands today as our most important and influential precursor. Thomas H. Johnson described how Dickinson adapted traditional meters found in her New England hymnal "to her own requirements of suppleness and variety, retardment and acceleration."[8]

> There's a certain Slant of light, (7 syllables)
> Winter Afternoons— (5)
> That oppresses, like the Heft (7)
> Of Cathedral Tunes— (5)
>
> Heavenly Hurt, it gives us— (7)
> We can find no scar, (5)
> But internal difference, (7)
> Where the Meanings, are— (5)
>
> None may teach it—Any— (6)
> 'Tis the Seal Despair— (5)
> An imperial affliction (7 or 8)
> Sent us of the Air— (5)
>
> When it comes, the Landscape listens— (8)
> Shadows—hold their breath— (5)
> When it goes, 'tis like the Distance (8)
> On the look of Death— (5)
>
> "258"

In this poem, and indeed throughout Dickinson's work, syntax is everything, syntax as ordering agent and engine propelling meditative speculation to a somber, yet oddly comforting, conclusion. Variety is injected through key distortions of the syllable count, capital letters (for emphasis), dashes governing the poem's pacing much as the placement of musical notes determines a score, and omission of words ("Sent us of the Air"). The anapest and iambs of the first line whisk us into the poem, but we are swiftly reined in by the headless, emphatic "Winter afternoons." We experience the dismal weight and gloom of that overcast day; our physical uneasiness finds a spiritual locus, the "Heavenly Hurt" the scene inspires. Our speculation deepens, bringing us almost in view of a definite answer, but the surprising caesura in the middle of line 8's last foot interrupts our progress, slowing us down in preparation for the emphatic line with its extra syllable, "None may teach it—Any." The answer, of course, is that there *is* no answer, no ultimate grasping of "An imperial affliction." There is, however, endurance and quiet counsel, awareness that the landscape that listens and holds its breath also includes us. Most of the abrupt halts and word omissions are dropped in the final stanza's perfectly parallel syllabics and grammar, in keeping with the formal exhalation that accompanies acceptance. Few poets have so dramatically harnessed feeling to form.

In a sense, Dickinson set out in her prosodic mission to dismantle traditional metrics. But unlike Hopkins, she remained inside tradition's framework, reinventing it from within. Through innovations in rhyme, emphasis, and syntactical arrangement, she restored vigor to patterns that had long been abused by pedestrian practitioners.

> There is a solitude of space
> A solitude of sea
> A solitude of death, but these
> Society shall be
> Compared with that profounder site
> That polar privacy
> A soul admitted to itself—
> Finite infinity.
>
> "1695"

Baldly reduced, this exquisite expression of Know Thyself, presented in a syllable count of alternating eights and sixes, achieves its integrity through parallelism (lines 2, 3, and 7), relative lack of punctuation (but for critical moments of pause and transition), full rhyme, and key word choice unique to the vocabulary Dickinson brings to her poetry. "That polar privacy" defines to perfection the isolated condition of spiritual loneliness in the moment of total self-awareness. The expression of this existential view, as much as her bold, prosodic innovations, has made Dickinson increasingly important to modern and postmodern writers.

ᴈᴖ *IV. Gerard Manley Hopkins*

Hopkins, like Whitman, violated "prosodic nature" and originated a rhythmic form that cannot be scanned by syllable and foot. Long after Hopkins had died, but a decade before his influence was even vaguely felt, Saintsbury was aware of his troubled and troubling spirit:

> Speaking prosodically, not of general poetry or literature, I do not know that Mr. Stevenson's verse requires special notice. Much more might be given to that of Father Gerard Hopkins, if it were not that, as his friend Mr. Bridges (who knew him long after I had lost sight of him, and with whose ideas on prosody he was much more in agreement than with mine) admits, he never got his notions into thorough writing-order. They belonged to the anti-foot and pro-stress division. But, even if it were not for old things and days, it would be unfair to criticize lines like
>
> > I want the one rapture of an inspiration
> >> [from the sonnet "To R. B."]
>
> —which you can, of course, scan, but where "one" seems to be thrust in out of pure mischief—or many others. He never published any; and it is quite clear that all were experiments.[9]

Since Hopkins's experiments in prosody have been so generally acknowledged as clear triumphs, and these triumphs loudly and with great confusion trumpeted to a prosodically naive world, it is refreshing to hear a slightly skeptical voice. Saintsbury touches, albeit briefly, on three major points: that Hopkins was engaged in experimentation; that his prosody "belonged to the anti-foot and pro-stress division"; that Hopkins was not above deliberate metrical distortion.

The experimental nature of Hopkins's prosody has given rise to much confused and contradictory theorizing. Consider the chewed-over matter of sprung rhythm. Paul F. Baum comes to the exasperated conclusion that "Sprung Rhythm is not a form of verse, to be scanned by feet, but a form of Prose Rhythm not amenable to scansion and therefore not to be explained as verse."[10] We partially agree. Hopkins's most sophisticated sprung rhythm cannot be scanned as syllable-stress meter; its prosodic character is nonmetrical. Hopkins drew a red herring of theory across the track of his achievements; he insisted that the nonmetrical form of sprung rhythm might be scanned from the strong syllable. Indeed, it can be, but so can any passage of rhythmical prose. In the poems in developed sprung rhythm, Hopkins discards the metrical foot and works with rhetorical rather than metrical units. We would not, however, say that Hopkins's poetry cannot be explained as verse. The bases of his prosody rest on complex matters of descent and development.

"Springing," as a metrical effect in English verse, probably owes its origin to early confusions between the older strong-stress meters and the post-Chaucerian syllable-stress meters. Measuring the line of verse, simply by counting the strong stresses and letting the unstressed syllables shift for themselves, was the native metrical tradition. The later syllable-stress meters eventually replaced the falling rhythms of accentual prosodies with the characteristic iambic—a rising rhythm. We find early verses that ambiguously teeter between strong-stress and syllable-stress metric:

> Old Mother Hubbard
> Went to her cupboard
>   To fetch her poor dog a bone
> But when she came there
> The cupboard was bare
>   And so the poor dog had none.

These lines do not scan comfortably. The rhyming couplets fall into strong-stress meter:

> Óld Mother Húbbard ‖ Wént to her cúpboard . . .
> But whén she came thére ‖ The cúpboard was báre.

Yet clearly there are metrical feet in the third and sixth lines:

> To fétch her póor dóg a bóne . . .
> And só the póor dóg had nóne.

How do these feet arrange themselves: do we have an iamb, an ana-
pest, and an iamb, in this distribution:

To fetch | her poor dog | a bone?

Mother Hubbard had not made up her metrical mind. Two principles
cross each other; the falling rhythm of "Old Mother Hubbard / Went
to her cupboard" is contradicted by "To fetch her poor dog a bone."

One kind of sprung rhythm results when the older stress metric
intrudes upon the "prosodic norm," or conventional syllable-stress
meter. This happens frequently in our poetry; a fine example is the
line quoted earlier from Yeats:

Speech af | ter long | sil | ence; it | is right.

Yvor Winters gives a similar example from Wyatt:

With na | ked foot, | stalk | ing in | my cham | ber.[11]

In both cases we have a monosyllabic foot in the third position.

In his poems in sprung rhythm, Hopkins makes this intrusion of
stress metric a deliberate principle of composition. Wyatt and Yeats
were composing in syllable-stress meter, and the crowding of accents
disturbs but does not shatter the metrical norm. Hopkins allows so
many heavy stresses to enter the normal syllable-stress line that even-
tually he writes a new metric. Sprung rhythm is not a sudden or consis-
tent development in Hopkins, nor is it sufficient to say that Hopkins
revives Old English meter and measures his verses by strong stresses
and dipodies. Like Old Mother Hubbard, individual poems scan
equally well as stress verse or syllable-stress verse:

INVERSNAID
This darksome burn, horseback brown,
His rollrock highroad roaring down,
In coop and in comb the fleece of his foam
Flutes and low to the lake falls home.

The rhythm is sprung because the lines contain stresses that cannot be
comfortably counted in normal scansion; we may rationalize them as
monosyllabic "feet":

> This da̍rk | some bu̍rn, ‖ ho̍rse back | bro̍wn . . .
> Flu̍tes | and lo̍w ‖ to the la̍ke | fa̍lls home.

Of course we may read these lines as stress verse pure and simple. We find the pronounced medial caesura, the four strong beats, and the alliteration that characterize the Old English meter.

Whether we measure these lines as syllable-stress or strong-stress meter, they are clearly metrical. Hopkins's poems in his characteristic, fully developed sprung rhythm move away from measured verse and into nonmetrical prosody. He arrived at his "new rhythm" through the native tradition of stress metric, through musical analogies, and by extending the practice of springing the line until all traces of syllable-stress meter vanish. "The Windhover," "Spelt from Sibyl's Leaves," or these fragments ("Ash-boughs"),

> Not of a̍ll my eyes see, wandering on the world,
>
> Is anything a milk to the mind so, so sighs deep
>
> Poetry to̍ it, as a tree whose boughs break in the sky

represent the most sophisticated form of sprung rhythm; they defy scansion as syllable-stress meter unless we are willing to admit into traditional metrical paradigms wholesale and indiscriminate use of the monosyllabic foot, paeons, and other anomalous structures.

To understand Hopkins's practice of sprung rhythm, we must make distinctions beyond those he makes in his author's preface. Sprung rhythm is obviously a matter of degree and a name given to a number of different prosodical techniques. Hopkins is himself not clear about his practice. He distorts the metrical base of "Spring and Fall" by placing inappropriate speech stresses on metrically unstressed syllables:

> Ma̍rgare̍t, are you gri̍eving
>
> Over Goldengrove unleaving?
>
> Le̍aves, li̍ke the things of man, you
>
> With your fresh thoughts care for, can you?
>
> A̍h! a̍s the heart grows older
>
> It will come to such sights colder.

Do we understand that Hopkins means us to say, "*Mar ge ret,* are you grieving . . . / *Ah! as* the heart grows older"? If so, Hopkins could not distinguish between metrical pattern and highly idiosyncratic reading. Despite Hopkins's markings, the lines are not sprung but trochees and dactyls in alternate trimeter and tetrameter:

> Mar ga ret, | are you | griev ing
>
> Ov er | Gol den | grove un | leav ing?
>
> Leaves, like the | things of | man, you
>
> With your | fresh thoughts | care for, | can you?

There is considerable evidence that Hopkins gave assent to the performative heresy. He was eager that poetry be reinstated as a spoken art: "above all remember what applies to all my verse, that it is, as living art should be, made for performance and that its performance is not reading with the eye."[12] Hopkins confuses the speaking of verse with meter, rhetorical stressing with basic structure. In his search for "instress" and "inscape," for rhythmic forms to express his excitements and exultations, he violates a simple meter. The result is not greater expressiveness but a puzzling dramatic distortion.

Hopkins's preface does not distinguish between metrical and nonmetrical sprung rhythm; we must deduce from his practice that poems as prosodically dissimilar as "The Wreck of the Deutschland" and "The Leaden Echo and the Golden Echo" embody different principles of versification. "The Wreck of the Deutschland" is composed in intricate strong-stress meter. Analogous lines in an expanding stanza contain identical numbers of stresses; composition is consistent throughout the poem, and the verse, though sprung, is metered:

Stresses per line	4
2	I am soft sift
3	In an hourglass—at the wall
4	Fast, but mined with a motion, a drift,
3	And it crowds and it combs to the fall;
5	I steady as a water in a well, to a poise, to a pane,
5	But roped with, always, all the way down from the tall

4   Félls or flánks of the vóel, a véin

6   Of the góspel próffer, a préssure, a prínciple, Chríst's gíft.

                                            6

2   Not óut of blíss

3   Spríngs the stréss félt

4   Nor fírst from héaven (and féw know thís)

3   Swíngs the stróke déalt—

5   Stróke and a stréss that stárs and stórms delíver,

5   That guílt is húshed by, héarts are flúshed by and mélt—

4   But it rídes tíme like ríding a ríver

6   (And hére the fáithful wáver, the fáithless fáble and míss).

We cannot, of course, scan these lines by feet; Hopkins is not think-
ing in syllable-stress meter, but in numbers of stresses per line. There is
no interplay between the precise expectations of foot prosody and
rhetorical stress; in sprung rhythm we find that close coincidence of
rhetorical and prosodical pattern that obtains in Old English verse.

Hopkins meters "The Wreck of the Deutschland" on stress prin-
ciples. "The Leaden Echo and the Golden Echo" has no metrical base.
Its prosody is close to Whitman's practice; rhythmic periods are
defined by syntactical arrangement, repetitions, and musical imita-
tion. Here is the coda of the "Golden Echo":

O then, weary then why should we tread? O why are we
    so haggard at heart, so care-coiled, care-killed, so fagged,
    so fashed, so cogged, so cumbered,
When the thing we freely forfeit is kept with fonder a care,
Fonder a care kept than we could have kept it, kept
Far with fonder a care (and we, we should have lost it) finer,
        fonder
A care kept.—Where kept? Do but tell us where kept, where.—
Yonder,—What high as that! We follow, now we follow.—
    Yonder, yes yonder, yonder,
Yonder.

Sound overrides sense as words serve as abstract musical structures; the movement of words is obviously meant to suggest the slowly fading echo. Gertrude Stein comes to mind; but more insistently, the end of "Anna Livia Plurabelle," composed by another poet who brought musical method to bear on English prosody:

> Night! Night! My ho head halls. I feel as heavy as yonder stone. Tell me of John or Shaun? Who were Shem and Shaun the living sons or daughters of? Night now! Tell me, tell me, tell me, elm! Night night! Telmetale of stem or stone. Beside the rivering waters of, hitherandthithering waters of. Night![13]

Joyce's "prose" can be scanned according to strong-stress principles:

> Níght! Níght! ‖ My ho héad hálls.
> I féel as héavy ‖ as yón der stóne.
> Whó were Shém and Sháun
> the líving sóns ‖ or dáughters óf?

Which brings us full circle. Hopkins has told us, in so many words, that sprung rhythm can be rhythmic prose: "Sprung Rhythm is the most natural of things . . . it is the rhythm of common speech and written prose, when rhythm is perceived in them." To dichotomize prose and verse, however, compounds confusion; I call sprung rhythm one of the many kinds of modern nonmetrical prosodies. Thus we can see that Hopkins's experiments parallel Whitman's assault on syllable-stress metric. Unlike Whitman, Hopkins broke down traditional metric by counterpointing and intruding upon it lines built on strong-stress principles. We can see the gradual disintegration of syllable-stress metric in these examples, selected from the twenty-year period of Hopkins's development:

> Elected Silence, sing to me
> And beat upon my whorlèd ear.
> "The Habit of Perfection," 1866

Lovely the woods, waters, meadows, combes, vales,
All the air things wear that build this world of Wales.
"In the Valley of the Elwy," 1877

Not, I'll not, carrion comfort, Despair, not feast on thee;
Not untwist—slack they may be—these last strands of man
In me o̍r, most weary, cry *I can no more.* I can.
"Carrion Comfort," 1885

Earnest, earthless, equal, attunable, vaulty, voluminous, . . .
    stupendous
Evening strains to be time's vast, womb-of-all, home-of-all,
    hearse-of-all night.
"Spelt from Sibyl's Leaves," 1885

Yes I can tell such a key, I do know such a place,
Where whatever's prized and passes of us, everything
    that's fresh and fast flying of us, seems to us, sweet of us and
    swiftly away with, done away with, done away with, undone . . .
"The Golden Echo," 1882

"The Habit of Perfection" scans as regular iambic tetrameter. The lines from "In the Valley of the Elwy" are strongly counterpointed; the second line should be noted for its spondee and monosyllabic foot:

Áll | the aír | things wéar | that búild | this wórld | of Wáles.

The next three examples are not amenable to foot scansion. "Carrion Comfort" is perhaps closest to traditional metric with its strongly varied hexameter lines. The last two examples are prosodically nonmetrical: sprung rhythm in its characteristic form.

ᨠ v. Toward the Twentieth Century

Browning, Whitman, Dickinson, and Hopkins forecast the four major prosodic developments of the modern period. Though now we can see them more clearly as influences, they established no schools, attracted no immediate disciples. Whitman's effect has been so various and far-reaching that it is nearly impossible to assess. Dickinson and

Hopkins had no impact on modern poetry until the late 1920s and early 1930s. It is true that Pound caught Browning's rhythms and owes much to Browning's adaptation of blank verse to modern speech. But our four Victorians were prophets, rather than practical reformers; their prosodies point a way rather than specify a program. Poets who start from the basic iambic, who, in expanding or tightening traditional meter, work toward looser rhythms, descend from Browning. Poets who compose to the music of syntactical arrangement, who pursue "the figure of grammar," follow Whitman; those who would distort that figure, staying with the lines yet turning their rhythm inside out, follow Dickinson. And those poets whose rhythm is marked by the energy of strong stressing are the spiritual, if not actual, heirs of Hopkins.

Our convenient categories do not account for all modern prosodies; the webs of practice are a tangle of individual development and often untraceable influence. Eliot knew Pound and had read Browning; his prosody changed after he came to Europe, but some of its essentials were worked out while he was still an undergraduate at Harvard. Pound himself was wildly eclectic, blown about in the winds of his shifting enthusiasms. Yet the main streams of modern prosody flow in the directions indicated by our Victorian ancestors. Despite all the smoke screens of propaganda thrown up by Pound, he and Eliot start from traditional meter. Pound began as a disciple of Provence and assimilated the colloquial iambics of Browning to the complex Provençal patterns. Whitman is the source of most contemporary "free verse." Even the imagists, who maintained a strict policy of non-recognition toward Whitman, often based their rhythms on the principles of syntactical parallelism.

Free verse is still the prosodist's most troublesome term. It frequently designates prosodic fads or gaucheries: certain kinds of imagistic vers libre, Whitmanized prose, bad iambic pentameter. Many readers link free verse with particular subject matter and associate unscannable poetry with atheism and anarchism. Since our aim is to provide categories of technical distinction and historical descent, we might better avoid *free verse* as a generic term and speak rather of *nonmetrical prosody.* *Nonmetrical prosody* has social and political neutrality; we should be able to say that one writes nonmetrically without implying anything about the poet's politics or sex life. *Nonmetrical* also possesses technical neutrality; we need not think of a nonmetrical poet as an anarchist of poetic form. And by the nineties of our benighted century, *free verse* and *free-verse* poet are irrevocably dated. To the young of 1910, *free verse* was written by international eccentrics who had the air of danger and privilege about every aspect of their lives and work; today's young often begin with the assumption that everyone writes free verse. Not that it is always easy to make distinctions; we have quasi-metrical prosody, such as Delmore Schwartz's:

IN THE NAKED BED, IN PLATO'S CAVE

In the naked bed, in Plato's cave,
Reflected headlights slowly slid the wall,
Carpenters hammered under the shaded window,
Wind troubled the window curtains all night long,
A fleet of trucks strained uphill, grinding,
Their freights covered, as usual.
The ceiling lightened again, the slanting diagram
Slid slowly forth.

These lines are set to a highly varied but unmistakable blank-verse rhythm; they recall the energetic forward motion and sudden compressions of "Gerontion." Although Schwartz's lines "are as well written as good prose," they no more resemble prose than these:

We hear the earth and the all-day rasp of the grasshoppers:
It was we laid the steel on this land from ocean to ocean:
It was we (if you know) put the U.P. through the passes . . .

It was we did it: hunkies of our kind:
It was we dug the caved-in holes for cold-water:
It was we built the gully spurs and the freight sidings.
        Archibald MacLeish, "Frescoes for Mr. Rockefeller's City"

Behind Schwartz's lines stand the practice of Eliot and ultimately Browning and the Jacobean dramatists; MacLeish's prosody here is 100 percent American with its end-stopped lines, repeated syntax, and primitive-sounding enumerations—Whitman *redivivus*.

Nonmetrical prosody appears in many forms: modified traditional metric, Whitmanesque syntactical cadence, fractured and emphatic fragmentation, and Hopkinsesque sprung rhythm. Modern poets will

mix their prosodic modes; Auden combines strong-stress and iambic
in these lines:

> Doom is dark and deeper than any sea-dingle:
> Upon what man it fall
> In spring, day-wishing flowers appearing,
> Avalanche sliding, white snow from rock-face,
> That he should leave this house . . .

Pound experimented with a number of nonmetrical prosodies, but
his free verse approaches a quantitative norm. His line always carefully
measured and weighed syllabic durations—before he gave up prosody
for economics. In the lines below, the rhythms are controlled by a
musician's sense of syllabic length:

> DANCE FIGURE
>
> Dark eyed,
> O woman of my dreams,
> Ivory sandalled,
> There is none like thee among the dancers,
> None with swift feet.
>
> I have not found thee in the tents,
> In the broken darkness.
> I have not found thee at the well-head
> Among the women with pitchers.

Pound's ear for quantity has been justly celebrated; but we must also
recognize the parallelisms or "rhythmic constants" of the Authorized
Version:

> I have not found . . .
> In the . . .
> I have not found . . .
> Among the . . .

We examined in chapter 3 some of the great modern poetry written
in traditional metric. We turn now to the aggressively and subtly "mod-
ern" prosodies. Much twentieth-century verse (though not necessarily
the best) does not turn on the armature of syllable-stress meter. Some

of it seems without immediate prosodical ancestry; the visual rhythms of the imagists, Language poets, and others strike the analyst as unprecedented technical innovation—until one takes a historical bearing and remembers the pattern poems of the Metaphysicals or the arguments of the Russian theorists. But a prosody need not be nonmetrical to be modern. Traditional metric, to be sure, is foot measured; however, modern prosodies may be measured by strong-stress and syllabic count. Since 1912 we have witnessed myriad attempts to energize language with new rhythms; we have heard and seen a spate of new prosodies: some strict, some "free," some berserk. Time allows us to see that if experimentation with nonmetrical prosodies has led into blind alleys, it has also opened out into wildly beautiful landscapes and pleasant meadows.

V

Imagism and Visual Prosody

What we ordinarily think of as "modernist poetry" begins with the imagist movement. Details of the movement's history and politics need not concern us here; we discover a zeal for poetic reform and experimentation tangled in a mesh of self-advertisement and energetic feuding. Critical opinion has been cautious about the leading personalities of imagism and who contributed what to theory and practice. Eighty years later, three figures emerge from the fog obscuring forgotten controversy. T. E. Hulme the idea man; Ezra Pound the public-relations man; Amy Lowell the business manager. Around this trinity is clustered a host of names, angels of greater and lesser brightness. H.D., D. H. Lawrence, F. S. Flint, John Gould Fletcher; even Yeats and T. S. Eliot were known, willingly and unwillingly, and at one time or another, as imagists.

Wide divergence exists between imagist theory and practice. The poetry published in the four imagist anthologies (1914–17) and the critical principles, issued like military commands in the various forewords and manifestos, scarcely make up a body of coherent doctrine and practice. Imagism was not a school of poetry but a visitation of the Zeitgeist; like all spectral phenomena, it soon faded after its first exciting appearances. But during the brief period of imagism's active life, modern poetry developed two of its leading conventions: the use of precise, sometimes startling images, and the programmatic use of the nonmetrical prosodies.

The imagists were loud propagandists for vers libre, though there was considerable disagreement about exactly what made vers libre. In one of his earliest pronouncements, Pound offers a famous musical analogy: "As regarding rhythm: to compose in sequence of the musical phrase, not in sequence of the metronome."[1] Pound later urges upon the would-be poet the intensive study of music to develop his sense of duration: the relative time values of syllabic length. Hulme also recommends free verse, but for reasons contradictory to those Pound advances.

Hulme believes the essence of the new poetry lies in the visual: "This new verse resembles sculpture rather than music; it appeals to the eye rather than to the ear."[2] Free verse, Hulme argues, is less musical than metered verse; for this reason it should carry the new poetry. The crudity of Hulme's thought is revealed in his speculations on meter and verse:

> I quite admit that poetry intended to be recited must be written in regular metre, but I contend that this method of recording impressions by visual images in distinct lines does not require the old metric system.
>
> The older art was originally a religious incantation: it was made to express oracles and maxims in an impressive manner, and rhyme and metre were used as aids to the memory. But why, for this new poetry, should we keep a mechanism which is only suited to the old?
>
> The effect of rhythm, like that of music, is to produce a kind of hypnotic state, during which suggestions of grief or ecstasy are easily and powerfully effective, just as when we are drunk all jokes seem funny. This is for the art of chanting, but the procedure of the new visual art is just the contrary. It depends for its effect not on a kind of half sleep produced, but on arresting the attention, so much so that the succession of visual images should exhaust one.
>
> Regular metre to this impressionist poetry is cramping, jangling, meaningless, and out of place. Into the delicate pattern of images and colour it introduces the heavy, crude pattern of rhetorical verse.[3]

Hulme's major heresy, which has been of considerable consequence to subsequent poetry and poetics, inheres in his belief that poetry must be primarily "this method of recording visual images in distinct lines." Hulme goes so far as to deny that sound is the basic material of verse. "This material . . . of Aristotle, is image and not sound. It builds up a plastic image which it hands over to the reader, whereas the old art endeavoured to influence him physically by the hypnotic effect of rhythm."[4] Hulme's insensitivity to music—Michael Roberts reports, "It seemed to him time spent in listening to music would have been better spent in conversation"[5]—and his overwhelming interest in painting and sculpture must be partly responsible for Hulme's indifference to sound values in poetry. Hulme talks of poetry as if it were a spatial and not a temporal art. This confusion about the basic material of poetry—language, which is organized sound moving in time—dismisses prosody as of no central importance in poetic structure.

Many poets, such as e. e. cummings and the Pound of the later Cantos, explored the poetry of a purely visual surface, but it did not require a Hulme to call attention to vers libre; vers libre and modern French poetry had thoroughly permeated the pre–World War I atmosphere. The impact of symbolist and later French poetry had been everywhere felt: by Eliot at Harvard, by Hulme and Pound in Europe. Hulme observed that it was vers libre itself that released and stimulated the extraordinary French poetic activity during the decades preceding World War I: "With the definite arrival of this new form of verse in 1880 came the appearance of a band of poets perhaps unequalled at any time in the history of French poetry."[6]

Two articulate proselytes of the new French prosody, the poets Georges Duhamel and Charles Vildrac, published in 1910 a brief treatise on vers libre, *Notes sur la technique poétique*. Amy Lowell, a close student of the modern French poets, mentions Duhamel and Vildrac's work; Pound refers to it repeatedly.[7] Others in the imagist group were undoubtedly familiar with this seminal little book. The *Notes* are an excited defense and analysis of vers libre method, written in a series of aphorisms—much like Pound's treatises and ABCs.

Duhamel and Vildrac explain how syntactical manipulation rhythmically energizes free verse. They name the various "figures of grammar" the *constante rythmique,* the *équilibre rythmique,* and the *symétrie rythmique.* In French the rhythmic constant may be merely a sequence of phrases containing equal numbers of syllables. More frequently, the structure of vers libre shows the familiar syntactical parallelisms. Vers libre does not rest on a controlling metric of syllabic count but is formed on syntax, and on the forms of grammar.

Who among the later nineteenth-century French poets first wrote vers libre is something of a historical mystery. Gustave Kahn was among the earliest practitioners of the new form; by the 1890s a group including Verhaeren and Vielé-Griffin were publishing as *vers librists*. But both Rimbaud and Laforgue had earlier written verse that breaks the old prosodic forms.

The political leaders of imagism, Pound, Flint, and Amy Lowell (Hulme dropped out in 1914 to pursue another enthusiasm, war), were generally at odds with each other about fundamental principles. Flint objected to the restrictions on subject matter proposed by Lowell; Pound believed in the image and in the principle of verbal precision, but felt that imagism was more a corrective to the deliquescence and sentimentality of post-Victorian poetry than a complete formula for the new verse. Only Amy Lowell, in her theories, and H.D., in her poetry, kept close to the letter of original imagist law. And by 1915, three years after the movement's founding, imagism finally became a matter of prosody:

> The 1915 preface [to Amy Lowell's *Some Imagist Poets*] not only accepted *vers libre* as Imagistic but elevated it to a position of central importance in its doctrine. That Imagist attention was now fixed primarily upon the rhythms of poetry is further indicated by the explanation given this principle in the 1916 anthology: "Poetry is a spoken and not a written art."[8]

❧ *II. Des Imagistes*

"Poetry is a spoken and not a written art." Yet when we examine imagist poetry we are struck by how often the poem's appearance on the page constitutes its chief prosodic feature. Typography, not sound, controls the rhythms in these lines:

> The trees are like a sea;
> Tossing,
> Trembling,
> Roaring,
> Wallowing,
> Darting their long green flickering fronds up at the sky,
> Spotted with white blossom-spray.
>
>   John Gould Fletcher, "Green Symphony"

A similar example from Amy Lowell's "An Aquarium":

> Streaks of green and yellow iridescence,
> Silver shiftings,
> Rings veering out of rings,
> Silver-gold-
> Grey-green opaqueness sliding down,
> With sharp white bubbles
> Shooting and dancing,
> Flinging quickly outward.
> Nosing the bubbles,
> Swallowing them,
> Fish.

The length of line contracts with the syntax, until we get the subject noun, "Fish," in clean visual isolation. Lowell does not neglect sound values; we have harshly stressed lines,

> With sharp white bubbles . . .

as well as the smoothly modulating vowels in

> Grey-green opaqueness sliding down.

The line also serves to isolate each separate image and hold it up to the eye for contemplation. Syntax is fragmentary; we have participles and nouns but no authentic verbs.

The dislocation of syntax generates a prosody of sorts in Lowell's "Violin Sonata by Vincent D'Indy":

> A little brown room in a sea of fields,
> Fields pink as rose-mallows
> Under a fading rose-mallow sky.
>
> Four candles on a tall iron candlestick,
> Clustered like altar lights.
> Above, the models of four brown Chinese junks
> Sailing round the brown walls,
> Silent and motionless.

Again we have free-floating images without grammatical orientation. By carefully suppressing all verbs, Lowell presents rather than comments on an experience. Such method denies the importance of human action in poetry and limits it to perceptual reporting.

None of the above, however, is true of H.D., the best poet, other than Pound, in the imagist group. H.D. follows the imagist practice of writing in short lines; she concentrates on visual detail and keeps careful control of the emotion that delicately moves between her imagery. Her prosody articulates rather than fragments the elements of her poetry. While she is aware of the effect of visual rhythms, she orders her prosody primarily by means of sound and active verbs. Our example is a complete poem, "Along the Yellow Sand":

> Along the yellow sand
> above the rocks,
> the laurel-bushes stand.
>
> Against the shimmering heat,
> each separate leaf
> is bright and cold,
> and through the bronze
> of shining bark and wood,
> run the fine threads of gold.
>
> Here in our wicker-trays,
> we bring the first faint blossoming
> of fragrant bays:
>
> Lady, their blushes shine
> as faint in hue,
> as when through petals
> of a laurel-rose,
> the sun shines through,
> and throws a purple shadow
> on a marble vase.
>
> (Ah, love,
> so her fair breasts will shine
> with the faint shadow above.)

H.D. does not follow the imagist practice of writing in sentence fragments; her syntax is complete and active. Note the verbs: "stand," "run," "bring," "shine," "throws." Metrically, the lines are dominated by iambic movement and punctuated by occasional rhymes. Individual lines are mainly trimeter or dimeter:

> and through | the bronze
> of shin | ing bark | and wood,
> run the | fine threads | of gold.

A train of Greek votive maidens brings offerings of laurel to Aphrodite,

> so her fair breasts will shine
> with the faint shadow above.

The subtle rhythmic shift in the last line emphasizes the suppressed excitement, the breath suddenly withdrawn, as the girls become aware of Lady Aphrodite's physical beauty. Unlike many imagist poems "Along the Yellow Sand" has recognizable plot; H.D. is not fixing an image in a moment of time but recording significant human action.

H.D.'s Hellenism shapes both the spirit and form of her work. Her long poem, *Helen in Egypt*, is written in a stanza of three short lines, evidently suggested by the cryptic *Palinode* of Stesichorus:

> Οὐκ' ἔστ' ἔτυμος λόγος οὗτος·
> οὐδ' ἔβας ἐν ναυσὶν εὐσέλμοις,
> οὐδ' ἵκεο πέργαμα Τροίας.

> That story is not true.
> You never sailed in the benched ships.
> You never went to the city of Troy.
>   translation by Richmond Lattimore

"According to the Palinode, Helen was never in Troy. She had been transposed or translated from Greece into Egypt. Helen of Troy was a phantom, substituted for the real Helen, by jealous deities. The Greeks and Trojans alike fought for an illusion."[9]

H.D.'s technique transcends the limitations imposed on narrative by imagist theory. Pound's doctrine of the image does not provide for connections between images; poetry is to proceed by a series of instantaneous, intense perceptions, a "sense of sudden growth."[10] Traditional narrative is nearly impossible within this canon, though a narrative of indirection and accretion may sometimes come into being. This is reflected, to a degree, in H.D.'s procedure in *Helen in Egypt*. She is, like Pound, essentially a lyric poet whose gifts do not include the epic grasp. *Helen in Egypt* has its own form: a series of visions or scenes, held together by brief connecting links in prose. Each vision is a lyric meditation; and the voices (Helen, Achilles, Paris, Theseus) shift as they dream in remembrance or prophesy the future. The prose links preserve the narrative line, yet allow Helen to "encompass infinity by intense concentration on the moment. . . . She will bring the moment and infinity together 'in time, in the crystal, in my thought here.' " Such a method is a delicious compromise; it allows H.D. to keep her cake of poetry and at the same time take sustenance from the prose. She can sustain poetic intensity and maintain narrative coherence.

The three-line stanza gives firmness to the prosody and solves the problem of a "carrying metric." The lines are short, but within the limitations of two to four stresses, H.D. gets considerable expressive variety:

> few were the words we said,
> but the words are graven on stone,
> minted on gold, stamped upon lead;
>
> he, Achilles, piling brushwood,
> finding an old flint in his pouch,
> "I thought I had lost that";
>
> few were the words we said,
> "I am shipwrecked, I am lost,"
> turning to view the stars,
>
> swaying as before the mast,
> "the season is different,
> we are far from—from—"
>
> *let him forget,*
> *Amen, All-father,*
> *let him forget.*

The easy prose movement tightens into a strong-stress pattern when the language thickens into metaphor:

       mínted on góld, ‖ stámped upon leád.

Another kind of movement images the actions of Achilles,

> turning to view the stars,
>
> swaying before the mast.

The section concludes with Helen's prayer in two-stress lines. At one point Helen remembers the scenes and noises of the Trojan War; the lines lengthen into English heroic measure, blank verse:

> whether they floundered on the Pontic seas
> or ran aground before the Hellespont,
> whether they shouted Victory at the gate,
>
> whether the bowmen shot them from the Walls,
> whether they crowded surging through the breach,
> or died of fever on the smitten plain . . .

H.D. wisely avoids attempting the English hexameter to render a sense of Greek meter.

     Richard Aldington, a member of the original imagist group and H.D.'s husband, also wrote verse to visual rhythms. Length of line gives prosodic shape to his verse, emphasizing important words and syntactic groups:

> THE FAUN SEES SNOW FOR THE FIRST TIME
> Zeus,
> Brazen-thunder-hurler,
> Cloud-whirler, son-of-Kronos,
> Send vengeance on these Oreads
> Who strew
> White frozen flecks of mist and cloud
>
> Over the brown trees and the tufted grass
> Of the meadows, where the stream
> Runs black through shining banks
> Of bluish white.

The expanding rhythm of the first stanza makes an especially strong impression on the ear; the heavy stressing in lines 2 and 3 is resolved by the smooth iambics of

White fro | zen flecks | of mist | and cloud.

We also hear rhythmic echoes: the iambics in line 6 are heard, with lessened dynamic intensity, in line 4:

Send ven | geance on | these O | re ads.

Within a basic iambic pattern such echoing would be inaudible; where the verse moves freely, a line in regular meter becomes suddenly arresting—as when we glimpse the shadowy form of a tree or a man in the paintings of the abstract expressionists.

Most free verse shows these appearances of regular metric. In good free verse a metrical line will intensify an image or an idea, or mark the climactic point of the rhythm. Such marking must be subtle; if the poet strains too hard for an "absolute rhythm," or attempts a literal matching of rhythm to the emotion or situation, the effect can be highly artificial. The final lines of Amy Lowell's "Patterns" move to obviously contrived rhythms; one line (the sixth below) has a completely inappropriate swing:

> I shall go
> Up and down,
> In my gown.
> Gorgeously arrayed,
> Boned and stayed.
> And the softness of my body will be guarded from embrace
> By each button, hook, and lace.

The swaying of the amphimacers (I shall go / Up and down, / In my gown. / . . . Boned and stayed) rather naively suggests the lady walking in her heavy gown; the sixth line, in the unmistakable trochaic meter of "Locksley Hall," unfortunately suggests:

> As the husband is, the wife is; thou art mated with a clown,
> And the grossness of his nature will have weight to drag
>   thee down.

In the open territory of free prosody, occasional metrical lines are often crudely and dangerously intrusive; the especially strong trochaic line coupled to the silly sentiments about the lady's chastity destroys the poem's emotional unity. If Amy Lowell had been working in a conventional meter, such a solecism as "And the softness of my body" would have been glaringly apparent. As these lines stand, they have neither the rhythmic force of strong prose nor the meaningful intensities of well-handled meter.

❧ III. *Marianne Moore*

Marianne Moore saw the need for greater prosodical discipline than that offered by imagist vers libre. Early and loosely associated with the imagist group (Richard Aldington was her "discoverer"), she developed a metrical idiom that had no immediate source and has had no successful imitators; in her punctuation, use of dashes, emphasis on rhyme, attention to syllable count, and careful construction of complex syntax, Moore follows the example of Emily Dickinson. The distinction of her verse scarcely lies in its "freedom" but in its studied complexity. Her meter combines imagist concern for the visual shape of line and stanza with careful syllabic count and the systematic use of rhyme. The result is a prosody of highly technical contrivance that beautifully works. We can see and hear its workings in some stanzas from "In the Public Garden":

> Boston has a festival—
> compositely for all—
> and nearby, cupolas of learning
> (crimson, blue, and gold) that
>   have made education individual.
>
> My first—an exceptional,
> an almost scriptural—
> taxi-driver to Cambridge from Back Bay said
> as we went along, "They
>   make some fine young men at Harvard." I recall
>
> the summer when Faneuil Hall
> had its weathervane with gold ball
> and grasshopper, gilded again by
> a -leafer and -jack
>   till it glittered. Spring can be a miracle

there—a more than usual
bouquet of what is vernal—
"pear blossoms whiter than clouds," pin-
oak leaves barely showing
    when other trees are making shade, besides small

fairy iris suitable
for Dulcinea del
Toboso; O yes, and snowdrops
in the snow, that smell like
    violets. Despite secular bustle . . .

An almost breathless anecdotal rhythm—the talk of an intelligent
and observant person rapidly leaping from description to idea and
back again—is held in check by the formal metrical elements. Moore
counts syllables, more or less strictly; the pattern in analogous lines is
seven, six, nine, six, eleven. A rhyme scheme binds the entire poem
together: the first and second and final lines of each stanza end with
either a light or heavy stress on the syllable *l*. Moore also measures as
well as counts her syllables, adding a consort of vowels to the orchestra-
tion of her lines:

Toboso; O yes, and snowdrops
in the snow.

The end of "In the Public Garden" grows more intense in its music;
the strict syllabism and severe stanzaic shape break down, and in their
place we hear the more immediate effects of assonance and consecu-
tive rhyming:

There are those who will talk for an hour
without telling you why they have
    come. And I? This is no madrigal—

no medieval gradual—
but it is a grateful tale.
Without that radiance which poets
are supposed to have—
    unofficial, unprofessional, still one need not fail

to wish poetry well
where intellect is habitual—
glad that the Muses have a home and swans—
that legend can be factual;
   happy that Art, admired in general,
   is always actually personal.

Madrigals are part songs with intricate contrapuntal textures; graduals are liturgical hymns sung from the steps of the altar. Moore modestly tells us her poem has neither richness nor authority; it is a simple tale told with Muses and swans and gratitude.

   An earlier poem, "The Monkeys," deals in aesthetics and the nature of poetry. The poetry Moore talks about in these lines is like her own: fastidious in craft and "malignant / in its power over us." We quote the whole poem; its prosody begins with the title and carries the poem to its last word:

THE MONKEYS

winked too much and were afraid of snakes. The zebras,
   supreme in
their abnormality; the elephants with their fog-coloured skin
   and strictly practical appendages
     were there, the small cats; and the parakeet—
      trivial and humdrum on examination, destroying
     bark and portions of the food it could not eat.

I recall their magnificence, now not more magnificent
than it is dim. It is difficult to recall the ornament,
   speech, and precise manner of what one might
    call the minor acquaintances twenty
     years back; but I shall not forget him—that
      Gilgamesh among
     the hairy carnivora—that cat with the

wedge-shaped, slate-gray marks on its forelegs and the
   resolute tail,
astringently remarking, "They have imposed on us with
   their pale
   half-fledged protestations, trembling about
    in inarticulate frenzy, saying

it is not for us to understand art; finding it
all so difficult, examining the thing

as if it were inconceivably arcanic, as symmet-
ricaly frigid as if it had been carved out of chrysoprase
or marble—strict with tension, malignant
in its power over us and deeper
than the sea when it proffers flattery in exchange
for hemp,
rye, flax, horses, platinum, timber and fur."

The scene of the poem is the zoo; the monkeys are offered as a synec-
doche for the other animals. Children always remember the vividness
of the monkeys; adults tend to be oppressed by their human re-
semblances. (The poem was originally titled "My Apish Cousins.") The
monkeys, like their human cousins, find art and poetry disturbing,
even—to use Moore's neologism—arcanic: possessed of strange, per-
haps curative, powers. Poetry frightens them because the understand-
ing of poetry requires some submission to its influence. Monkeys, like
people, prefer things as they are. Poetry offers, in exchange for real
goods (vegetable, animal, mineral), only a dubious flattery.

We must read the whole poem before we understand why the
monkeys feared the snakes. Snakes are like poems: frigid, tense, and
symmetrical. Moore's characteristic syllabic prosody enforces
symmetry—even in the ironic splitting of this word (first line, last
stanza) to maintain her syllabic equivalence. The first two lines of the
last stanza abandon the prevalent rhyme: as if to assert the freedom of
poetry immediately after submitting to its formal exactions. Moore
regards the limitations of her prosodic method as means rather than
ends; the strictness of the form must be broken if subject and feeling
demand ampler latitude for expression. Basic to Moore's aesthetic is
"the principle of accommodation": that even meticulous good taste
and craftsmanship can be carried to excess,

that excessive conduct augurs disappointment,
that one must not borrow a long white beard and tie it on
and threaten with the scythe of time the casually curious:
to teach the bard with too elastic a selectiveness
that one detects creative power by its capacity to conquer
one's detachment;

that while it may have more elasticity than logic,
it knows where it is going.
> "The Labours of Hercules"

Poetry and its form must balance the opposing requirements of logic and elasticity; "it knows where it is going," yet it must, in its own special and precise way

> convince snake-charming controversialists
> that it is one thing to change one's mind,
> another to eradicate it—that one keeps on knowing
> "that the Negro is not brutal,
> that the Jew is not greedy,
> that the Oriental is not immoral,
> that the German is not a Hun."
> > "The Labours of Hercules"

In "The Labours of Hercules" Moore makes many accommodations. The verse adjusts to the seemingly casual movements of Moore's mind and interests, but displays no prosodical uncertainty. Her prosody closely follows "the figure of grammar," mapping its course along a series of repeated verbal and modifier word groups. If we skeletonize the grammatical structure in a manner analogous to the two-voice framework of musical analysis, the prosodical scheme becomes apparent. As in all of Moore's poems, we begin with the title:

THE LABOURS OF HERCULES [ARE]
To popularize the mule . . .

to persuade one of austere taste . . .

that the piano is . . . that his "charming tadpole notes" . . .

to persuade those self-wrought Midases . . .

that excessive conduct . . .
that one must not . . .

to prove to the high priests of caste
that snobbishness is a stupidity . . .
> . . . —that we are sick of the earth,

sick of the pig-sty, wild geese and wild men

etc. Syntax like music, we say. The poem is built on two motifs, the verbal group beginning with *to* (infinitive), and the modifier group beginning with *that* (dependent clause). Modern structural linguistics calls both infinitives and dependent clauses *head-tail* groups and describes the similarity of their rhythmic structure.[11] The overall grammatical structure consists of the title as subject, the copula *are,* and the poem itself as a complex complement.

The poem is a single sentence, and since here Moore does not count syllables or construct stanzas, the syntax carries the chief prosodical burden. The method is a refinement on Whitman's more obvious syntactical parallelisms. Moore acknowledges no debt to Whitman, but rather to their common source, Hebrew poetry:

> "Hebrew poetry is
> prose with a sort of heightened consciousness." Ecstasy affords
> the occasion and expediency determines the form.
>
> "The Past Is the Present"

We may be puzzled by Moore's statement about expediency and ask what can be expedient about a method so carefully contrived and formally exact. But remembering that expedients are simply means and resources, we understand that syllable, stanza, and grammatical arrangement enable the poet to gain advantages in the kingdom of language. Moore is cunningly adept in the game of getting the most out of every word she uses. Hers is a limited ecstasy—her reference to Hebrew poetry strikes the mind as calculated irony. The unemphatic movements of her prosody suit the demands of her feeling and subject. A syllabic-syntactic prosody gives no "beat"; it resembles certain songs by Campion and Dowland where rhythm has nothing to do with bar lines and accents. Moore's rhythms proceed without strong accentuation (a key distinction between her verse and Dickinson's); they convince our minds and ears that rhythms are not crass patterns of phonetic recurrence but definitions of time. The spatial elements, the heritage of imagism in her prosody, help arrange the illusion of time; they are expedients to a calculated end. Too heavily an accented foot or stress prosody would impede the quick and delicate movements of her feeling; it would clot the fineness of her observations, slow down the darting and sensible eye of her intelligence.

❧ *IV. William Carlos Williams*

Our first contact with William Carlos Williams's verse makes us jump; nothing, and certainly nothing in the way of a deliberate metric, seems to intervene between us and the sensibility of this extraordinary man. Our first example, a fragment Williams reprints from *Paterson*,[12] delights both ear and eye with its carefully spaced lines and young girl voice:

> I bought a new
> bathing suit
>
> Just pants
> and a brassiere—
>
> I haven't shown
> it
>
> to my mother
> yet.

As in imagist poetry, the lines are arranged for rhetorical emphasis; the half-rhymes ("suit" / "it" / "yet") mark slight hesitations in the young lady's brief and pithy discourse. (We must suppress, as being critically undemonstrable, our inclination to see in the shape of the poem an emblem of its subject: both poem and bathing suit share a tantalizing brevity.) Williams was early associated with the imagists; his first literary friends were Pound and H.D., and Pound included a poem by Williams in *Des Imagistes* (1914). But Williams never officially joined the imagists nor signed their manifestos. He went to Europe on trips, preferring to remain an American sightseer rather than take up the uncertain life of an expatriate. His aggressive and positive Americanism resembles Pound's aggressive, *negative* Americanism.

Both Williams and Pound take an antihistorical stand. Williams shows his contempt for history simply by ignoring it; he tells us again and again he prefers direct experience to the ash heaps of the past. Pound's antihistoricism makes more devious but nevertheless followable tracks. He became a scholar, digested what he needed, and rejected the rest. The "philosophy of history" informing the *Cantos* retells history as Pound, from his odd angle of vision, sees it. We find no "history," of course: only mythology animated by demonology. Pound brought his American brashness to Europe and started a poetic revolution; Williams stayed home, practiced medicine in Rutherford, and cultivated his sensibility.

We see a clue to Williams's position, both technical and spiritual, in his tirade against Eliot. We quote from *The Autobiography of William Carlos Williams:*

> To me especially *[The Waste Land]* struck like a sardonic bullet. I felt at once that it had set me back twenty years, and I'm sure it did. Critically Eliot returned us to the classroom just at the moment when I felt that we were on the point of escape to matters much closer to the essence of a new art form itself—rooted in the locality which should give it fruit. . . .
>
> If with his skill he could have been kept here to be employed by our slowly shaping drive, what strides might we not have taken! We needed him in the scheme I was half-consciously forming. I needed him: he might have become our advisor, even our hero. By his walking out on us we were stopped, for the moment, cold. It was a bad moment. Only now, as I predicted, have we begun to catch hold again and restarted to make the line over. This is not to say that Eliot has not, indirectly, contributed much to the emergence of the next step in metrical construction, but if he had not turned away from the direct attack here, in the western dialect, we might have gone ahead much faster.[13]

After discounting Williams's considerable personal antipathy for Eliot,[14] we understand his cry against the calculated craftsmanship, the dazzling metrical virtuosity of *The Waste Land*. To Williams, *The Waste Land* seemed a step backward into the prosodical past; it returned the poet "to the classroom." Williams found no use for Eliot's meters: which scarcely demolishes Eliot but helps to explain Williams. We need not quarrel with Williams about Eliot's repudiation of America; Eliot *had* to go to Europe just as Williams *had* to remain in New Jersey. Matters of temperament determined their location as well as their style. Style is the writer; and the writer is the air one breathes, the food one eats, the ground on which one's house is built.

Williams built his poetic line on "the western dialect" and on the idea that the poem assumes a rhythmic shape congruent to its shape as a presented *object*. The objectivist theory argued the poem, like every other form of art, is an object, an object that in itself formally presents its case and its meaning by the very form it assumes. Therefore, being an object, it should be so treated and controlled—but not as in the past.[15]

Williams did not make clear whether the poem-object existed in space or time; he implies the poem exists in time *and* space ("like a symphony or cubist painting"). Objectivist theory emphasized the concreteness of the poem, the "thingness" of its words; Williams discovered in the writings of Gertrude Stein a "feeling of words themselves, a curious immediate quality quite apart from their meaning, much as in music different notes are dropped, so to speak, into a repeated chord one at a time, one after another—for itself alone."[16] A word in a poem must function as a discrete perceptual entity; it must be given, with all its physical immediacy, to hearing, vision, or touch. The poet and the reader must revive their childhood belief that words are indeed the things and qualities they symbolize; words like *rough, smooth, round* possess for the mind perceptual roughness, smoothness, roundness.

Objectivist theory represents another variety of the spatial heresy and the attempts of modern poets to fight the medium. Language is stubbornly conceptual; poets must resist abstraction and struggle to make their words vivid to eye, ear, and touch. The objectivist poem achieves its vividness by stopping time; the poem sits on the page in its unmoving "thingness":

> BETWEEN WALLS
> the back wings
> of the
>
> hospital where
> nothing
>
> will grow lie
> cinders
>
> in which shine
> the broken
>
> pieces of a green
> bottle.

Nothing happens; the verbs ("lie," "shine") present little action and function nearly as copulas. The poem's significance is implied, not stated. We understand that the back of the hospital, the infertile cinders, and the shattered bottle add up to a feeling of sudden desolation. The sun, catching the green glass, points up the bleak surroundings.

Such a poem requires a bare minimum of prosodic means. The lines are alternately long and short and hold two and one stress, respectively. Important words stand by themselves or at the ends of lines: "nothing," "cinders," "broken," "green." The poem is composed in space, and the eye comes to rest on "green." Perhaps green suggests fertility, in contrast to the barren back of the hospital. But Williams would probably snort at this "interpretation" and maintain "The feeling of words themselves, a curious immediate quality, quite apart from their meaning." But as words detach themselves from their meanings, prosody becomes static. Rhythmic structure moves in time, but the objectivist poem does not move; like the Gumbie Cat it "sits and sits and sits and sits," maintaining its inscrutability.

Not all of Williams's poems, however, sit motionless, pinned down by typography and visual form. "The Dance" has a boisterous, even catchy, swing:

> In Breughel's great picture, The Kermess,
> the dancers go round, they go round and
> around, the squeal and the blare and the
> tweedle of bagpipes, a bugle and fiddles
> tipping their bellies (round as the thick-
> sided glasses whose wash they impound)
> their hips and their bellies off balance
> to turn them. Kicking and rolling about
> the Fair Grounds, swinging their butts, those
> shanks must be sound to bear up under such
> rollicking measures, prance as they dance
> in Breughel's great picture, The Kermess.

The lines stomp along in heavily accented triple time: the German *Ländler* with its ONE-two-three, OOM-pah-pah. Interior rhyme and a firm anapestic meter hold the poem together:

their híps | and their bél | lies off bál | ance

to túrn | them. Kíck | ing and ról | ling a bóut |

the Fair Gróunds, | swíng | ing their bútts, | those

shánks | must be sóund.

We cannot miss the obvious music of "The Dance." Williams's eye is sharp, but his ear is equally sharp. We hear finer, more intricate music in other poems. Hoagy Carmichael reads "Tract" ("I will teach you my townspeople / how to perform a funeral") over a pulsing jazz accompaniment; his soft Southern voice gracefully picks out the rhythms and we know that Williams writes for the ear as well as the eye.

Most of Williams's poems are composed in characteristic short lines. However, he wrote a number of poems using a longer, and more conventional, line. These are the concluding tercets from "The Yachts":

> Arms with hands grasping seek to clutch at the prows.
> Bodies thrown recklessly in the way are cut aside.
> It is a sea of faces about them in agony, in despair
>
> until the horror of the race dawns staggering the mind,
> the whole sea becomes an entanglement of watery bodies
> lost to the world bearing what they cannot hold. Broken,
>
> beaten, desolate, reaching from the dead to be taken up
> they cry out, failing, failing! their cries rising
> in waves still as the skillful yachts pass over.

The lines approximate blank verse—the modern, loosened kind with free use of substitution and hypermetrical effects. Rhythmic beauty is achieved by a long rallentando, a gradual slowing down of prosodic movement. The first tercet has the normal rising rhythm of blank verse, but beginning with the last line of the second tercet, the rhythm begins to shift. A pattern of trochaic words, "Broken," "beaten," "reaching," "failing," "rising," crosses the rising iambic base; like the waves themselves, we have a rocking movement generated by the falling metrical units of trochee and dactyl:

béat en. | dé so late, | reách ing from | the déad | to be tá | ken úp

they crý | óut, fáil | ing, fáil | ing! their críes | rí sing.

The final lines evoke a nearly unbearable pathos—nearly, but not quite; the passionately well-ordered metric keeps the feeling manageable, within human bounds.

❧ *v. e. e. cummings*

Imagist techniques pushed first the image, then the individual word toward prosodic isolation. The typographical prosody of e. e. cummings is a by-product of imagism; however, cummings goes a step further. Not only does he break down the line into visual shapes and give the separate word rhythmic autonomy, but he fragments words themselves. Each letter of the alphabet assumes importance in the rhythmic scheme. In the following poem cummings distorts typography, but does not paint a picture of the poem's ostensible subject. The typographical derangements, the capital *O*s evidently enhance the *moon*-ness of the poem; it is a matter of quality, not photography:

> mOOn Over tOwns mOOn
> whisper
> less creature huge grO
> pingness
>
> whO perfectly whO
> flOat
> newly alOne is
> dreamest
> oNLY THE MooN o
> VER ToWNS
> SLoWLY SPRoUTING SPIR
> IT

1 from No Thanks

Even when the typographic fit is upon him, cummings is a more versatile technician than he is usually given credit for. He is the master of several visual styles. The well-known grasshopper poem works like a cubist painting; we must piece together the shattered words and disarranged punctuation to discover what the poem *says*. (It reads, as near as we can make out, "The grasshopper, who as we look up now, gathering into PPEGORHRASS, leaps! arriving to become, rearrangingly, grasshopper!") We are unable to discover what rationale lies behind the poem's punctuation. What the poem is *doing* is leaping, flying apart in midair, and rearranging itself on the page:

r-p-0-p-h-e-s-s-a-g-r
who

a)s w(e loo)k
upnowgath
     PPEGORHRASS
         eringint(o-
aThe):l
   eA
      !p:
S   a
    (r
rIvInG   .gRrEaPsPhOs)
                        to
rea(be)rran(com)gi(e)ngly
,grasshopper;

13 from *No Thanks*

The poem apparently resembles its subject: the disintegrating and reintegrating grasshopper. Actually, the poem does not so much *look like* the grasshopper's action as give the feel of action. cummings uses an elaborate technique of synaesthesia, a complex visual and aural derangement, to signify emotional meaning. We must, in order to read this poem, "see" sounds and "hear" shapes.

Synaesthesia is, of course, nothing new to poetry. Blake can see sound,

> And the hapless Soldier's sigh
> Runs in blood down Palace walls.

or Dame Edith Sitwell hear light,

> Jane, Jane, tall as a crane,
> The morning light creak down again.

The equation for successful synaesthesia takes this general form: a stimulus, perceived by one sense, is metaphorically apprehended by another. The method of synaesthesia holds considerable potential for emotional violence; the sigh that runs in blood affects us with great and peculiar power—peculiar, because the sensuous derangement of a Blake or a Sitwell conducts a shock of sudden insight.

Such is the intention of the grasshopper poem. But we have shock without the suddenness; it takes time to construe the anagrammatized words and the disjunct punctuation and syntax. What should be grasped in an instant must be slowly deciphered. Our reaction is not passionate surprise but that cummings is a very clever fellow. The poem lacks one term of the equation for workable synaesthesia. We have the visual stimulus, the poem's eccentric shape, but the metaphorical gap between eye and ear remains unfilled. The poem exists without significant aesthetic surface: apprehensible phonetic qualities.

Which is not to say that cummings's work with typography has no merit. Poetry has been, for a long time, also a printed art; unless we read on a primitive level, most of us do not move our lips to form the words our eyes meet on the page (though in reading poetry, perhaps we should). But with visual symbols only, which cannot be transformed and perceived by the ear, the poet severely limits his range of feeling. Ultimately our admiration for cummings's shape poetry is intellectual; the pattern or hieroglyphic poem belongs to the genre of the poetry of wit. George Herbert before cummings "possessed the fantastic idea that a poem should resemble its subject in typographical appearance."[17] The poem's printed appearance forms a metaphorical structure, a conceit; we question whether to interpret the shape of the pattern poem rhetorically or rhythmically. Is the shape a matter of figurative language or prosody?

In Metaphysical shape poetry we have no doubt what is intended. The visual element in Herbert's "Easter-wings" is metaphorical; the length of line is both metaphorical and prosodical:

> My tender age in sorrow did beginne;
> And still with sicknesses and shame
> Thou didst so punish sinne,
> That I became
> Most thinne.
> With thee
> Let me combine

> And feel this day thy victorie:
> For, if I imp my wing on thine,
> Affliction shall advance the flight in me.

The line thins down from pentameter to monometer, then expands back to full pentameter again. Meter controls rhythmic structure; the phonetic pattern is prosodically dominant. Shape functions rhythmically but does not by itself carry the prosody.

Cummings also writes the kind of shape poem where meter as well as visual pattern make a prosody. The poet is explaining to a talkative, obtuse woman that war is not glorious. He counts out his feelings in lines of one to nine syllables—as he might show a child a problem in simple arithmetic on his fingers. The expanding and contracting shape of the poem conducts the reader through the dynamics of feeling; the longest line lengthens to an irritated "O / what the hell"; the last, short lines drop down to a hopeless "i am / dead." The poem's triangular shape indicates, like the crescendo fork of musical notation, where the reader must raise and lower the intensity of his voice:

> i'm
> asking
> you dear to
> what else could a
> no but it doesn't
> of course but you don't seem
> to realize i can't make
> it clearer war just isn't what
> we imagine but please for god's O
> what the hell yes it's true that was
> me but that me isn't me
> can't you see now no not
> any christ but you
> must understand
> why because
> i am
> dead

"40" from *XAIPE*

Cummings had a technical advantage over the Metaphysical pattern poets: he composed on the typewriter. We should note here that

the typewriter exerted significant influences on modern writing, af-
fecting the rhythms of modern prose. Certainly the iconographic
effects cummings achieved with the distribution of individual letters
and punctuation would have been impossible without it. With the
typewriter, and now the word processor, the poet can fully exploit the
spatial possibilities of a blank sheet of white paper; the page itself
enters into the composition of the poem. Since poets began compos-
ing on the typewriter, many have used the blank space, the isolated
line or word, and the pregnant indentation to poetic and rhythmic
advantage.

๛ VI. *"The Visual in the Verbal"*

By itself, the notion of "the visual in the verbal" was a lively, needed,
fructifying heresy.[18] As with Language poetry, New Formalism, and the
resurgence of narrative in our present time, imagism stimulated in-
terest once again in the problems of poetic form and technique; the
new visualism brought a discipline of seeing with precision and
recording with accuracy. A new technique, as Hulme pointed out, be-
became a source of creative excitement and urged poets to new
themes and subjects. The concern with sharp images strengthened
certain textural features of the new verse; although these lines are
iambically based, we feel a rhythmic hardness not found in Georgian
poetry:

> Wipe your hands across your mouth, and laugh;
> The worlds revolve like ancient women
> Gathering fuel in vacant lots.
>
> T. S. Eliot, "Preludes"

Eliot was never a card-carrying imagist; in his poetry seeing, feeling,
and thinking fuse in ways that transcend mere poetic doctrine.

The limitations of imagism prevented prolixity and rhythmic flabbi-
ness. A successful imagist poem was, by definition and decree, a short
poem usually composed in short lines. Such brevities discouraged
dealings in abstractions and unrealized emotion. If the imagist poet
were going to treat ideas as well as sense impressions, his or her eyes
had to see what the brain formulated. As a result, imagist poets had few
transactions with the world of ideas; orthodox imagism began and

ended with recording acts of simple perception. A man could hardly be sentimental in a poem such as this:

Black swallows swooping or gliding
In a flurry of entangled loops and curves;
The skaters skim over the frozen river.
And the grinding click of their skates as they impinge
　　upon the surface,
Is like the brushing together of thin wing-tips of silver.
　　　　　　　　　　　　　　John Gould Fletcher, "The Skaters"

But the impact of imagism on prosody proved, in the historical long run, more of a force for confusion and weakness than a stimulus toward new and useful rhythmic forms. A poetic so committed to what the eye saw rather than what the ear heard was doomed, from the very beginning, to run "upstream, against / The grain of language and the course of change."[19] Imagist rhythms relaxed, almost inevitably, into the slackness of prose; the line rather than the sentence or paragraph became the verse unit. Most of Whitman's lines end with a full rhythmic cadence; so do the vers libre poems of Pound:

Go, my songs, to the lonely and the unsatisfied,
Go also to the nerve-wracked, go to the enslaved-by-convention,
Bear to them my contempt for their oppressors.
Go as a great wave of cool water,
Bear my contempt of oppressors.
　　　　　　　　　　　　　　　　　　　"Commission"

The methods of syntactical manipulation, practiced by Whitman and the French *vers librists* and recommended by Duhamel and Vildrac, have only limited rhythmical interest.

Imagist poetry favored a dislocated syntax, a network of images unrelated by strict grammatical connections. While it is possible that a metrical prosody can support syntactical looseness—Hart Crane and Dylan Thomas are both poets who, though careless of their syntax, maintain a regular metric—the combination of free verse and free syntax shatters the continuity of poetic structure. The long poem becomes impossible; the prosodical forms of imagism prevent both discursive and narrative movement. Imagism, at least in theory, dedicated itself to new freedoms of ear and eye; vers libre and immediate visual perception were the new orders in poetry.

But these orders were in fact destructive elements. Without the support of close syntax and with only the very weak support of vers libre, imagist poetry relied more and more on visual effects. Imagist theory, in the speculations of Hulme, and, for a brief period, imagist practice, tried to make poetry a spatial art: to turn words into pictures and rhythms into palpable surfaces. Many poems by cummings, Williams, and Pound elevated orthography and the minor eccentricities of print to leading features of poetic structure: such poems are the logical and absurd reductions of Hulme's belief that the newest poetry must resemble painting and sculpture. Poetry becomes a species of picture writing scarcely requiring a prosody of phonetic surface. A further step would be poetry without language, the abandoning of the larger aural symbolism of which prosody is an integral part. Even Hulme and Pound would hardly consciously countenance such a violation. But with the persistence of Language poetry, which rejects the signifying aspect of words, one might ask: have the ideogram and "the ideogrammatic method," the apotheosis of "the visual in the verbal," replaced syntax and prosody, the rational structures of poetry? We shall return to this question in a later chapter, but before we do, let us look closely at the most influential modern and late-modern poets and their verse practices.

VI

The "Celebrated Metric" of
Ezra Pound

No poet has been more lavishly admired for prosodical skill than Pound; no poet has elicited such praise for his ear. It was Eliot who first anticipated the subtleties of Pound's music. In 1917 he published anonymously ("I was so completely unknown that it seemed more decent that the pamphlet should appear anonymously")[1] *Ezra Pound: His Metric and Poetry*. This, Eliot's first critical book, might serve as a model for prosodical criticism; its twenty-five pages define Pound's method in precise aphorisms:

> The freedom of Pound's verse is rather a state of tension due to constant opposition between free and strict. There are not, as a matter of fact, two kinds of verse, the strict and the free; there is only a mastery which comes of being so well trained that form is an instinct and can be adapted to the particular purpose in hand.[2]

Metric precedes *poetry* in the title; Eliot comments little on Pound's subjects but centers his observations on the technical accomplishment of the verse. Eleven years later Eliot takes the same tack in his introduction to the Faber edition of Pound's *Selected Poems*. He praises the *Selected Poems* as a "textbook of modern versification," and brilliantly generalizes on vers libre, technique and inspiration, and "the relation of a poet's technical development and his personal development."[3] Similarly, Eliot professes admiration for the versification of the *Cantos*, though he expresses distaste for their "philosophy."

Most of the pieties heard about Pound's metric echo what Eliot said so long ago. The reluctance to deal directly and critically with Pound's verse can be traced to Eliot's sensitive and authoritative remarks; few trust their own ears sufficiently to quarrel with Eliot's judgments. But we know that Eliot's criticism was hardly disinterested. During the years 1917–22 Pound and Eliot worked together; what they then said must be understood in a context of mutual defiance of the Philistines. The two were utterly engaged in nothing less than the admirable task of resurrecting the poetry of their time. Into the 1990s, Pound's disciples were still fighting many of the battles of the teens and twenties; most of the talk about Pound's metric was charged with outdated polemic and unnecessary apology. The arguments have subsided considerably in succeeding years, though they have not completely died out. But now—as then—few take the trouble (or have the ability) to submit Pound's lines to careful prosodic scrutiny.

We shall attempt to examine Pound's verse as if we had heard none of the propaganda of his disciples. We shall take with sufficient salt what Pound himself has said about prosody: statements often made in jest, in irritation, or in the querulous voice of the "village explainer."[4] In his *Treatise on Metric* Pound tells us that the supposed rules of prosody cannot teach us to become poets: "Prosody and melody are attained by the listening ear, not by an index of nomenclatures, or by learning that such and such a foot is called a spondee."[5] No poet has ever been seriously injured by learning the craft of versification and discovering which foot is called a spondee. Pound himself bothered to learn a great deal about prosody—including the nonexistent rules. He studied, with professorial thoroughness, the forms of Provençal verse; he learned how to write English quantity and strong-stress meter.

I

A persistent melomania dominates Pound's statements on prosody. In one of his early exhortations, he urged the poet to "behave as a musician, a good musician, when dealing with that phase of your art that has exact parallels in music."[6] At the same time, and perhaps unaware of the contradiction, Pound proclaimed first the image, and later the ideogram the essence of the poetic. Curiously, as he increasingly made musical knowledge a sine qua non for the aspiring poet, his own prosody forsook musical virtues and became steadily more visual. The early lyrics aspire happily toward the condition of music ("Pound quotes approvingly the dictum of Pater");[7] the later *Cantos* are marked by the famous Chinese characters and other appeals to the eye.

Pound's own musical gifts and his relationship to musical art are perplexing matters. There exist numerous stories about his musical talents; Yves Tinayre reports that Pound had no ear (!), could not carry a tune, but "sang rhythmically."[8] William Carlos Williams corroborates Tinayre's report and observes that Pound's interest in music lay in the rhythm, "the time variants," and that "Tones, I am certain, meant nothing to him, can mean nothing."[9] Whatever handicaps of tone deafness Pound suffered, they did not deter him from writing an opera or "composing" a violin sonata.[10] He even tried his versatile hand at music theory and wrote *Antheil and the Treatise on Harmony* (1927). It is in this book that Pound expatiates most fully on music, rhythm, and their relationships to prosody, and offers his idea of a musically inspired poetic doctrine:

I believe in an absolute rhythm.
E. P. 1910 with explanations.

In 1910 I was working with monolinear verbal rhythm but one had already an adumbration that the bits of rhythm used in verse were capable of being used in musical structure, even with other dimensions.

———

I am inclined to think that the horizontal merits faded from music, and from the rhythm of poetry, with the gradual separation of the two arts. A man thinking with mathematical fractions is not impelled toward such variety of rage as a man working with the necessary inequalities of words. But the verbal rhythm is monolinear. It can form contrapunto only against its own echo, or against a developed expectancy.

———

Again, I emphasize the value of these different rhythm roots as above that of a tired and mechanical accent-metric.

———

A rhythm is a shape; it exists like the keel-line of a yacht, or the lines of an automobile engine, for a definite purpose, and should exist with an efficiency as definite as that which we find in yachts and automobiles.[11]

Pound reacts, at least in theory, against traditional syllable-stress metric. An earlier injunction warned the aspiring poet, "Don't chop your stuff into separate *iambs*. Don't make each line stop dead at the end, and then begin every next line with a heave."[12]

Pound composed, of course, in iambic verse—which does not invalidate his remarks about suppleness and variety. He has never favored a heavily stressed line; his translation of "The Seafarer" keeps to the strong-stress quadruple meter, but offers melody rather than emphatic beat:

> Storms, on the stone-cliffs beaten, fell on the stern
> In icy feathers; full oft the eagle screamed
> With spray on his pinion.

The rhythm overrides the metrical divisions as a good tune will move across the bar lines.

The statements about "absolute rhythm," "monolinear rhythm," and "contrapunto" (if we properly understand them) refer to the problem of finding a rhythmical form for a long poem. Pound had already begun composition of the *Cantos;* the early poems were behind him. An "absolute rhythm" worked for the shorter poems—especially the ones in Pound's imagistic manner. But absolute rhythm can sustain itself only for a limited number of lines; Pound was considering a musical method for the *Cantos:* "bits of rhythm used in verse were capable of being used in musical structure, even with other dimensions." Pound is evidently proposing the use of "bits of rhythm" thematically, as short motifs are repeated in a musical work. "[E]ven with other dimensions" puzzles us: unless Pound had a sudden insight that the structure of the *Cantos* was going to collapse into a jigsaw puzzle of visual forms.

Perhaps unwittingly, Pound admits the impossibility of the method he proposes. Verbal rhythm can form "contrapunto only against its own echo"; this means that similar rhythmic structures must be quite close together if we are going to experience any "contrapuntal" effect. Verbal rhythm also forms counterpoint "against a developed expectancy," that is, against a regular meter. "The necessary inequalities of words" must be welded into rhythmic form either by strong, close syntax or by regular meter; neither obtains in the *Cantos.* Close syntax—using repeated, parallel, or incremental grammatical forms—makes rhythmic echoes possible; a regular meter allows the greatest possible variety of echoes "against a developed expectancy." These are irrefutable lessons that too many contemporary practitioners have ignored altogether.

The Treatise on Harmony explains, not clearly, that music inheres in the verbal surface of poetry, and also affords larger, architectonic possibilities. Pound recognizes that rhythmic forms of music and poetry move in time and vary in intensity and duration. The later *Treatise on Metric* hammers home the importance of rhythm as a *shape in time:*

> Rhythm is a form cut into TIME, as a design is determined SPACE . . .
>
> In making a line of verse (and thence building the lines into passages) you have certain primal elements:
> That is to say, you have the various "articulate sounds" of the language, of its alphabet, that is, and the various groups of letters in syllables.
> These syllables have differing weights and durations
> A. original weights and durations
> B. weights and durations that seem naturally imposed on them by the other syllable groups around them.
>
> Those are the medium wherewith the poet cuts his design in TIME.[13]

Pound's *Treatises* admonish the poet to use one's ears, to pay the closest possible attention to the aural surface of one's art. The tenor of all Pound's statements on rhythm and meter indicates a preference for a quantitative prosody; he does not, however, advocate Greek and Latin meters in English. The poet must exercise care in the handling of syllables, not make the impossible attempt, as Bridges did, of devising grammatical rules for English quantity. An early statement (1917) *Re Vers Libre* warns the poet against trying to imitate the Greek and Latin meters:

> I think the desire for vers libre is due to the sense of quantity reasserting itself after years of starvation. But I doubt if we can take over, for English, the rules of quantity laid down for Greek and Latin, mostly by Latin grammarians.

... I think progress lies rather in an attempt to approximate classical quantitative meters (NOT to copy them) than in carelessness regarding such things.[14]

A still earlier statement (1913)—it is remarkable that the further back we dig in Pound's critical work, the more lucid and detailed are his perceptions—sums up everything of value in Pound's doctrine of *ut musica poesis:*

> The movement of poetry is limited only by the nature of syllables and of articulate sound, and by the laws of music, or melodic rhythm. Space forbids a complete treatise on all the sorts of verse, alliterative, syllabic, accentual, and quantitative. And such treatises as the latter are for the most part useless, as no man can learn much of these things save by first-hand untrammeled, unprejudiced examination of the finest examples of all these sorts of verse, of the finest strophes and of the finest rhyme-schemes, and by a profound study of the art and history of music.[15]

II

Our first example, from the 1909 *Personae,* descends from Yeats and the Pre-Raphaelite line; we have the sound of Yeats's fin de siècle mood music. Pound's world-weariness, however, has more exuberance than languor:

> O smoke and shadow of a darkling world,
> These, and the rest, and all the rest we knew.
> 'Tis not a game that plays at mates and mating,
> 'Tis not a game of barter, lands and houses,
> 'Tis not "of days and nights" and troubling years,
> Of cheeks grown sunken and glad hair gone grey;
> There *is* the subtler music, the clear light
> Where time burns back about th'eternal embers.
> We are not shut from all the thousand heavens:
> Lo, there are many gods whom we have seen,
> Folk of unearthly fashion, places splendid,
> Bulwark of beryl and of chrysoprase.

———

Thou hooded opal, thou eternal pearl,
O thou dark secret with a shimmering floor.

"The Flame"

Most readers will notice that Pound is trying hard for the rich, full effect:

Of cheeks grown sunken and glad hair gone grey . . .

Folk of unearthly fashion, places splendid,
Bulwark of beryl and of chrysoprase.

Rhythmically, the lines are static; one line stops dead "at the end," the next begins "with a heave." But some lines "go" with a strikingly individual movement:

These, and the rest, and all the rest we knew . . .

There *is* the subtler music, the clear light
Where time burns back about th'eternal embers.

In the first line above, Pound splits the inverted first foot with a caesura; in the next two lines, we find the rising Ionic flowing over the end of the line and into the next:

There *ís* | the súb | tler mú | sic, the cleár líght

Where tíme | *búrns* báck | a bóut | th'_e tér | nal ém | bers.

We note the holding effect of the unstressed long syllable in the second foot of the line above; the length of "burns" is approximately twice that of "back," on which the ictus falls. We have blank verse in *tempo rubato;* the right hand, freely moving and pausing among the quantities, plays over the steady syllable-stress base line.

A new rhythm distinguishes a somewhat later example of Pound's blank verse; here is the opening of the second part of "Near Perigord" (*Lustra,* 1915):

End fact. Try fiction. Let us say we see
En Bertrans, a tower-room at Hautefort,
Sunset, the ribbon-like road lies, in red cross-light,

> Southward toward Montaignac, and he bends at a table
> Scribbling, swearing between his teeth; by his left hand
> Lie little strips of parchment covered over,
> Scratched and erased with *al* and *ochaisos.*
> Testing his list of rhymes, a lean man? Bilious?
> With a red straggling beard?
> And the green cat's eye lifts toward Montaignac.

The rhythmical tune sounds familiar; we heard it before in *The Ring and the Book:*

> To stop song, loosen flower, and leave path . . .

Pound stretches the line both tighter and looser than Browning does. We have blank verse compressed to four beats—a strong-stress line:

> The dull round towers encroaching on the field,
> The tents tight drawn, horses at tether
> Farther and out of reach, the purple night,
> The crackling of small fires, the bannerets,
> The lazy leopards on the largest banner.

We have the verse flowing out in hexameters:

> Stray gleams on hanging mail, an armourer's torch-flame.
>
> "Say that he saw the castles, say that he loved Maent!"

The brilliant metrical surface of "Portrait d'une Femme" strikes the ear differently; many individual lines scan as blank verse, but the movement is highly varied and frequently a matter of vocal cadence:

> Great minds have sought you—lacking someone else.
> You have been second always. Tragical?
> No. You preferred it to the usual thing:
> One dull man, dulling and uxorious,
> One average mind—with one thought less, each year.

This kind of "irregularity" does not clash with other rhythms. Pound leads up to a metrical half-close by gradually bringing each line nearer to the iambic norm. The verse period begins with a half-line,

And takes strange gain away,

works into three lines where trisyllabic and trochaic feet unsettle the verse,

> Trophies fished up; some curious suggestion;
> Fact that leads nowhere; and a tale or two,
> Pregnant with mandrakes, or with something else,

and then slips back into regular iambic,

> That might prove useful and yet never proves,
> That never fits a corner or shows use,
> Or finds its hour upon the loom of days.

Pound demonstrates his prosodical brilliance in other than syllable-stress meters; *Ripostes* (1912) contains the strong-stress "The Seafarer" and the quantitative "Apparuit." There is little point in arguing whether "The Seafarer" is translation or "re-creation"; such lines as

> Cuckoo calleth with gloomy crying
> He singeth summerward, bodeth sorrow,
> The bitter heart's blood. Burgher knows not—

combine Ye Olde Englishe with Pound's favorite pidgin Eskimo. The use of the definite article—"*The* burgher knows not"—would hardly disturb the rhythm. It is not Pound's occasional mistranslations that set the reader's teeth on edge, but his lapses occasioned by straining after "flavor." His translation of

> þaer mec oft bigeat
> near nihtwaco   aet nacan stefnan
> þonne he be clifum cnossað

is close enough to satisfy even the dustiest Old Reader:

> and there I oft spent
> Narrow nightwatch nigh the ship's head
> While she tossed close to cliffs.

But why the archaic and cute "oft" and "nigh"? *Near* would be the subtler orchestration, with its modulated vowel and its delicate alliteration with "narrow."

All criticism, however, seems mean and carping given the poem's rhythmic magnificence. The strong-stress meter describes the slow arc of feeling; the continuous falling movement is the perfect vehicle for Pound's favorite theme, "Time is the evil. Evil" (*Canto 30*). Pound handles the meter more strictly than not, maintains a norm of three alliterated and four stressed syllables in each line, and varies the position of the medial pauses:

> Waneth the watch, but the world holdeth.
> Tomb hideth trouble. The blade is layed low.
> Earthly glory ageth and seareth.

"Waneth the watch, but the world holdeth" reproduces the meter of the original quite faithfully but mistakes the meaning of

> wuniað þa wacran   and þas woruld healdaþ,

"Weak men endure and inherit the earth." Perhaps Pound relied in this case on his ear. But the ear triumphs and only pedants regret the loss of the original meaning.

We offered a stanza from "Apparuit" in chapter 2 as an example of pseudoquantitative meter. Pound uses the Sapphic stanza whose paradigm is

$$— \, \smile \mid — \, \underline{\smile} \mid — \, \smile\smile \mid — \, \smile \mid — \, \underline{\smile}$$

repeated for three lines, followed by a short line (the adonic):

$$— \, \smile\smile \mid — \, \underline{\smile}$$

We see how closely Pound adheres to the pattern; we give the last two stanzas:

> Half the graven shoulder, the throat aflash with
> strands of light inwoven about it, loveli—
> est of all things, frail alabaster, ah me!
>   swift in departing.
>
> Clothed in goldish weft, delicately perfect,
> gone as wind! The cloth of the magical hands!

> Thou a slight thing, thou in access of cunning
> dar'dst to assume this?

Stress underlines quantity; the normal word accent coincides with (but in only one place, "access," combats) the length of vowel. The suppleness and ease of Pound's handling may be contrasted to Swinburne's—one of Pound's acknowledged masters. Swinburne's "Sapphics" are stiff and uncomfortable, the lines nearly awkward:

> All the night sleep came not upon my eyelids,
> Shed not dew, nor shook nor unclosed a feather,
> Yet with lips shut close and with eyes of iron
> Stood and beheld me.
>
> Then to me so lying awake a vision
> Came without sleep over the seas and touched me,
> Softly touched mine eyelids and lips; and I too,
> Full of the vision . . .

Pound's sapphics are unquestionably superior in syntax and in rightness of the quantities; they catch the rhythm—and hence the spirit—of their great original:

> κὰδ δέ μ'ἴδρως κακχέεται, τρόμος δὲ
> παῖσαν ἄγρει, χλωροτέρα δὲ ποίας
> ἔμμι, τεθνάκην δ' ὀλίγω' πιδεύης
> φαίνομ' ἀλαία.
>
> Sappho, "To a Bride"

> And the sweat breaks running upon me, fever
> shakes my body, paler I turn than grass is;
> I can feel that I have been changed, I feel that
> death has come near me.
>
> translation by Richmond Lattimore

❧ *III*

Pound's nonmetrical prosody comes in several varieties. "The Alchemist," from *Ripostes,* plays variations on a number of rhythmic constants. The poem is subtitled "Chant for the Transmutation of Metals" and is a catalog of exotic proper names collected from Pound's reading on medieval alchemy. The rhythms are established through enumerations, anaphora, and repeated syntax:

> Sail of Claustra, Aelis, Azalias,
> As you move among the bright trees;
> As your voices, under the larches of Paradise
> Make a clear sound . . .
>
> Bring the saffron-coloured shell,
> Bring the red gold of the maple,
> Bring the light of the birch tree in autumn
> Mirals, Cembelins, Audiarda,
>   Remember this fire . . .
> Midonz, with the gold of the sun, the leaf of the
>   poplar, by the light of the amber,
> Midonz, daughter of the sun, shaft of the tree,
>   silver of the leaf, light of the yellow of the
>   amber,
> Midonz, gift of the God, gift of the light, gift of
>   the amber of the sun,
>   Give light to the metal . . .

Pound uses a great variety of enumerative and parallel techniques in the *Lustra* volume. "Salutation," "Salutation the Second," and "Commission" all descend prosodically from Whitman; Pound, with some surliness, acknowledges his debt in "A Pact":

> I make a pact with you, Walt Whitman—
> I have detested you long enough.
> I come to you as a grown child
> Who has had a pig-headed father . . .
>
> We have one sap and one root—
> Let there be commerce between us.

Evocative handling of quantity sustains the syntactic rhythms; the first two lines of "Surgit Fama" suggest Virgilian hexameters:

> There īs ā | trŭce ā mŏng | the gŏds, / Kŏrē īs |
>
> seēn īn thĕ | North

The last lines echo the rhythm of the first with Pound's favorite mixture of spondees and dactyls:

> Once more in Delos, once more is the altar a-quiver.
> Once more is the chant heard.

Other poems in *Lustra* that move to free quantitative measures include "Dance Figure" and "Gentildonna."

A number of the imagist poems in *Lustra* approximate the syllabic haiku. The following examples contain nineteen and twenty, instead of the prescribed seventeen, syllables:

> FAN PIECE . . .
> O fan of white silk,
>   clear as frost on the grass-blade,
> You also are laid aside.

> LI PO
> And Li Po also died drunk.
> He tried to embrace a moon
> In the Yellow River.

The prosody of Pound's imagist period relies little on visual effects, line arrangement, stanzaic shaping, and other vagaries. The permanent, and probably damaging—we shall speak of this below—contribution of Pound's 1912–15 years was the fashioning of "prose song." Pound reviewed Ford Madox Ford's *Collected Poems* and praised lines like these for their "leisurely, low toned" qualities:

> 'Though you're in Rome you will not go, my You,
> Up to that Hill . . . but I forget the name.
> Aventine? Pincio? No, I never knew . . .
> I was there yesterday. You never came.
>
> I have that Rome; and you, you have a Me,
> You have a Rome, and I, I have my You.[16]

Pound's affection for Ford must have deafened his ears; if this is "the prose tradition in verse," then flatness and ineptness must be virtues.

At the time (1915) Pound's own practice hardly follows Ford's; music, not ineptness, created "The River Song." This is an adaptation (through Fenollosa) from the Chinese poet Li Po:

At the time (1915) Pound's own practice hardly follows Ford's; music, not ineptness, created "The River Song." This is an adaptation (through Fenollosa) from the Chinese poet Li Po:

> This boat is of shato-wood, and its gunwales are cut magnolia,
> Musicians with jewelled flutes and with pipes of gold
> Fill full the sides in rows, and our wine
> Is rich for a thousand cups.
> We carry singing girls, drift with the drifting water,
> Yet Sennin needs
> A yellow stork for a charger, and all our seamen
> Would follow the white gulls or ride them.
> Kutsu's prose song
> Hangs with the sun and moon.

This may be poetry "as well written as prose," but its rhythm depends on the delicate balancing of the metrical with the nonmetrical. Only a poet who wrote well in regular meter could have written the superb hexameter:

> We carry singing girls, drift with the drifting water.

The iambic movement is softly muted by the inverted fourth foot and the feminine ending. To call this "prose song" was misleading to all the Poundlings who never learned to sing. Just as many poets thought they wrote like Whitman because they began each line with the same sequence of words, so some thought they wrote like Pound because they stitched together lines of varying length and stultifying flatness.

It is a misnomer to call "The River Song" free verse; the lines, in scansion, fall easily into metrical feet. No line in our example has more than two consecutive unstressed syllables—which reduces the authentic prose effect. We hear a more obvious prose movement in "Villanelle: The Psychological Hour." This poem relies on line arrangement for deliberate rhetorical emphasis; Pound also uses an italicized refrain:

> I had over-prepared the event,
>   that much was ominous.
>   With middle-ageing care

> I had laid out just the right books.
> I had almost turned down the pages.
>
> *Beauty is so rare a thing.*
> *So few drink of my fountain.*
>
> So much barren regret,
> So many hours wasted!
> And now I watch, from the window,
>   the rain, the wandering busses.

The refrain is metered in trochees and fits smoothly with the freer, nonmetrical lines. A falling rhythm predominates, lightening the lugubrious self-pity:

> *Beauty would drink of my mind.*
> Youth would awhile forget
>   my youth is gone from me.

The dying fall of the last line

>   my yoúth | is góne | from mé

gives the necessary ironic tone to the voice. A man barely thirty cannot be discovered, in all seriousness, lamenting his fled youth.

❧ IV

When Pound and Eliot were new friends, benefiting from each other's stimulation, they resolved to do something about the general state of English prosody circa 1918–20. Pound recommended a return to traditional meters:

> at a particular date in a particular room, two authors, neither engaged in picking the other's pockets, decided that the dilution of *vers libre,* Amygism, Lee Masterism, general floppiness had gone too far and that some counter current must be set going . . . Remedy prescribed "Émaux et Camées" (or the Bay State Hymn Book). Rhyme and regular strophes.
>
>   Results: Poems in Mr. Eliot's second volume . . . also "H. S. MAUBERLEY."[17]

Mauberley displays an overall rhythmical hardness combined with an accomplished freedom. Its metrical *cantus firmus* derives, as Pound explains, from the octosyllabic couplet used in Gautier's *vers de société, Émaux et Camées.*

Pound does not copy Gautier's stanza but adapts it to English meter. He measures accents rather than syllables; the opening section of *Mauberley* moves in four- and five-stress lines:

> For three years, out of key with his time,
> He strove to resuscitate the dead art
> Of poetry; to maintain "the sublime"
> In the old sense. Wrong from the start—
>
> No, hardly, but seeing he had been born
> In a half-savage country, out of date;
> Bent resolutely on wringing lilies from the acorn;
> Capaneus; trout for factitious bait . . .

The rhyming is *abab* in sections 1 and 2; in section 3 Pound changes to a more relaxed scheme of rhyming only the second and fourth lines:

> Faun's flesh is not to us,
> Nor the saint's vision.
> We have the Press for wafer;
> Franchise for circumcision.
>
> All men, in law, are equals.
> Free of Pisistratus,
> We choose a knave or an eunuch
> To rule over us.
>
> O bright Apollo,
> τίν ἄνδρα, τίν' ἥρωα τίνα θεὸν,
> What god, man, or hero
> Shall I place a tin wreath upon!

The use of macaronic rhymes (θεὸν, "upon") can also be traced to Gautier.

Mauberley's rhyming deserves detailed scrutiny. Some of the double-rhymed unstressed endings strike the note of comic doggerel:

> Knowing my coat has never been
> Of precisely the fashion
> To stimulate, in her,
> A durable passion;
>
> Doubtful, somewhat, of the value
> Of well-gowned approbation
> Of literary effort,
> But never of The Lady Valentine's vocation.

Pound rhymes with Byronic slap and dash; *Mauberley* has yet to be recognized as essentially comic; not only in theme but in details of technique. John Espey minimizes the comic and Byronic impulses in *Mauberley*,[18] but lines like these are out of *Don Juan:*

> Nothing, in brief, but maudlin confession,
> Irresponse to human aggression,
> Amid the precipitation, down-float
> Of insubstantial manna,
> Lifting the faint susurrus
> Of his subjective hosannah.

A romantic ironist, Pound turns the weapons of satire and ridicule upon himself. The rhythms trickle into sand in the above passage; the rhymes, "confession"/"aggression," "manna"/"hosannah," are tired inspirations. These are intended effects; Pound makes fun of himself—up to a point. Self-pity replaces self-ridicule in the next quatrain:

> Non-esteem of self-styled "his betters"
> Leading, as he well knew,
> To his final
> Exclusion from the world of letters.

How much of Pound is Mauberley, or whether Mauberley bears *any* resemblance to Pound, has been a critical ass's bridge. Mauberley's complaint of "Exclusion from the world of letters" has no biographical relevance. After his arrival in Europe, Pound quickly entered literary circles, experienced little difficulty in getting published, was friend and equal to Yeats, Joyce, and Eliot. The character Mauberley is a fiction, compounded out of Pound's fragile ego, some shrewd self-criticism, and much projective rhetoric. The versification testifies to this compounding. Gautier's quatrain supplies the basic metrical melody, but we hear this melody only briefly. The opening quatrains are heavily counterpointed; indeed, scansion shows no regular foot:

> For thrée | yeárs, out | of key | with his tíme . . .
> In the old sénse. | Wróng from | the stárt—
> In a hálf-sáv | age coún | try, oút | of dáte . . .

Nonmetrical lines fit easily into this scheme:

> Bent resolutely on wringing lilies from the acorn . . .
>
> The chopped seas hid him, therefore, that year.

The stanza shrinks down to two beats; the rhythm diminishes:

> Turned from the "eau forte
> Par Jacquemart"
> To the strait head
> Of Messalina:
>
> "His true Penelope
> Was Flaubert,"
> And his tool
> The engraver's.

In the recapitulation ("THE AGE DEMANDED") rhythm is augmented; the movement leisurely, Whitmanian:

> Incapable of the least utterance or composition,
> Emendation, conservation of the "better tradition,"
> Refinement of medium, elimination of superfluities,
> August attraction or concentration.

Here Pound builds his rhythm by the enumeration of Latin polysyllables. Mauberley enters tropical waters and slowly drifts into nonexistence. The metric meanders and murmurs, finally settles in an epitaph of slow dimeter and monometer:

"I was
And I no more exist;
Here drifted
An hedonist."

All that remains of Gautier's stanza is the rhyme, "exist"/"hedonist."

The persona Mauberley, beauty struck and fashionably alienated, was described by Pound himself as "mere surface. Again a study in form, an attempt to condense the James novel."[19] The metrical surface is similarly condensed. The rhythm moves toward extreme compression; the tempo is quick, nervous with "Syncopation from the Greek."[20] The base rhythm, provided by the Gautier stanza, holds together the loose texture of images, impressions, and *vignettes de société*. Without this carrying rhythm, the poem would break apart into unshored and ruinous fragments. With it, the poem achieves a special vitality and coherence and a place in the canon of twentieth-century poetry.

Although the *Homage to Sextus Propertius* (1917) precedes *Mauberley* in composition, its overall poetic method and specific prosodical character bring it close to the *Cantos*. We regard the *Homage,* as Eliot does, as "the necessary prolegomena to the *Cantos*": their immediate technical and spiritual precursor. Its sudden transitions, oblique references, and entanglement of mythological and personal allusion are the familiar devices of Pound's epic. The *Homage* also resembles the *Cantos* in versification. Pound adapts from Propertius's elegiac meter a loosely dactylic line with its falling rhythm. The *Cantos* are an extreme prosodic mixture and in many sections forsake formal versification, but what traces we discern of a carrying metric sound like Pound's favorite dactylic-spondaic—the basic feet in the elegiac paradigm. In both the *Homage* and the *Cantos* the rhythm is wide open, of course; it can accommodate the freest cadence of slang or the most elegantly polished hexameter.

Pound found in Propertius a kindred spirit. Propertius is enigmatic, gloomy, "difficult," and given to contradictory and violent moods. Like Pound he is a historical pessimist, believing in the imminent collapse of civilization, and complaining, like any contemporary *poete maudit,* of a culture hostile to poets and poetry. He also displays Pound's odd emotional polarity: a sense of absolute personal defeat alternating with wild and extravagant hopes. He argues, as Pound

argued in the teens and twenties, that the poetry of the latest age is
distended and overblown, that it has sacrificed craft to "Caesar's
affairs":

> Annalists will continue to record Roman reputations,
> Celebrities from the Trans-Caucasus will belaud
>   Roman celebrities
> And expound the distentions of Empire,
> But for something to read in normal circumstances?
> For a few pages brought down from the forked hill unsullied?

And like Pound, Propertius believes fate has destined him to purify the
Muse:

> Now if ever it is time to cleanse Helicon;
>   to lead Emathian horses afield.

Propertius shows amusing ambivalence toward the epic. However
much he mocks the Virgilian organ tones and imperial stance, he
yearns to sing the larger strain and change from reeds to trumpets. He
projects a poem celebrating the excitements of Caesar Augustus's
expanding empire:

> The primitive ages sang Venus,
>   the last sings of a tumult,
> And I also will sing war when this matter of a girl is exhausted.
> I with my beak hauled ashore would proceed in a more stately
>   manner,
> My Muse is eager to instruct me in a new gamut, or gambetto,
> Up, up my soul, from your lowly cantilation,
>   put on a timely vigour.
>
> O august Pierides! Now for a large-mouthed product.

This is *Propertius through Pound*. The *Homage* paraphrases and fills out
Propertius's text with the emotional contents of Pound's tempera-
ment. Pound enlarges and applies to himself the self-mockery and
heavy irony he discovers. The originality of the *Homage* rests in this
technique of expanding the feeling, of making something intensely
personal out the Latin. Pound also wanted to move from personal

involvement and lyric form—*Mauberley* is essentially a suite of lyrics—to larger themes.

Propertius writes in the meter common to Latin, and earlier Greek, elegiac poets. An elegiac poem consists of a series of couplets; each couplet is made up of a line of hexameter followed by a line of pentameter. Like its English cousin, the heroic couplet, the elegiac holds in two lines a complete thought in a finished syntactical unit. Propertius handles the couplet with great expressiveness and colloquial vigor.

Pound freely renders Propertius's meter and catches the abrupt syntactical patterning, the quick turns of speech, and the overall descending movement. Pound makes no attempt to reproduce the quantitative structure but rather demonstrates his usual genius in handling syllabic weights and durations. This is Pound's version of Propertius:

> Midnight, and a letter comes to me from
>   our mistress:
> Telling me to come to Tibur:
>   *At* once!!
> "Bright tips reach up from twin towers,
> "Anienan spring water falls into flat-spread pools."
>
> What is to be done about it?
>   Shall I entrust myself to entangled shadows,
> Where bold hands may do violence to my person?

Pound maintains Propertius's dialectic: the sudden pause and question, the balance of one line against the other. Pound gets the sense of extreme compression that the Latin conveys and the sense of exact rhythmic balancing. Pound also balances "bits of rhythm": "Midnight;" "At once"; "Bright tips." The spondee becomes a structural element. Sound values also carry over into the English.

What prosodic inspiration Pound takes from Propertius can be seen in comparing other passages. The exquisite balance of the Latin, the give and take of hexameter and pentameter stand behind these lines:

> The moon will carry his candle,
>   the stars will point out the stumbles,
> Cupid will carry lighted torches before him
>   and keep mad dogs off his ankles.

Behind these, the magnificent sonority of the Latin vowels:

> For long night comes upon you
> > and a day when no day returns.
> Let the gods lay chain upon us
> > so that no day shall unbind them.
>
> > Nox tibi longa venit nec reditura dies.
> Atque utinam haerentes sic nos vincire catena
> > Velles, ut numquam solveret ulla dies!

Occasionally Pound falls into the actual swing of the Latin, and we have the best English equivalents of the quantitative hexameter:

> Death has his tooth in the lot,
> > Avernus lusts for the lot of them,
> Beauty is not eternal, no man has perennial fortune,
> Slow foot, or swift foot, death delays but for a season.

& *V*

The *Cantos* enlarge upon the material and method of the *Homage*. Pound's scope widens from Augustan Rome to nearly all history. Anachronism, which has merely local and comic functions in the *Homage*—

> My cellar does not date from Numa Pompilius,
> Nor bristle with wine jars,
> Nor is it equipped with a frigidaire patent

—develops into a major principle of composition in the *Cantos*. The mingling of myth and personal history, of gossip and chronicle, of indisputable fact with the wildest prejudice has qualitative affinities with the adaptations from Propertius. But in length and intention the *Cantos* loom as a monstrous expansion; their sheer bulk dwarfs the earlier poem. We stress the importance of length; the *Cantos* raise special questions of syntax and prosody, and more crucially than the *Homage*, questions of structural coherence. We also stress Pound's "history" and his anachronistic mode of presenting it.

Pound's intended purpose in the *Cantos* is to tell the truth about History; the jacket of *Section: Rock Drill, Cantos 85–98* announces that the *Cantos* are the tale of the tribe . . . it is their purpose to give the true meaning of history as one man has found it: in the annals of ancient China, in the Italian Renaissance, in the letters and diaries of Jefferson, the Adamses and Van Buren, in the personalities of his own time. The lies of history must be exposed; the truth must be hammered home by reiteration, with the insistence of a rock-drill.

The *Cantos are* history: completely, aggressively, staggeringly so. They bulge with facts and supposed facts, teem with people and events. Much of the substance of the *Cantos* we recognize as direct chronicle, the matrix out of which rational histories have been written. Pound gives the documents, letters, papers, and anecdotes. It would be hard to deny that the *Cantos* are "the tale of the tribe."

Pound's peculiar telling of the tale, however, creates vexing formal difficulties and becomes an instrument for destroying the *Cantos* as poetry. Pound sets out to annihilate sequential time in his epic by fixing events in deliberate temporal disorder. His compositional method depends on the wholesale use of anachronism; in the prophetic mind of the poet, "All ages are contemporaneous."[21] Queen Elizabeth I, von Moltke, Andrew Jackson, and St. Ambrose, the fourth-century bishop of Milan, simultaneously live in a timeless world:

> "JESUS ! !"
> quoth the Queen, 1584 anno Domini, "sterling,
> pound sterling how much? 13,000. It is not to be looked for."
> From ploughing of fields is justice,
>   and if words be not solid
> Von Moltke, Fontainebleau, 1867, "a stag hunt"
>   "In locis desertis
>
> "laetamur, silvis in mediis.
>   "tondentur, occiditis, mulgentur
> "quibus agrum colitis.
>   "Cruorem funditis,
>   "carnes intrinsecus vos onerant
>   "Corporum sepulcra mortuorum viventia."
>   Ambrose "De Brachmanorum."
> "That Virginia be sovreign," said Andy Jackson
>   "never parted with . . ."
>   Oh GAWD ! ! ! that tenth section . . .

"any portion of . . ."
            DAMN IT.

Canto 100

This passage is an extreme example of temporal distortion and historical compression. But an earlier instance, from *Canto 3*, illustrates Pound's odd historiography: that the past need not be considered in its conventional chronological order and its putative pattern of cause and effect.

> My Cid rode up to Burgos,
> Up to the studded gate between two towers,
> Beat with his lance butt, and the child came out,
> Una niña de nueve años,
> To the little gallery over the gate, between the towers,
> Reading the writ, voce tinnula:
> That no man speak to, feed, help Ruy Diaz,
> On pain to have his heart out, set on a pike spike
> And both his eyes torn out, and all his goods sequestered,
> "And here, My Cid, are the seals,
> The big seal and the writing."
> And he came down from Bivar, My Cid,
> With no hawks left there on their perches,
> And no clothes there in the presses,
> And left his trunk with Raquel and Vidas,
> That big box of sand, with the pawn-brokers,
> To get pay for his menie;
> Breaking his way to Valencia.
> Ignez da Castro murdered, and a wall
> Here stripped, here made to stand.
> Drear waste, the pigment flakes from the stone,
> Or plaster flakes, Mantegna painted the wall.
> Silk tatters, "Nec Spe Nec Metu."

The passage deals with three eras: eleventh-century Spain, fourteenth-century Portugal, and fifteenth-century Italy. There is a probably accidental progression from the eleventh to the fifteenth century; but it is not chronology that affords this passage unity. The historical instances exemplify pathetic change; we witness the Cid's

frustrated heroism, the cruel and senseless murder of Ignez da Castro, and the slow decay of a fresco by Mantegna. Emotion and rhythm hold these lines together. As long as Pound maintains rhythmic force, a prosody that the ear can hear, the *Cantos* possess at least the unity of tone and sound.

The opening of *Canto 1* augurs well for the prosodic health of the whole poem. The measure is that of "The Seafarer," strong-stress meter with four heavy beats to the line. The strong-stress line sustains narrative and modulates with easy fluency from formal to gamey speech. While it is hard to say what exactly the carrying prosody of the *Cantos* is, it is easy to discover what it is not. Blank verse or any variation on the iambic norm figure minimally in the *Cantos*. We have occasional passages of Browningesque "stretched blank verse,"

> We also made ghostly visits, and the stair
> That knew us, found us again on the turn of it,
> Knocking at empty rooms, seeking for buried beauty

but the iambic movement is worried by trisyllabic substitution.

Pound combines the strong-stress meter with other, freer rhythms. Canto 3 opens in Pound's most luminous and limpid "quantities":

> I sat on the Dogana's steps . . .
>
>   Gods float in the azure air,
> Bright gods and Tuscan, back before dew was shed.
> Light: and the first light, before ever dew was fallen.
> Panisks, and from the oak, dryas,
> And from the apple, maelid,
> Through all the wood, and the leaves are full of voices.

The same rhythms move through Canto 4:

> The silver mirrors catch the bright stones and flare,
> Dawn, to our waking, drifts in the green cool light;
> Dew-haze blurs, in the grass, pale ankles moving.
> Beat, beat, whirr, thud in the soft turf
>   under the apple trees.

We recognize Pound's prosodical signature, the dactylic-anapestic and spondaic paradigms:

Líght: and the | fírst líght, | before év | er déw | was fáll | en . . .

Dáwn, to our | wák ing, | drifts in the | gréen cóol | líght . . .

Béat, béat, | whirr, thúd, | in the sóft túrf . . .

This signature is written on almost any page of the *Cantos;* for random verification we cite and scan lines from all sections of the poem:

Évil and | fúrther | évil, and a | cúrse cúrsed |

on our chíl | dren.

Canto 2

And the síl | ver béaks | rí sing and | cróss ing.

Stóne trées, | whíte and | róse-white | in the dárk | ness.

Canto 17

And in Aú | gust that yéar | díed Pópe | Al es sán | dro Bór | gia.

Canto 30

The shá dow | of the tent's péak | tréads on its | cór ner peg

márk ing the | hóur. The | móon splít, | no clóud | néarer

than | Lucca.

Canto 78

Till the blúe gráss | turn yél | low

and the yél | low léaves | float in | áir.

Canto 99

Chárity | Í have had | sóme tímes

Í cannot | máke it | flów thrú.

Canto 116

Our "scansions" lay the lines down in Procrustean beds; we are not reading structural meter but showing an approximate rhythmical direction. A predominant dactylic-spondaic foot generates a falling rhythm—which prevails in the *Cantos* when rhythm is present.

We have already seen the literal reverse of this type of movement, the accumulative, building rhythm in the long lines of Robinson Jeffers. Working quite independently of one another, the two poets, each cut from prophetic cloth, discovered many of the same solutions in constructing the long poem. The major differences between the two lie in Jeffers's respect for the portrayal of events in sequential time, and his rejection of deliberate temporal disorder.

Throughout the *Cantos* the sustaining movement is intermittent. No unifying mode of versification establishes itself. Beginning with *Canto 30*, the initial rhythmic impetus begins to falter and is broken by large blocks of prose. Beginning with *Canto 52*, Chinese ideograms and other visual devices gradually supplement audible prosodic means. Without an overall sounding rhythm, syntax (never Pound's strong point) staggers. An audible rhythm can cover the lack of syntactical closeness: truncated word groups, omitted articles, and shorthand grammar may have charm when rhythmically supported:

> Sun up; work
> sundown; to rest
> dig well and drink of the water
> dig field; eat of the grain
> Imperial power is? and to us what is it?
>
> The fourth; the dimension of stillness.
> And the power over wild beasts.
>
> *Canto 49*

As long as we hear spondees and dactyls, the lack of syntactical closeness is not serious. But when the rhythm peters out and no longer carries Pound's disconnected syntax, we have this as historical narrative:

> Lord North, purblind to the rights of a
> continent, eye on a few London merchants . . .
> no longer saw redcoat
> as brother or as a protector
> (Boston about the size of Rapallo)
> scarce 16,000,
> habits of freedom now formed

> even among those who scarcely got so far as analysis
> so about 9 o'c in the morning Lard Narf wuz bein'
>   impassible.
>
>   *Canto 62*

We have for a prosody a tone of voice, for syntax a tangle of uncon-nected references.

Pound's defenders have advanced the theory of the ideogram to uncover the method and justify the coherence of the *Cantos.* Hugh Kenner tells us for the *Cantos,* "Plot, in the Dickensian sense, is ob-solete." Kenner also tells us that "a philosophical system, a chronologi-cal or geographical ordering of events . . . would be no more relevant to the *Cantos* than a chain of anagrams."[22] Instead of narrative or discursive structure, an authentic syntax, the *Cantos* achieve structural unity through the ideogrammatic method. Pound does not present merely abstract words, emptied of their "thingness" and yoked to-gether by the sterile articulations of formal grammar; he presents ideograms.

The application of the ideogram to English language and poetic frankly baffles us. Yet many admirers of the *Cantos* argue their "ideo-grammatic unity." It is as if the poem were written in pictures, not words. "Thinking by ideogram," as Pound actually practices it, means a poetry of vivid images and strong ideas functioning with a minimum of syntax. Ideas and images can achieve a structure of sorts through mere juxtaposition:

> IN A STATION OF THE METRO
> The apparition of these faces in the crowd;
> Petals on a wet, black bough.

Here "ideogrammatic method" means poetry without complete sen-tences. The absence of verb and preposition enhances both rhythm and significance; a certain mystery evaporates if we supply the implied copula and relational word:

> The apparition of these faces in the crowd
> [Is like] Petals on a wet, black bough.

No harm comes if we want to see this as vaguely analogous to Chinese writing; the two images have spatial and emotional relationships.

Grammar, however, is not missing; it is automatically supplied by the reader.

"In a Station of the Metro" comes from Pound's 1912–14 period and is often quoted as the characteristic imagist poem. Later, when ideogrammatic method takes over in the *Cantos,* we see that the long poem continually breaks down into shorter imagist poems, often no longer than one or two lines:

> a man on whom the sun has gone down
> the ewe, he said had such a pretty look in her eyes;
> and the nymph of the Hagoromo came to me,
>   as a corona of angels
> one day were clouds banked on Taishan
>   or in glory of sunset
>   and tovarish blessed without aim
> wept in the rainditch of evening
>   Sunt lumina

Canto 74

Each line or two articulates a single image; nothing, not even an implied grammar or an emotional consistency, articulates one image with another. To say that the coherence of this passage devolves on the method of Chinese writing gives assent to the notion that language can be manipulated like brightly colored bits of glass, or that the description of language used in a certain way can be anything, finally, the speaker wishes it to be.

The ideogrammatic method parallels the anachronistic historiography of the *Cantos.* A programmatically anachronistic history throws events together regardless of their chronological syntax; the ideogram denies that the formal syntax of language is necessary to poetic logic. Together, ideogram and anachronism turn the *Cantos* into myth, "where past, present, and future are still tied up together; they form an undifferentiated unity and indiscriminate whole. Mythical time has no definite structure; it is still an 'eternal time.' From the point of view of the mythical consciousness the past has never passed away; it is always here and now."[23] In the undifferentiated unity and indiscriminate whole of the *Cantos,* the destruction of chronology makes all history contemporary history and all reality phantasmagorically "present."

As mythical and ideogrammatic method becomes pervasive in the *Cantos,* Pound more and more forgets that significant rhythms must have an aural shape in time. We previously noted the intermittent nature of the initial rhythmic impetus. Pound occasionally recovers the rhythm, as in sections of *The Pisan Cantos*. We find passages in Pound's loveliest "English quantities":

> No glass is clearer than are the globes of this flame
> what sea is clearer than the pomegranate body
>   holding the flame?
>   Pomona, Pomona.
>
> *Canto 79*

We also find Pound in one rare iambic pentameter mood, writing in the stanza and rhythm of *The Rubáiyát:*

> Tudor indeed is gone and every rose,
> Blood-red, blanch-white that in the sunset glows
> Cries: "Blood, Blood, Blood!" against the gothic stone
> Of England, as the Howard or Boleyn knows.
>
> *Canto 80*

or blank verse with irregular rhyme:

> The ant's a centaur in his dragon world.
> Pull down thy vanity, it is not man
> Made courage, or made order, or made grace,
>   Pull down thy vanity, I say pull down.
> Learn of the green world what can be thy place
> In scaled invention or true artistry,
> Pull down thy vanity,
>   Paquin pull down!
> The green casque has outdone your elegance.
>
> *Canto 81*

But these are infrequent intervals; the dominant rhythm that falters after *Canto 31* is undetectable after *Canto 84*. From *Cantos 85* to *109* the "prosody" is oppressively visual, depending on line arrangements, spacing, and stunts. *Canto 75* is a page of music; *Cantos 85, 86,* and *98* are largely printed ideograms; *Cantos 93* and *97* fiddle with hiero-glyphics. The greater "unity" of *Section: Rock Drill, Cantos 85–95* and

Thrones (*Cantos 96–109*) lies in their orthography. What audible versification exists has little structural power because it affects the ear too faintly to set up verbal echoes or create a pattern of expectation.

In an early 1960s interview for *The Paris Review*, Donald Hall questioned Pound about the progress of his epic. Pound's replies were poignant, pointing out his recognition of the need for greater clarity, and for a wide revision, which he knew he would not live to accomplish:

Interviewer

Since your internment, you've published three collections of *Cantos*, *Thrones* just recently. You must be near the end. Can you say what you are going to do in the remaining *Cantos*? . . . Are you more or less stuck?

Pound

Okay, I am stuck. The question is, am I dead, as Messrs. A.B.C. might wish? In case I conk out, this is provisionally what I have to do: I must clarify obscurities; I must make clearer definite ideas or dissociations. I must find a verbal formula to combat the rise of brutality—the principle of order versus the split atom. . . .

I don't know. There's need of elaboration, of clarification, but I don't know that a comprehensive revision is in order. There is no doubt that the writing is too obscure as it stands, but I hope that the order of ascension in the *Paradiso* will be toward a greater limpidity. . . .[24]

Cantos 115 and *116*, published in the same issue of *The Paris Review*, do achieve a greater limpidity and a new measure of coherence. The ideograms and other visual contrivances have disappeared; in their place we find some of Pound's magical quantities:

> I have brought the great ball of crystal,
>   who can lift it?
> Can you enter the great acorn of light?
>
> but the beauty is not the madness
> Tho my errors and wrecks lie about me.
>
>   and I cannot make it cohere.

Canto 116

"I cannot make it cohere . . ." *Canto 116* laments Pound's inability to bring the *Cantos* into clarity and

> affirm the gold thread in the pattern.

And no better criticism of the *Cantos* exists than these last lines with their pathos, agony, and essential honesty:

> Charity, I have had sometimes,
>   I cannot make it flow thru.
> A little light like a rush light
>   to lead back splendour.

੨ VI

Before Pound returned to Italy, he made a recording of *Cantos 1, 4, 36,* and *84*.[25] The recording is proof that Pound was a remarkable reader: his voice is vigorous and extraordinarily well modulated. He affects an Irish brogue, heavily trilling the *r*s and allowing his voice to fall at the ends of lines. The effect is a beautifully stylized chant that holds firmly to metrical bedrock—when such bedrock is offered.

Pound's voice emphasizes the four-beat structure of *Canto 1*. In these lines

> Bore sheep aboard her, and our bodies also
> Heavy with weeping, and winds from sternward
> Bore us out onward with bellying canvas,
> Circe's this craft, the trim-coifed goddess.

he marks with slight but perceptible stresses the alliterated *b*s of the first line and the repeated *c*s of the fourth line. He holds the caesuras for at least the length of a stressed syllable, carefully balancing the half-lines. In the line

> Thus with stretched sail, we went over sea till day's end

Pound pauses significantly on the stressed *sea* and reads the four light syllables *we went ov-er* with quick, even precision. He declaims, also with significant pauses and emphases:

> But first Elpenor came, our friend Elpenor.

The line startles with its unforeseen expressiveness. The labials *f* and *p* are the metrical checkpoints; Pound trills the *r*s of "first" and "friend" and pronounces "Elpenor" in the Greek fashion, Ἐλπήνορ, prolonging the stressed πή (which is pronounced *pay*).

Canto 4 is a suite of natural sounds. We hear a chorus of nymphs and satyrs:

> Beat, beat, whirr, thud, in the soft turf
>   under the apple trees.

We hear the swallows crying in the tongueless voice of Procne, mourning her slaughtered son Itys. By homonymic metamorphosis *Itys* becomes "It is":

> "All the while, the while, swallows crying:
> Itys!
>   "It is Cabestan's heart in the dish."
>   "It is Cabestan's heart in the dish?"

Unwitting cannibalism links the myth of Tereus and the story of Guillaume de Cabestan. Procne fed the flesh of Itys to her murderous husband Tereus; the jealous husband of Marguerite fed her the heart of Cabestan, her troubador lover. Pound's reading catches the eerie cry of the swallows:

> 'Tis. 'Tis. Ytis!

Pound unvoices the *s* of "'Tis," hissing the syllables in sharp onomatopoeia.

Two superb lines of Canto 4 become audible rhythmic echoes as Pound's voice takes full account of their prosodic form: first the eleven syllable

> The empty armour shakes as the cygnet moves

and its answer, in nearly equal syllables twenty lines later,

> A scarlet flower is cast on the blanch-white stone.

The two lines are completely realized imagist poems related to each other by their rhythmic form: music for syntax once again.

Pound's delivery of *Canto 84* tries to compensate for its prosodic disorder. Since he no longer has an audible metric to guide him— neither the strong-stress lines of *Canto 1* nor the quantities of *Canto 4*—he reads dramatically. His mimicry of a Southern senator's dialect is very funny:

> "an' doan you think he chop an' change all the time
> stubborn az a mule, sah, stubborn as a MULE."

A tone of ironic deprecation, projected by heavily falling cadences, characterizes these political and personal sallies:

> Thus the solons, in Washington,
> on the executive, and on the country, a.d. 1939
>
> and Mr Sinc Lewis has not
>   and Bartók has left us
>
> and that Vandenberg has read Stalin, or Stalin, John Adams
> is, at the mildest, unproven.

Canto 84 ends with an often-quoted couplet: we find relief in this sudden shift back to metrical stability:

> If the hoar frost grip thy tent
> Thou wilt give thanks when night is spent.

The music returns to Pound's voice as it briefly rediscovers formal poetic diction and the security of rhymed tetrameter. Pound descends from the soapbox and once again is the poet, affirming the thread in the pattern and entering the circles of light.

VII

T. S. Eliot and the Music
of Poetry

❧ *I*

Eliot has given us unforgettable rhythms—rhythms that echo and reecho in the mind's ear. We need only go to our memories for prosodical touchstones: lines grasped long ago by the "auditory imagination" and never lost. They recover an emotion from personal or racial origins, recall some shuddering gesture of the spirit, or catch the flat intonation of a bored voice. It is the heard rhythms that animate these lines:

> Where worried bodies of drowned men drift down in the green
> silence . . .

> Whispers and small laughter between leaves and hurrying feet
> Under sleep, where all waters meet.

> The awful daring of a moment's surrender
> Which an age of prudence can never retract

> Let Mr. Sweeney continue his story.
> I assure you, Sir, we are very interested.

Eliot's rhythms, capable of such variety in movement and sonority, return us to the musical function of prosody. No modern poet has so effectively used rhythm to evoke a "knowledge of how feelings go"; no rhythms have shown such power to summon emotion to the forefront of consciousness.

Eliot was aware of prosody-as-music. Whether he speaks, dry-mouthed and stammering,

And no rock
If there were rock
And also water
And water
A spring,

The Waste Land

or smoothly sings of a frozen moment, "suspended in time,"

In windless cold that is the heart's heat,
Reflecting in a watery mirror
A glare that is blindness in the early afternoon,

Little Gidding

the patterns of stress and pause, quantity, dynamics, and syntax reach down and "make conceivable" the richness of the inner life of feeling. Eliot quarreled with Pater's ethical notions, but Eliot's prosody—the function of the "auditory imagination"—aspires toward the condition of music.

Eliot does not approach the condition of music in order to submerge his ideas in his form or merely to create pleasing sounds. To Eliot "the music of poetry" means a great deal more than melodious verse, achieved through smooth textures and verbal tone color. The music of poetry is not "the elemental sound of brasses, strings, or wood-winds, but the intellectual and written word in all its glory—music of perfect fullness and clarity, the totality of universal relationships."[1] Alliteration and assonance, or such onomatopoeia as "Forlorn! the very word is like a bell" are not the essential music of poetry: it lies in "the totality of universal relationships."

Eliot's verse first establishes these relationships through the articulating structures of syntax. Syntax, the order of words as they arrange themselves into patterns of meaning, is the analogue to harmony in music. Like harmony, syntax generates tension and relaxation, the feelings of expectation and fulfillment that make up the dynamics of poetic life. Susanne Langer remarks:

The tension which music achieves through dissonance, and the reorientation in each new resolution to harmony, find their equivalents in the suspensions and periodic decisions of propositional sense in poetry. Literal sense, not euphony, is the "harmonic structure" of poetry; word melody in literature is more akin to tone color in music.[2]

Syntax gives us the arc of "literal sense," the articulations of meaning. Like harmony in music, syntax makes connections, strengthens ideas, and relates thematic material. Eliot himself emphasizes that music in poetry does not inhere in word melody and tone color, but in the harmony of meanings and connections:

> It would be a mistake, however, to assume that all poetry ought to be melodious, or that melody is more than one of the components of the music of words. . . . The music of a word is, so to speak, at a point of intersection: it arises from its relation first to the words immediately preceding and following it, and indefinitely to the rest of its context; and from another relation, that of its immediate meaning in that context to all the other meanings which it had in other contexts, to its greater or less wealth of association.[3]

The reverberation of words, their semantic resonances, are the shifting tones in the harmony of intersections and associations.

Eliot's syntax carries the bass line of his prosody. Through a deliberate and idiosyncratic use of repeated grammar and repeated words, Eliot achieves qualities common to both music and poetry—the feelings of arrest and motion, of beginnings and endings, of striving and stillness. "Musical syntax" forms a basic element in the Eliotic style and method. Although Eliot had experimented with musical forms and techniques in his earlier verse, we can hear the richest and most moving syntactical music in *Four Quartets*. We offer the opening lines of *Burnt Norton:*

> Time present and time past
> Are both perhaps present in time future,
> And time future contained in time past.
> If all time is eternally present
> All time is unredeemable.

These lines present neither images nor metaphors, the supposed quintessential materials of poetry. Everything is handled through the silent rhythms of syntax and the audible rhythms of isochronism and strong-stress meter. We hear the echoing repetitions of individual words and phrases; we hear the more subtle repetitions of syntactical structure, the persistently unvarying grammatical forms. The syntax is static: the noun "Time," the modifiers "past," "present," "future," the copulatives "is" or "are" all follow in strict order. We hear the literal sense modified by each repetition of word and phrase; we hear how each repetition fits into an overall pattern of incantation.

Note the grammatical marking time in these lines:

> If all time is eternally present
> All time is unredeemable

Eliot tells how time can be immovable, without direction. But there comes a point where Eliot must resolve his meaning, where a composer would introduce a cadence to tell us where his music is going, harmonically speaking. Then Eliot changes his syntax; he drops the copulatives and allows the movement of the preceding lines to pivot on the transitive verb point:

> What might have been and what has been
> Point to one end, which is always present.

Eliot has suspended syntactical movement by using only the verbs *is* and *are* for nine lines running. The verb point releases us into a new idea, and we modulate into a new syntactical unit:

> Footfalls echo in the memory
> Down the passage which we did not take
> Towards the door we never opened
> Into the rose-garden. My words echo
> Thus, in your mind.

Now the verbs are active; the repeated echo develops a special burden of sound and meaning. And we hear again a haunting syntactical melody: "Down the passage . . . Towards the door . . . Into the rose-garden."

Another kind of music is heard in the lyrical fourth section of *Burnt Norton:*

Will the sunflower turn to us, will the clematis
Stray down, bend to us; tendril and spray
Clutch and cling?
Chill
Fingers of yew be curled
Down to us? After the kingfisher's wing
Has answered light to light, and is silent, the light is still
At the still point of the turning world.

We have the insistent repetitions as in the first section: "turn to us . . . bend to us . . . Down on us." These are the melodies. We have, however, an effect which, to quote Langer again, involves "the suspense of literal meaning by a sustained ambiguity resolved in a long-awaited key word."[4]

Reading the penultimate line, we briefly rest on the word "still." Meter and rhyme (with "Chill") enforce our usual tendency to pause slightly at the end of the line, and we understand "still" as an adjective modifying "light." Moving down to the next line, we see that "still" is more exactly an adverb whose effect is strong enough to modify the sense of both lines. The light is even yet "at the still point of the turning world."

We realize the ambiguity here, and how the world functions as a grammatical pivot on which the movement and meaning of the lines turn. The effect is analogous to an ambiguous harmonic structure that hovers between tonalities, a structure that might take any of a number of possible directions, but which is suddenly resolved by an unexpected cadence.

In *East Coker* we note another "effect of harmony"; we might call it "the illusion of tonality." The poem opens in this key:

In my beginning is my end. In succession
Houses rise and fall, crumble, are extended,
Are removed, destroyed, restored, or in their place
Is an open field, or a factory, or a by-pass.

At the end of the first section, we have:

Dawn points, and another day
Prepares for heat and silence. Out at sea the dawn wind

Wrinkles and slides. I am here
Or there, or elsewhere. In my beginning.

Again Eliot builds tension through repeated syntax: "or in their place . . . or a factory . . . or a by-pass." This pattern is repeated, in diminution, just before Eliot restates his theme: "I am here / Or there, or elsewhere. In my beginning." The familiar, almost expected, syntax acts as a return section, preparing us for the new entrance of the theme in its initial "tonality." We stress this musical preparation through syntax. Many have recognized Eliot's use of repeated thematic material without realizing how complex Eliot's musical procedures actually are. At the end of *East Coker,* we hear the same hesitant syntax announcing the theme, in inversion:

The wave cry, the wind cry, the vast waters
Of the petrel and the porpoise. In my end is my beginning.

The striking effect created by each return of the theme is not gained through simple verbal repetition or modification. It is gained through the manipulation of syntax that gives this "illusion of tonality." Eliot's procedure parallels sonata form, where the principal tonality is reestablished at the end of the movement, and the main theme makes its final appearance.

We "hear" Eliot's music in the meanings of words and the structures of grammar. We qualify *hear* with quotes because the rhythms of meaning and syntax are silent; they achieve tension and resolution not in phonological but in intellectual realms. The explicit, heard music of Eliot's verse sounds in Eliot's meters and the rhythmic effects occurring within the context of formally ordered metrical patterns. We shall treat later the more technical aspects of Eliot's meters: his varied handling of syllable-stress and strong-stress meter; his uses of open rhythm and nonmetrical techniques. However, we return to *Burnt Norton* for a moment to examine the musical aspects of Eliot's explicit sound patterns and the rhythm they inspire.

The falling strong-stress lines of *Burnt Norton*'s opening develop a single rhythmic idea, a motif that slowly accumulates emotional force. Individual word groups form themselves into apparent isochronic units; the four-beat strong-stress line resembles common measure (4/4) in music.

In the latter part of this chapter, we hope to show more precisely the musicality of *Four Quartets*. The point we wish to establish is that Eliot, through prosody, and a syntax so intricately patterned that it must be reckoned a part of Eliot's prosody, evokes a complexity of feeling in ways that music evokes comparable states in the minds of sensitive listeners. Eliot extends the limitations of language by entering the domain of another art. He uses syntax and prosody like music to enlarge the available means of expression. *Four Quartets* represents Eliot's most conscious and deliberate attempt to use musical method; but from the very beginning of his career, Eliot used sounds and rhythms in specifically musical ways.

This music has sounded in a predominantly metrical context. Some early and obviously deaf critics labeled Eliot a "free-verse poet," and since first misconceptions, like first impressions, doggedly persist, many still think of Eliot as a writer of unmetered verse.[5] Perhaps the general naïveté about matters prosodical has never been so clearly displayed as when the critics wondered at the "faintness" of the verse of *The Cocktail Party*. Some even suggested that Eliot's writing in lines was snobbish convention: *The Cocktail Party* was prose, and why not write it as such? Yet it contains lines as thumping in their metrical effect as any Eliot wrote:

> *Peter* I like that story.
> *Celia*   I love that story.
> *Alex*   *I'm* never tired of hearing that story.

Eliot gave occasional encouragement to the notion that he was, after all, really a simple fellow, unlearned in the techniques of his craft: "I have never been able to retain the names of feet and metres, or to pay the proper respect to the accepted rules of scansion."[6] But the Eliotic pose of unsophistication fools no one. In other critical writings Eliot makes clear he knows an iamb from a spondee; *Old Possum's Book of Practical Cats* displays Eliot's amazing virtuosity in rarely used, complicated meters that Eliot may not be able to name but certainly uses in accordance with whatever the "accepted rules of scansion" may be. And in an early essay, "Reflections on *Vers Libre*," Eliot explains the principles informing his own prosodical practices.

The essay attacks vers libre as a negative phenomenon. Eliot points out that vers libre, as practiced by the imagists, was not a verse form, but often a name used to rationalize verse that had no form: "and we conclude that the division between Conservative Verse and *Vers Libre* does not exist, for there is only good verse, bad verse, and chaos." Eliot's conclusion is similar to his often-quoted "no verse is libre for the man who wants to do a good job." Art allows no easy freedom. The poet, to achieve a masterly prosody, cannot abjure meter; the poet may work toward formal metric or away from it, but

> the ghost of simple metre should lurk behind the arras in even the "freest" verse; to advance menacingly as we doze, and withdraw as we rouse. Or, freedom is only truly freedom when it appears against the background of an artificial limitation.
>
> So much for metre. There is no escape from metre; there is only mastery.[7]

Sister Mary Martin Barry, after carefully scanning a significant body of Eliot's verse, confirms that Eliot never escaped from meter: "his general practice is well within the limits of metrical verse."[8] While many readers have long suspected what Sister Barry has painstakingly proven, it is good to have her statistical confirmations. Even Yvor Winters, who spoke contemptuously of Eliot's prosody, might have been reassured to discover that Eliot wrote scannable verse.[9]

Eliot trained himself on the meters of the late-nineteenth-century poets; a stanza from "Circe's Palace," one of Eliot's undergraduate pieces of 1908, has the unmistakable Swinburnean swing:

> Around her fountain which flows
> With the voice of men in pain,
> Are flowers that no man knows.
> Their petals are fanged and red
> With hideous streak and stain;
> They sprang from the limbs of the dead.—
> We shall not come here again.

The mixture of iambs and anapests is characteristic, as is the delicate ambiguity of stress in the last line:

We shall | not | come here | *again.*

Prufrock's despairing observations gain in pathos and uncertainty through similar metrical "hovering":

I do | not | think | that they | will sing | to me.

The metrical forms of Tennyson and Swinburne serve Eliot in his earliest volumes—with, of course, a difference. "Prufrock," "Portrait of a Lady," the "Preludes," and "La Figlia che Piange"—the most considerable pieces in the 1917 volume—have a base in the iambic verse of the later nineteenth century. But iambic pentameter exists to be evaded and approximated: "the most interesting verse which has yet been written in our language has been done . . . by taking a very simple form, like the iambic pentameter, and constantly withdrawing from it."[10] The evasion and approximation of iambic pentameter define Eliot's earliest prosodic style; scansion of a short passage from "Portrait of a Lady" gives the technical essentials:

Now | that li | lacs are | in bloom
She has | a bowl | of li | lacs in | her room
And twists | one in | her fin | gers while | she talks.
"Ah, | my friend, | you do | not know, | you do | not know
What life | is, you | who hold | it in | your hands";
(Slow ly | twist ing | the li | lac stalks)
"You let | it flow | from you, | you let | it flow."

The passage opens in trochaics (we scan it as iambs with an initial catalexis), but the falling rhythm quickly gives way to regular iambic pentameter in the second line. The sixth line again introduces trochaics with particularly expressive effect.

The opening of "Prufrock" offers a notable example of iambic evasion:

Let us go then, you and I,
When the evening is spread out against the sky
Like a patient etherized upon a table;

> Let us go, through certain half-deserted streets,
> The muttering retreats
> Of restless nights in one-night cheap hotels.

Not until the sixth line do we have unambiguous iambics. Four lines begin with two trochaic feet:

> Lét us | gó then . . .
>
> Whén the | évening . . .
>
> Líke a | pátient . . .
>
> Lét us | gó, through . . .

Like the passage from "Portrait of a Lady," we may read these lines of falling rhythm as iambic with initial catalexis:

> Lét | us gó | then, yóu | and Í.

Since the total metrical context is iambic, the above scansion is technically "correct," but hardly gives the rhythmic feel of the line.

Lines in "Prufrock" and "Portrait of a Lady" expand away from the pentameter; we find hexameters and even fourteeners:

> The yellow fog that rubs its back upon the window-panes,
> The yellow smoke that rubs its muzzle on the window-panes . . .

> Among the smoke and fog of a December afternoon
> You have the scene arrange itself—as it will seem to do.

Evidently smoke and fog drifted in Eliot's mind to a septenary rhythm. More interesting than the long lines per se are occasional incursions of lines that to the careless reader appear to be prose, yet are intricately crafted verse.

> It is impossible to say just what I mean!

> Except when a street piano, mechanical and tired . . .

> "And so you are going abroad; and when do you return?"

Eliot seems here to escape the "artificial limitation" of metrical control. But only seems. The first line above is anchored by rhyme to the line that follows it:

> It is impossible to say just what I mean!
> But as if a magic lantern threw the nerves in patterns on a
>   screen . . .

The secret lies in balance and tact. Eliot follows a lightly metered line
(it can be scanned: It is | im pos | si ble | to say | just what | I mean) with
a strong, almost ponderous line of eight feet. The delay until we hear
the rhyme creates a characteristic tension, of "indecisions and
revisions."

The meter of the "Preludes" is a tight iambic tetrameter. The heavi-
ly accented opening lines gain density by emphatic alliteration:

> The winter evening settles down
> With smell of steaks in passageways.
> Six o'clock.

Eliot's "evasions" of his meter consist largely of half-lines, lines of
trimeter,

> Of faint | stale smells | of beer . . .
> One thinks | of all | the hands . . .

or lines where substituted feet predominate:

> And the light crept up between the shutters
> And you heard the sparrows in the gutters,
> You had such a vision of the street
> As the street hardly understands;
> Sitting along the bed's edge, where
> You curled the papers from your hair.

Scanning, we find in the first two lines initial anapests and "feminine"
endings; the third line is the ambiguous iambic-trochaic

> You | had | such | a | vi | sion | of | the | street,

which we recognize as a metrical signature in Eliot's early verse. The
fourth line apparently "springs" out of syllable-stress meter; the two

contiguous and nearly equal stresses of the second foot combine with
the initial inverted foot to unsettle the metrical base:

As the | street hard | ly un | der stands.

We hear metrical echoes of this line in "La Figlia che Piange," a
poem about a lover's parting. An essentially romantic theme is compli-
cated by Laforguian ironies and a Jamesian point of view. We have a
triangular affair, involving the girl, her lover, and the poet-observer.
The poet turns out to be the lover; he "distances" the painful parting
by elaborate staging and a final rhetorical bravado: an affected irony
that tries to say—"I really don't care—much!"

> Sometimes these cogitations still amaze
> The troubled midnight and the noon's repose.

The poem's metric betrays an underlying emotional intensity—so
carefully concealed by the poet's disguises of attitude and setting. The
observer's final "cogitations" settle into regular iambics—his "pose of
repose"—but not until after significant disturbances of the meter. The
excitement of the opening invocation approaches romantic violence;
the third line moves toward the freedom of stress verse without losing
its metrical orientation:

Weave, | weave, | the sun | *light* in | your hair—

Eliot's fingering of the vowels, the unaccented long syllable in the
fourth foot, and the equalizing pauses disclose an ear for the music of
English quantity as fully accomplished as Pound's. Quantity does not
assume in Eliot's verse a point of departure; the norm that is ap-
proached or evaded is traditional syllable-stress meter. Pound, whose
verse gravitates toward quantitative norms, chides Eliot for not recog-
nizing "metres depending on quantity, alliteration, etc.; Eliot writes as
if all metres were measured by accent."[11]

Meters measured *by accent*, however, bear along Eliot's half-
submerged but nonetheless vehement feelings; these nervously
"sprung" and counterpointed lines belie the poet's surface detach-
ment:

As the | soul leaves | the bo | dy torn | and bruised,
As the | mind | de serts | the bo | dy it | has used . . .
Her hair | o ver | her arms | and her arms full | of flow | ers . . .

Springing and counterpointing are possible only in syllable-stress contexts. It is interesting that Pound, who prefers the suavities of a quantitative line, rarely wrote verse marked by feelings in strong conflict. Pound's emotions are simple; rage and hate and love are relatively unmixed and require direct presentation. Eliot, whose moods and passions are rich, subterranean, complex, and uncertain, finds "metres measured by accent" more sensitive to the shifting and subtle movements of the inner life.

❧ III

"Gerontion," the opening poem of Eliot's 1920 volume, ranks as a prosodic triumph. The poem so skillfully blends the rhythms of prose and iambic pentameter that we are unaware of the shifts into metered verse until we analyze them. Rhythms grow out of syntactical repetitions:

> Nor fought in the warm rain
> Nor knee deep in the salt marsh, heaving a cutlass . . .

The first pentameter line is

Blis tered | in Brus | sels, patched | and peeled | in Lon | don . . .

Eliot accurately describes the prosodic method of "Gerontion" as "taking no form at all, and constantly approximating to a very simple one."[12]

Eliot's verse shows extreme care in its distribution of secondary accents and lesser syllables. A "rhythmic constant," constructed out of these secondary accents and syllables, develops into a prosodic tune. A grouping of two unstressed syllables followed by two stressed syllables (the minor Ionic) recurs with obsessive frequency (a preference for this Greek meter that Eliot shares with Jeffers): "in a dry month . . . at the hot gates . . . in the warm rain . . . in depraved May . . . in the next room . . . of a dry brain . . ." This repetition functions thematically and gives the poem musical coherence.

When "Gerontion" pleads for understanding, the metric tightens; it is in these passages that we hear the loosened blank verse of the Jacobean dramatists:

> After such knowledge, what forgiveness? Think now
> History has many cunning passages, contrived corridors
> And issues, deceives with whispering ambitions,
> Guides us by vanities. . . .
>
> I that was near your heart was removed therefrom
> To lose beauty in terror, terror in inquisition.
> I have lost my passion: why should I need to keep it
> Since what is kept must be adulterated?
> I have lost my sight, smell, hearing, taste and touch:
> How should I use them for your closer contact?

These great "didactic" passages fall into something less than Marlovian regularity, but they clearly establish the direction of blank verse. The movement is restless; trisyllabic feet, trochaic feet, and hypermetrical syllables occur at many points in the line. "Gerontion" makes a prosodic leap; its advance over the earlier rhymed monologues is considerable. It is in "Gerontion," where Eliot abandons the plangent rhyming of "Prufrock" and "Portrait of a Lady," that his studies in the Jacobean dramatists yielded important metrical results.[13]

The decision to give up rhyme is signaled in "Reflections on *Vers Libre:*" "Rhyme removed, much ethereal music leaps up from the word." Rhymed verse directs attention to the ends of lines, to the obvious music of chiming sounds. Unhampered by rhyme, the mind is free to linger and construe the meanings of *juvescence,* and *concitation,* and to dwell on *History* with its *issues.* In "Gerontion" Eliot argues a position, assumes an attitude toward history. The poem makes a public statement on what we now like to call the "cultural situation." The looser prosodic form Eliot uses reduces the merely sensuous resources of language; "Gerontion" echoes with none of the music that "is successful with a 'dying fall,'" easy alliteration or that legacy of the 1890s, the lush hexameter:

> Afternoon grey and smoky, evening yellow and rose . . .

The music of "Gerontion" is heard as the metric releases "The word within a word." The open rhythms of conversation flow easily between the formal set speeches; prose phrasing and repeated syntax create unmistakable, characteristic "Eliotic" effects. And the whole prosodic direction of "Gerontion" is manipulated by the politic ghost "of some simple metre": the iambic pentameter lurking behind the arras.

The other English poems in the 1920 volume are all written in the Gautier stanza, urged upon Eliot by Pound. These poems are more nasty than witty, more clogged with irrelevant pedantry than flowing with gracious learning. ("Burbank with a Baedeker: Bleistein with a Cigar," a poem of thirty-two lines, contains at least twenty-one separate allusions to literature.) [14] The stanza permits epigrammatic brilliance or an ironic appraisal of Grishkin's charms:

> Grishkin is nice: her Russian eye
> Is underlined for emphasis;
> Uncorseted, her friendly bust
> Gives promise of pneumatic bliss.

Like Pound in *Mauberley,* Eliot modifies Gautier's stanza and rhymes only the second and fourth lines. (The exception, where Eliot follows Gautier's scheme exactly and rhymes *abab,* is "The Hippopotamus.") But Eliot does not use the stanza as a prosodic theme for a set of far-ranging variations; he works close to the form and brings off passages of the strictest virtuosity.

IV

The Waste Land assimilates every prosodic advance Eliot made in his earlier verse; it also points toward newer methods, especially the strong-stress techniques of *Four Quartets* and the plays. Because of its length, *The Waste Land* raises the question of a carrying metric. If we believe Yvor Winters, *The Waste Land* fails in unity because Eliot establishes no metrical cohesiveness; the poem falls "into lyrical fragments." We contend that Eliot succeeded in establishing a prosodic tone, a metric that is systematically a part of the poem's structure, and that this success gives *The Waste Land* what unity it has.

To understand how Eliot's prosody works in *The Waste Land* means understanding the poem's dramatic structure. The symbol and myth hunters have attacked the poem as if it had a rational narrative. We need only to unravel the images and legends and see their relationships. Then we have the story! But there is no "story" in *The Waste Land;* if we try to fit together "the broken images," we discover contradictions and discrepancies. A more fruitful approach lies in reconstructing the poem's scenario; who is speaking; when does a character shift into another character; where are we, spatially, in the poem?[15] The poem speaks with many voices; we hear monologues, dialogues, and conversations from adjacent tables and nearby rooms. Students who have the greatest difficulty in understanding *The Waste Land* as a printed poem respond to Eliot's own recorded reading.

The dramatic convention of *The Waste Land* develops out of the earlier monologues; but in "Prufrock" or "Gerontion" we hear one, or at the most, two voices. We might hear women, in the next room, "talking of Michelangelo"; or the imagined voice of one, not wishing to be misunderstood, saying, "That is not what I meant, at all." In *The Waste Land* we are assaulted by the voices and the noises of a whole civilization. The poet walks through the streets of modern London, overhearing the prophecies of Madame Sosostris or a conversation in a pub between two Cockney women. Tiresias reports a squalid sexual encounter; voices come "singing out of empty cisterns and exhausted wells." At the end of the poem, the narrator is a victim of auditory hallucination; the rhythm of a children's singing game mixes with literary fragments from five languages.

Eliot meets the prosodic requirements of his complex dramatic scheme by a brilliant and simple expedient. He alternates two metrical modes; more precisely, he sets two limitations on prosodic freedom. At one pole he sets up a conversational idiom, which comprises the opening "April is the cruellest month, breeding" and the succeeding seventeen lines. The first important passage of exhortation swings from this line into blank verse, the other metrical pole of the poem:

> What are the roots that clutch, what branches grow
> Out of this stony rubbish? Son of man,
> You cannot say, or guess, for you know only . . .

There is no fixing of the meter in this passage; Eliot moves out of blank verse, into the relative four-beat line:

             I could not
Speak, and my eyes failed, ‖ I was neither
Living nor dead, ‖ and I knew nothing,
Looking into the heart of light, ‖ the silence.

Prosody shifts with the changing voices. Madame Sosostris gives way
to Tiresias, who again speaks blank verse. The modulations from com-
pressed conversational idiom to iambics and vice versa are accom-
plished with great technical subtlety. "A Game of Chess" opens in
blank verse modeled on Shakespeare's later metrical manner. Eliot
wants to move from description to dialogue: the hopeless conversation
between the lady of the dressing table and the man of Rats' Alley. Eliot
breaks the prevailing movement with a half-line,

> And still she cried, and still the world pursues,
> "Jug Jug" to dirty ears

and the verse gradually loosens:

> And the other withered stumps of time
> Were told upon the walls; staring forms
> Leaned out, leaning, hushing the room enclosed.
> Footsteps shuffled on the stair.
> Under the firelight, under the brush, her hair
> Spread out in fiery points
> Glowed into words, then would be savagely still.

We are now prepared, prosodically, for the neurotic rhythms of the
lady, and the sullen, mocking replies of the man.

Eliot preserves prosodic unity by careful preparation; the transi-
tions are never sudden. Mister Eugenides is introduced by a line of
blank verse:

> Under | the brown | fog of | a win | ter noon.

The two reversed feet, especially the trochee in the third place, un-
settle iambic direction so that the rest of the passage seems scarcely
different in rhythm:

Mr. Eugénides, || the Smýrna mérchant

Unsháven, || with a pócket fúll of cúrrants

C.i.f. Lóndon: || dócuments at síght.

A dazzling instance of rhythmic modulation occurs when Tiresias works gradually into the elegiac quatrains of the typist and clerk scene. After ten preparatory lines the verse settles into the familiar stanza of Gray's "Elegy":[16]

> The time is now propitious, as he guesses,
> The meal is ended, she is bored and tired,
> Endeavours to engage her in caresses
> Which still are unreproved, if undesired . . .

>   She turns and looks a moment in the glass,
> Hardly aware of her departed lover;
> Her brain allows one half-formed thought to pass:
> "Well now that's done: and I'm glad it's over."
> When lovely woman stoops to folly and
> Paces about her room again, alone
> She smoothes her hair with automatic hand,
> And puts a record on the gramophone.

Prosodic tone, strengthened in pathos by the lines' alternating stressed and unstressed endings, contrasts strikingly with the unpleasant subject matter. The elegiac effect adds a prosodic irony, climaxed as Eliot parodies not only the sense but the meter of Goldsmith's moral ditty:

"Wéll nów | that's dóne: | and | I'm glád | it's ó | ver."

When lóve | ly wó | man stóops | to fól | ly ánd

Pá ces | a bóut | her róom | a gáin, a lóne . . .

Goldsmith's original line is lengthened by a single syllable, the metrically emphatic "and." *And* also receives metrical stress in the line given to the erring typist. Tiresias mimics her bored relief: his *and,* appearing conspicuously at the end of the line, echoes hers with stinging contempt.

Tension returns in the finale of *The Waste Land,* where the prosody tightens once again into blank verse as we hear the prophet's voice in three lines of ringing anaphora:

> After the torchlight red on sweaty faces
> After the frosty silence in the gardens
> After the agony in stony places . . .

The earlier dramatic scenes are replaced by disconnected, broken visions. The prophet and the protagonist are united into a single voice; the mood is one of interrogation and insanity. Iambic movement predominates, although the famous passages of spiritual thirst are set in short, hesitating lines, as in the Indian episode:

> Gánga was súnken, ‖ and the límp leáves
> Wáited for ráin, ‖ while the bláck clóuds
> Gáthered fár distant, ‖ óver Hímavant.
> The júngle cróuched, ‖ húmped in sílence.

❧ V

The Waste Land's dramatic structure required a colloquial idiom not too far removed from prose; the poem's didactic and hortatory impulses needed the closer ordering of blank verse. Eliot wrote *Sweeney Agonistes* directly for the stage; its two brief scenes were meant as part of a longer play, *Wanna Go Home, Baby?* Eliot devised an immediately effective metric for the two *Fragments:* a metric supple enough to carry musical incantation. The style is repetitive, responsive; the subject matter, at first commonplace, later becomes sordid and comic-horrible. The metric is simplicity itself: a four-stress line sharply divided at the caesura. But unlike the clipped, shorter lines in *The Waste Land,* the percussive lines of "Sweeney" are carefully measured in time:

> *Dusty.* How about Pereira?
>   What about Pereira?
> *Doris.* I *don't care.*

> *Dusty.*   You don't care!
>   Who pays the rent?
> *Doris.*   Y*e*s, he pays the rent.
> *Dusty.* Well some men don't and some men do
>   Some men don't and you know who.

The antiphonal idiocies of Dusty and Doris follow duple time; the shifting of accents within the lines gives the characteristic jazzy effect. With the appearance of Sweeney in the second part, syncopation increases. Eliot occasionally italicizes the accents to insure a proper performance:

> *Doris.*   You'll carry me off? To a cannibal isle?
> *Sweeney.* I'll be the cannibal.
>   I'll be the missionary.
> *Doris.*   I'll convert you.
> *Sweeney.*   I'll convert *you!*

Eliot reads the "Fragment of an Agon" to an emphatic double beat—to what jazz musicians call "cut time." Over this timing, he sharply syncopates the accents; our scansion (if we may indulge for a moment in the Performative Heresy) corresponds as closely as possible to Eliot's reading:[17]

> *Doris.*   Thát's not lífe, ‖ thát's no lífe
>   Whý I'd júst as soón be deád.
> *Sweeney.* Thát's what lífe is. Júst is.
> *Doris.*   Whát is?
>   Whát's that lífe ís?
> *Sweeney.*   Life ís death.

Eliot heavily accents the offbeats when he delivers Sweeney's staggering revelation.

The rhythms of Sweeney turn up in *The Cocktail Party*. Perhaps Eliot is perpetrating a subtle, if not exactly tasteful, joke; after all, Celia Coplestone becomes a missionary, goes among the cannibals, and if not "converted" into missionary stew, is crucified and eaten by ants. Or perhaps the similarity of rhythms derives from the ritual bases of both plays; *The Cocktail Party* elaborates the sin and atonement theme of "Sweeney." The man-who-did-a-girl-in (who is probably Sweeney himself) suffers intolerable loneliness and delusions about what is real and imagined:

> When you're alone like he was alone
> You're either or neither . . .
> Death or life or life or death
> Death *is* life and life *is* death.[18]

Celia Coplestone, in language and rhythms reminiscent of Sweeney, wonders about love, and loneliness, and reality:

>   Can we only love
> Something created by our own imagination?
> Are we all in fact unloving and unlovable?
> Then one is alone, and if one is alone
> Then lover and beloved are equally unreal
> And the dreamer is no more real than his dreams.

More obviously Sweeney-like are passages where the speakers divide the line in stichomythia:

> *Julia.* And he had a remarkable sense of hearing—
>   The only man I ever met who could hear the cry of bats.
> *Peter.* Hear the cry of bats?
> *Julia.*   He could hear the cry of bats.
> *Celia.* But how do you know he could hear the cry of bats?
> *Julia.* Because he said so. And I believed him.
> *Celia.* But if he was so . . . harmless, how could you believe him?

A little of this goes a long way; Eliot wisely uses these rhythms thematically throughout the play: not as a carrying prosody but for heightening effects, at moments of levity or elation, or for simple conversational banter.

Eliot explains the verse technique of his plays in a loose and puzzling way. He makes clear he employs strong-stress metric:

What I worked out [for *The Family Reunion*] is substantially what I continued to employ: a line of varying length and varying number of syllables, with a caesura and three stresses. The caesura and the stresses may come at different places, almost anywhere in the line; the stresses may be close together or well separated by light syllables; the only rule being that there must be one stress on one side of the caesura and two on the other.[19]

Many passages in *The Family Reunion* correspond to Eliot's paradigm; especially the lyrical interchanges between Harry and Mary:

> *Mary.* The cold spring now is the time
> For the ache in the moving root
> The agony in the dark
> The slow flow throbbing the trunk
> The pain of the breaking bud . . .

> *Harry.* Spring is an issue of blood
> A season of sacrifice
> And the wail of the new full tide
> Returning the ghosts of the dead.

But more often than not, the verse of *The Family Reunion* settles into a four-stress line; this passage derives from a similar one in "Burnt Norton":

> The sudden solitude in a crowded desert
> In a thick smoke, many creatures moving
> Without direction, for no direction
> Leads anywhere but round and round in that vapour—
> Without purpose, and without principle of conduct.

We have an undisputed three-stress line,

> Without púrpose, and without prínciple of cónduct,

in a context largely made up of four-stress lines:

> In flíckering íntervals ‖ of líght and dárkness;
> The pártial anesthésia ‖ of súffering without féeling

And pártial obsérvation || of one's ówn autómatism

While the slów stáin sinks déeper || through the skín

Táinting the flésh || and discóloring the bóne.

However, this counting of stresses seems niggling. Eliot develops a metric for his plays that is unobtrusive in the passages of low dramatic intensity and powerful in the moments of incantation or exultation. Edmund Wilson ingeniously suggested that this metric is an adaptation of the classical iambic hexameter or "trimeter": the basic meter of Roman drama:

> That this ignorance of iambic hexameter (so confusingly called "iambic trimeter") is pretty generally prevalent in this country would seem to be indicated by the failure of writers on Eliot's plays to mention that the meter he uses is an adaptation of this. (He follows the loose Latin version—suggested to him, perhaps, by his study of Seneca—in which the line has come to depend mainly on three stresses; and he has even made a point of varying this, in the traditional Roman way, with passages written in trochaics.)[20]

Taken with Eliot's own account of his procedure, this makes good sense. The rhythmic effects of Latin quantity cannot be reproduced in English. An attempt would give us a line roughly divided into three major divisions or dipodies. Many such lines turn up in *The Family Reunion* and *The Cocktail Party;* many more in Eliot's later plays, *The Confidential Clerk* and *The Elder Statesman.* Actual Senecan influence on the prosody can be seen only in *The Family Reunion.* Like Seneca, Eliot uses a mixed metric: one line for dialogue and set speeches; another line, more fluid in movement, for choral and lyrical interludes.[21]

After *The Family Reunion* Eliot submerges obvious metrical design, abandons the formal rhyming techniques of *Murder in the Cathedral* and the intricate lyric patterns of *The Family Reunion,* and relies more and more for rhythmic interest on the repetition of phrase and syntactical echo:

> *Edward.* A common interest in the moving pictures
>   Frequently brings young people together.

    Peter. Now you're only being sarcastic:
        Celia was interested in the art of the film.
Edward. As a possible profession?
    Peter. She might make it a profession;
        Though she had her poetry.
Edward. Yes, I've seen her poetry—

We might note here a favorite rhythmic "tune" of Eliot's, the quadripartite

    A common interest in the moving pictures,

so like

    The awful daring of a moment's surrender . . .

    The infirm glory of the positive hour . . .

The carrying prosody of Eliot's later plays achieved a rhythmic blandness, a transparency, the kindest say; a tired and nerveless prosiness, the more realistic say. We might, for a moment, refer back to some general principles for writing dramatic verse that Eliot formulated. These are not principles a priori, but part "of the self-education of a poet trying to write for the theatre."[22] The first, and earliest, caveat was to avoid regular blank verse and its unfortunate propensity to mock-Shakespearean echoes. Eliot's three- and four-stress line, reviving the native English verse tradition, "sounds nothing like" Shakespeare because it is historically unrelated to blank verse. And with its persistent and variable coincidence of rhetorical and metrical stress, the strong-stress line is endlessly adaptable to the rhythms of contemporary speech.

    A second, and later, principle was "the ascetic rule to avoid poetry which could not stand the test of strict dramatic utility."[23] Eliot's asceticism led him to the verse of *The Elder Statesman,* of which the following is a fair sample:

Charles. And your father will come. With his calm possessive air
        And his kindly welcome, which is always a reminder
        That I mustn't stay too long, for you belong to him.
        He seems so placidly to take it for granted

> That you don't really care for any company but his!

Monica. You're not to assume that anything I've said to you
    Has given you the right to criticise my father.
    In the first place, you don't understand him;
    In the second place, we're not engaged yet.

Compared to "Sweeney," or even to parts of *The Cocktail Party,* this seems pretty pallid stuff. When Lord Claverton achieves the peace which passeth all understanding, the blessed illumination of the aged Oedipus at Colonus, there is scarcely a stir of feeling; abstractions, not music, heavily move the verse along:

> This may surprise you: I feel at peace now.
> It is the peace that ensues upon contrition
> When contrition ensues upon knowledge of the truth.
> Why did I always want to dominate my children?
> Why did I mark out the narrow path for Michael?
> Because I wanted to perpetuate myself in him.
> Why did I want to keep you to myself, Monica?
> Because I wanted you to give your life to adoring
> The man I pretended to myself that I was.

Confronted with the rhythmic neutrality of this passage, we might wonder whether Eliot's dramatic verse, while having gone in the right direction, has not (as Randall Jarrell said of a rival poet) gone a great deal too far. The verse of *The Elder Statesman* and *The Confidential Clerk* has been put "on a very thin diet in order to adapt it to the needs of the stage."[24] The result has not been a lean athletic prosodic style but one displaying woeful symptoms of malnutrition.

ᣠ *VI*

> When it appears, the study of the music
> Of *Ash-Wednesday* should compel the minds of all
> Poets; for in a hundred years no poem
> Has sung itself so exquisitely well.

> Karl Shapiro, *Essay on Rime*

Faced with Shapiro's encomium, we hesitate to submit "Ash Wednesday" to the barbarisms of metrical analysis. "Ash Wednesday" displays unsurpassed rhythmic power and control; the opening sections, all of section 3 ("Al som de l'escalina"), and the concluding section convince us no metric was ever devised that so closely follows a poet's mental and emotional posture. We find occasional lapses, where Eliot yields to his own facility:

> On the mainland, in the desert or the rain land,
> For those who walk in darkness
> Both in the day time and in the night time
> The right time and the right place are not here
> No place of grace for those who avoid the face . . .

> Will the veiled sister between the slender
> Yew trees pray for those who offend her
> And are terrified and cannot surrender . . .

The obsessive interior and feminine rhyming brings these overexcited lines close to the edge of doggerel. But these are flaws occasioned not by a failure but an excess of technique.

Ash Wednesday emphatically illustrates one of Sir Donald Tovey's most brilliant generalizations: that aesthetic form is movement.[25] A variety of rhythms of "vital import" are danced out in "Ash Wednesday"; in no other poem of Eliot do we find so much ritual movement and incantatory music. We have the opening gestures of "turning"; later we find ascents and descents, climbing, walking, "Stops and steps of the mind." The stiff iambics of the opening mirror an attitude of ceremony touched with despair:

> Because I do not hope to turn again
> Because I do not hope
> Because I do not hope to turn
> Desiring this man's gift and that man's scope
> I no longer strive to strive towards such things
> (Why should the aged eagle stretch its wings?)
> Why should I mourn
> The vanished power of the usual reign?

Movement falters and direction becomes uncertain in the second and third lines: the rhythmic vacancy is the result of defeated expectation as the pentameter of the first line still echoes in our metrical memory.

Eliot, moving between doubt and resolution, resembles a dancer slowly circling, stating a pattern, losing it, and finding it again. The lines of three and four feet,

> Because I do not hope
> Because I do not hope to turn,

are surprisingly resolved by the full pentameter line lifted from Shakespeare's Twenty-ninth Sonnet:

> Desiring this man's gift and that man's scope . . .

The prosodic smoothness of this line is now contradicted by

> I no lón | ger strive | to strive | tówards | such things.

Elision springs from the line at the fourth position; the wrench in rhythm mimes the striving, the hesitations of Eliot's inner struggle. (We are aware that this argument, in our time, may devour itself when it is called up to explicate lines that mime another author's mind and spirit, or when lines betray the lack of any significant inner struggle.)

The prose movement that opens section 2 interrupts the dance; the lady, the leopards, and the bones command our eyes rather than our ears. The music and the dance resume with the song of the bones, set to the rhythms of "Ave Maria":

> Lady of Silences
> Calm and distressed
> Torn and most whole
>
> Ave, Marie;
> gratia plena;
> Dominus tecum

A number of rhythms have now been heard as structural constants: the opening iambic; the long prose line, with its carefully placed caesural divisions,

> There, where trees flower, and springs flow, for
>   there is nothing again . . .

> On my legs my heart my liver and that which had
>   been contained
> In the hollow round of my skull . . .

and the various sections set to the liturgy of the Catholic service. There is continual shifting and interchanging of these rhythms but no sense of roughness or unprepared transition (and therein lies the greatness of an ear). Rhyme, used within and at the ends of lines, serves as binding material:

> At the first turning of the second stair
> I turned and saw below
> The same shape twisted on the banister
> Under the vapour in the fetid air
> Struggling with the devil of the stairs who wears
> The deceitful face of hope and of despair.

The stanza above introduces the third section, with its remarkable contrast between the dense, clotted rhythms of

> The same shape twisted on the banister

and the untroubled iambics of

> The broadbacked figure drest in blue and green.

Through the "slotted window bellied like the fig's fruit" is glimpsed a Maytime celebration, and the poet recalls one of those aching and exalted moments of sexual experience. Eliot breaks the iambic meter and allows a characteristic repetition to supply rhythmic interest. We hear this kind of repetition as another structural constant:

> In a white gown, to contemplation, in a white gown . . .

> Blown hair is sweet, brown hair over the mouth blown,
> Lilac and brown hair . . .

> White light folded, sheathed about her, folded.

Section 3 concludes with an extraordinary diminuendo; the ascent seemingly proceeds after the last word has been uttered, into the silence of imagined time:

> Distraction, music of the flute, stops and steps
>   of the mind over the third stair,
> Fading, fading; strength beyond hope and despair
> Climbing the third stair.

Paradoxically, the rhythm falls as the protagonist climbs. The last words of section 3, the *Domine, non sum dignus* from the Ordinary of the Latin Mass, are muttered in distraction as the speaker momentarily awakens from his vision.

The vision continues in section 4, but the pace has changed. The tempo is now the true andante, a moderate walking speed. The section is nominally iambic, with lines of varying length. Grover Smith suggests the influence of *The Faerie Queene;*[26] the lines do arrange themselves in periods resembling the Spenserian stanza, each period punctuated by longer lines. We have at least one authentic Alexandrine,

> Who then made strong the fountains and made fresh
>   the springs

an approximate hexameter,

> One who moves in the time between sleep and waking,
>   wearing

and Eliot's favorite septenary,

> Whose flute is breathless, bent her head and signed
>   but spoke no word.

However, the prosodic relevance of Spenser here is questionable; Eliot was always fond of the long line and richly musical vowel patterns. We find, in a new and more delicate orchestration, "the music with a dying fall":

> But the fountain sprang up and the bird sang down
> Redeem the time, redeem the dream
> The token of the word unheard, unspoken
> Till the wind shake a thousand whispers from the yew

> And after this our exile . . .

The interior rhyming, "sprang up . . . sang down / . . . redeem the dream / . . . token . . . unspoken," is exactly timed to create the tension of unfulfilled expectation. We must also note the silences indicated by the pregnant spacing between lines. These pauses for the eye, which note pauses for the ear, are like fermata in musical notation and are carefully observed by Eliot in his reading.[27]

The absence of full stops at the conclusion of section 4 has prosodic effect; the unresolved vision remains flickering before the mind's eye, "between the ivory gates."

The rhetorical clamor of section 5 stands in marked contrast to the rest of the poem. Granted that Eliot intends us to hear the noise of "the unstilled world," the onomatopoeic bustle and homonymic punning of

> Against the Word the unstilled world still whirled
> About the centre of the silent Word

is finally tedious, justifying Henry Reed's delicious parody:

> The wind within a wind unable to speak for wind . . .
> "Chard Whitlow"

However, we must note the rhythmic musculature of the concluding lines of section 5; they recall the classical logaoedic meter with its free mixture of anapestic and iambic feet:

> And affirm before the world and deny between the rocks
> In the last desert between the last blue rocks
> The desert in the garden the garden in the desert.

The last line but one, an Eliotic hexameter, possesses two caesuras, and a violently dactylic second foot:

> Of droúth, ‖ spit ting from | the moúth ‖ the wíth | ered
>
>   áp | ple-seed.

The appropriate harshness of the inverted second foot throws the line into falling rhythm, emphasized by the final fragment, set in trochees:

O my people.

Section 6 restores the iambic meter of the opening. The movements of deliberate hesitation quickly give way, and Eliot varies the metric with lines of different length and freer distribution of stresses:

> And the lost heart stiffens and rejoices
> In the lost lilac and the lost sea voices
> And the weak spirit quickens to rebel
> For the bent golden-rod and the lost sea smell
> Quickens to recover
> The cry of quail and the whirling plover
> And the blind eye creates
> The empty forms between the ivory gates
> And the smell renews the salt savour of the sandy earth.

The rhythmic animation of the lines makes vivid the sudden and intense longing for the things of this world; but "In memory only, reconsidered passion." A solemn movement of "English hexameters" preludes the concluding prayer:

> But when the voices shaken from the yew-tree drift away
> Let the other yew be shaken and reply.

The prayer briefly revives the two-stress "Ave Maria" meter; we venture to reset the lines into their metrical periods:

> Blessèd sister,
> holy mother,
> spirit of the fountain,
> spirit of the garden.

An especially expressive visual *fermata* provides actual separation between the final line and those preceding it:

> And the spirit of the river, spirit of the sea,
> Suffer me not to be separated
>
> And let my cry come unto Thee.

ও VII

But the abstract conception
Of private experience at its greatest intensity . . .

"Ash Wednesday" is at once the most obscure and the most imme-
diately musical of Eliot's major poems. The strain of attempting to
communicate the essence of religious vision occasions an inevitable
fineness in the meaning; it also occasions the music. An interval of five
years separates "Ash Wednesday" (1930) from the first of the *Four
Quartets*, "Burnt Norton" (1935). Eliot was now considering a new
music, a more "transparent" medium. In a lecture delivered in 1933,
Eliot remarked he wished to write poetry

> which should be essentially poetry, with nothing poetic about it,
> poetry standing naked in its bare bones, or poetry so transparent
> that we should not see the poetry, but that which we are meant to
> see through the poetry, poetry so transparent that in reading it we
> are intent on what the poem *points at,* and not the poetry, this seems
> to me the thing to try for. To get *beyond poetry*, as Beethoven, in his
> later works, strove to get *beyond music*. We shall never succeed, per-
> haps, but Lawrence's words mean this to me, that they express to
> me what I think that the forty or fifty original lines I have written
> strive towards.[28]

"Strive towards!" The burden of "Ash Wednesday" still sang in
Eliot's ears. But the music of *Four Quartets* differs from that of "Ash
Wednesday." We no longer hear the tone color, the rich intermingling
of rhyme and metrical sequence that distinguish the texture and
movement of "Ash Wednesday." The music of *Four Quartets* originates
at a deeper level than that of meter and rhyme; it is implicit, as we have
shown in our earlier analysis, in syntax, the rhythm of thought itself.

The syntactical music of *Four Quartets* represents Eliot's highest
technical achievement; hearing Eliot read the *Quartets* is as genuine a
musical experience as hearing the Budapest Quartet play Beethoven's
op. 132. Eliot's hint about Beethoven's later works provides an impor-
tant clue to the form and substance of *Four Quartets.* J. W. N. Sullivan,
whose influence on Eliot has been convincingly demonstrated by Her-
bert Howarth,[29] describes below Beethoven's Quartets in B-flat, op.

130, C-sharp Minor, op. 131, and A Minor, op. 132; he is also describing, with uncanny precision, Eliot's *Four Quartets:*

> In these quartets the movements radiate, as it were, from a central experience. They do not represent stages in a journey, each stage being independent and existing in its own right. They represent separate experiences, but the meaning they take on in the quartet is derived from their relation to a dominating, central experience. This is characteristic of the mystic vision, to which everything in the world appears unified in the light of one fundamental experience. In these quartets, then, Beethoven is not describing to us a spiritual history; he is presenting to us a vision of life. In each quartet many elements are surveyed, but from one central point of view. They are presented as apprehended by a special kind of awareness, they are seen in the light of one fundamental experience. It is not any kinship between the experiences described in the separate movements themselves, but the light in which they are seen, that gives to these works their profound homogeneity.[30]

The formal prosody of *Four Quartets* grows out of this "dominating central experience" and "profound homogeneity." Each movement, in Eliot's five-movement scheme, has its characteristic metric; yet, throughout the *Quartets,* Eliot sustains an overall consistency in metrical tone. This consistency is first established by the close musical structure, derived in all probability from Beethoven's Quartet in A Minor, op. 132.[31] Eliot had been using musical structures and techniques long before he composed *Four Quartets; The Waste Land* was an experiment in the use of repeated thematic material as well as being orchestral in its elaborate handling of contrasting sonorities. Eliot's methods in the *Quartets* are more strictly musical; we find the pervasive repetitions of themes, images, and rhythms. We find, in addition, devices Eliot may have absorbed in his listening to Beethoven: variation of theme, inversion, diminution, rhythmic contraction and expansion.

The metrical modes complement the musical form. The first movements of "Burnt Norton," "East Coker," and "Little Gidding" are set in Eliot's flexible strong-stress lines. Line lengths vary, but the number of stresses remains close to the normative four:

Drý the pool, ‖ drý concréte, ‖ brówn edgéd,

And the póol was fílled with wáter ‖ out of súnlight,

And the lótos róse, ‖ quíetly, quíetly,

The súrface glíttered ‖ out of héart of líght.

"Burnt Norton"

The measure is the same in "Little Gidding," but the alliteration gives an archaic flavor—a suggestion of "Piers Plowman":

Midwinter spring is its own season
Sempiternal though sodden towards sundown,
Suspended in time, between pole and tropic.
When the short day is brightest, with frost and fire,
The brief sun flames the ice, on pond and ditches,
In windless cold that is the heart's heat,
Reflecting in a watery mirror
A glare that is blindness in the early afternoon.

Again we discover that the principle of Eliot's metric resides in "the contrast between fixity and flux, this unperceived evasion of monotony, which is the very life of verse."[32] The opening of "The Dry Salvages" skillfully avoids the monotony usually occasioned by triple meter in English; although the lines move in almost regular trisyllabic feet, anapests and dactyls, there is neither the solemn torpor of "Evangeline" nor the galloping frenzy of "The Destruction of Sennacherib":

I do not know much about gods; but I think that the river
Is a strong brown god—sullen, untamed and intractable,
Patient to some degree, at first recognized as a frontier;
Useful, untrustworthy, as a conveyer of commerce;
Then only a problem confronting the builder of bridges.

Each line has five principal stresses and a strongly felt caesura; the meter is anapestic pentameter with dactylic and spondaic substitutions. But the ear is not assaulted by anapests and dactyls; it hears the slow and primitive music of the Mississippi as it flows through past and present, recalling Eliot to childhood memories. The ear hears the infinitely subtle inflections of human feeling.

METRICAL MODES IN *FOUR QUARTETS*

	I Landscape	II Lyric	III Didactic	IV Lyric	V Didactic
BURNT NORTON	Four-stress line	1. Irregularly rhymed tetrameter 2. Hexameters and septenaries 3. Loose blank verse and four-stress line	1. Four-stress 2. Three-stress	1. Irregular iambic, rhymed	1. Four-stress 2. Three-stress
EAST COKER	Four-stress line	1. Irregularly rhymed tetrameter 2. Four-stress	1. Hexameter 2. Irregular five- and four-stress	1. Regular tetrameter stanzas	1. "Hexameters" 2. Four-stress
THE DRY SALVAGES	1. Five-stress anapestic/dactylic 2. Four-stress	1. Adapted sestina 2. Probably non-metrical, merging into four-stress	1. "Hexameters" 2. Four-stress	1. Five-line stanza unrhymed; falling rhythm	1. Four-stress 2. Three-stress
LITTLE GIDDING	1. Four-stress 2. Irregular blank verse; four-stress	1. Regular trimeter and tetrameter stanzas 2. Blank verse in *terza rima*	1. "Hexameters" 2. Three-stress	1. Regular tetrameter and trimeter stanzas	1. Four-stress with irregular blank verse 2. Three-stress

The second movement of each quartet opens with a rhyming lyric. The precision of the natural order is "figured" in regular tetrameter,

> We move above the moving tree
> In light upon the figured leaf
> And hear upon the sodden floor
> Below, the boarhound and the boar
> Pursue their pattern as before
> But reconciled among the stars,
>
> "Burnt Norton"

as are the disturbances of the spring, "not in time's covenant":

> Comets weep and Leonids fly
> Hunt the heavens and the plains
> Whirled in a vortex that shall bring
> The world to that destructive fire
> Which burns before the ice-cap reigns.

The second movement of "The Dry Salvages" introduces a variation on sestina form. The pattern is complicated, and as it unfortunately turns out, clumsy and self-defeating.

> Where is there an end of it, the soundless *wailing,*
> The silent withering of autumn *flowers*
> Dropping their petals and remaining *motionless;*
> Where is there an end to the drifting *wreckage,*
> The prayer of the bone on the beach, the *unprayable*
> Prayer at the calamitous *annunciation?*

The end rhymes undergo an increasingly desperate metamorphosis until we get "sailing" and "bailing," and "devotionless," "oceanless," and "erosionless." The ineffable weariness here brings to mind Eliot's own parody of this mood:

> O when will the c*reaking heart* ease?
> When will the broken chair give ease?
> Why will the summer day delay?
> *When* will Time flow away?
>
> "Lines to a Persian Cat"

A longer section, of greater philosophic density, follows the lyrical interludes. In "Burnt Norton" Eliot penetrates to the unity of all experience; these lines, among all that Eliot has written, approach, for him, the *poetry beyond poetry:*

> At the still point of the turning world. Neither flesh
>   nor fleshness;
> Neither from nor towards; at the still point, there the
>   dance is,
> But neither arrest nor movement. And do not call it fixity,
> Where past and future are gathered. Neither movement from
>   nor towards,
> Neither ascent nor decline. Except for the point,
>   the still point,
> There would be no dance, and there is only the dance.

Though the lines contain six and seven principal stresses, they move, for many, with the ease and grace of the celestial dance they describe. Equally facile is the parallel section of "Little Gidding," the "Inferno" episode. Eliot's adaptation of Dante's stanza avoids rhyme but alternates masculine and feminine endings to achieve the interlocking effect of *terza rima:*

> In the uncertain hour before the morning
>   Near the ending of interminable night
>   At the recurrent end of the unending
> After the dark dove with the flickering tongue
>   Had passed below the horizon of his homing
>   While the dead leaves still rattled on like tin . . .

The pattern does lead Eliot into the weakness and strained image of line 5's last three feet, but these lines do follow Dante's *endecasillabo,* even to observing the elision of a final vowel before *h:*

> Had passed below *th' horizon* of his homing.

We are not dealing, however, with syllabic meter but blank verse. Eliot's "familiar compound ghost" speaks in grave, measured pentameter:

> Let me disclose the gifts reserved for age
>   To set a crown upon your lifetime's effort.
>   First, the cold friction of expiring sense
> Without enchantment, offering no promise
>   But bitter tastelessness of shadow fruit
>   As body and soul begin to fall asunder.

The final allusion to *Hamlet* reminds us that Eliot's versification owes as much to Shakespeare as to Dante; it may also be Old Possum's little joke that the "compound ghost," ingeniously fashioned from a dozen literary sources, is only that sad spook, the ghost of Hamlet's father:

> The day was breaking. In the disfigured street
> He left me, with a kind of valediction,
> And faded on the blowing of the horn.

Some readers have been dismayed by Eliot's weariness, his repetitive circling of ideas, and his flaccid rhythms in the *Quartets*. Karl Shapiro complains

> Eliot
> Himself in the *Quartets* (in my opinion
> His most depressing prosody) makes shift
> Of rhythms one thought he had exhausted ten
> Or fifteen years before. Symptoms of doubt
> Lie in reiteration; we sense confusion,
> The anxiety of the sensitive to mistakes.
>
> *Essay on Rime*

Donald Davie, in a devastating analysis of "The Dry Salvages," speaks of its "stumbling, trundling rhythms . . . inarticulate ejaculations of reach-me-down phrases . . . debased currency of the study circle."[33] Exhaustion and even clumsiness certainly mar passages in "East Coker" and "The Dry Salvages"; the two inner *Quartets* suffer the most from Eliot's bemused prosiness and the grinding futility of disillusion chasing its tail—

> The loud lament of the disconsolate chimera.

We agree with Davie that these lines are dismal in every respect:

It seems, as one becomes older,
That the past has another pattern, and ceases to be
    a mere sequence—
Or even development: the latter a partial fallacy
Encouraged by superficial notions of evolution.

Eliot allows too many weak syllables to intervene between strong stresses:

    ˘ ´   ˘   ˘ ´   ˘ ´   ˘ ´   ˘   ˘   ˘   ˘ ´ ˘

En cour aged by su per fi cial no tions of e vo lu tion.

Since it is nearly impossible to tell which syllables are dynamically strong, the metrical checkpoints are obscured. The obsessive parenthetical qualification disrupts syntactical movement, and there are sections of "The Dry Salvages" when Eliot, usually so precise, loses control of his grammar.

But we need not judge the *Quartets* by their arid or tired moments. Far from containing Eliot's "most depressing prosody," "Little Gidding" concludes the *Quartets* with a consistently strong and unbroken rhythmic impulse. While the other *Quartets* struggle with definition and direction, "Little Gidding" reaches a resolution of both technique and idea. The larger formal rhythm (the five-movement divisions of landscape, lyric, didactic, lyric, didactic) is firmly settled as a pattern; the gestalt of the other three *Quartets* is impressed on our minds. The expected sequence of metrical modes (see the chart on p. 195) now seems inevitable; we react with a sense of prepared surprise to the changes from four-stress verse to regular iambics, and from irregular pentameter to regular three-stress verse. Within each movement Eliot achieves his surest rhythms against an always discernible controlling meter.

The opening, with its balance between strong-stress and pentameter verse, offers these superb lines:

And glow more intense than blaze of branch, or brazier,
Stirs the dumb spirit: no wind, but pentecostal fire
In the dark time of the year. Between melting and freezing
The soul's sap quivers. There is no earth smell
Or smell of living thing. This is the spring time
But not in time's covenant.

The lines at first expand toward five stresses and blank verse; as the overall rhythm turns downward, reaching toward conclusion, the line turns back to four stresses:

> But this is the nearest, in place and time,
> Now and in England.
> > If you came this way . . .
>
> Is England and nowhere. Never and always.

The lyrics of sections 2 and 4 have the simple regularity of songs; their mixture of iambic with trochaic and anapestic feet derives largely from the examples of Blake and Tennyson—and their great example, the Shakespearean song:

> Ash on | an old | man's sleeve
> Is all | the ash | the burnt ro | ses leave.
> Dust in | the air | sus pen | ded
> Marks | the place | where a sto | ry en | ded.

As in many of Shakespeare's songs, the iambic line begins on the strong syllable (trochaic or monosyllabic substitution): where the musical beat would naturally fall.

A hiatus, indicated by a visual pause, intervenes between the two strophes of section 5:

> > So while the light fails
> On a winter's afternoon, in a secluded chapel
> History is now and England.
>
> With the drawing of this Love and the voice of this Calling
>
> > We shall not cease from exploration
> And the end of all our exploring
> Will be to arrive where we started
> And know the place for the first time.

The break is charged with silent energy; the poet stops, catches his breath for his final statement. The concluding movement (in three-

stress lines) draws together motifs from all the *Quartets;* the falling
rhythm of

> Quick now, here, now, always—

is transformed upward:

> When the tongues of flame are in-folded
> Into the crowned knot of fire
> And the fire and the rose are one.

As God's testing fire merges with the Rose of his Love, the rhythm
slowly rises and ends the sequence of the *Quartets* in quiet triumph.

VIII

Stevens, Frost, and Jeffers: Three Who Stayed Home; Hart Crane: One Who Found No Home

Unlike Eliot and Pound (and noting the fact that Frost for a time moved to England where he found a publisher for his first book), these four poets chose to spend most of their creative lives working in their home country. In doing so, they can be said to have both possessed and given voice to the American sensibility. Certainly Stevens and Frost, especially, continue to influence the field of contemporary mainstream poetry; and after early celebrity and later exclusion from the canon, Jeffers's poems have begun to demand our attention again. The prodigious influence on later generations of the former, and the recent resurrection of the latter, will become clearer in a later chapter, but here we will focus on the considerable artistry of these three. As poets they are as different in technique and temperament as Tennyson and Browning. Their dissimilarity, in fact, may serve critical generalization; in the dialectic of extreme opposition, Red and White, Left and Right, often exhibit comparable qualities.

In his poetry Wallace Stevens kept a fastidious distance between himself and "real life." Often, he has been referred to as alienated. We may often wish that Stevens's poetry were less ephemeral, less of the sun and the moon, of "the formulations of midnight"; that it admit a subject larger than poetry itself. But the wishes of critics, set against the achievement of all of these poets, are paltry things; they gave themselves magnificently, and it is ungrateful to ask for something else. With this understanding, we can say that Stevens had no gift for the "plain style"; he sought after the incantatory power of words, the authority of rich and rhythmic language. In attempting to characterize his style, the word *rhetorical* comes immediately to mind. Although rhetoric's stock has risen, fallen, and risen again—many poets misunderstood Pound to have said poetry should be as flatly written as prose—twentieth-century poetry has often made use of resounding rhetoric; Yeats, Eliot, Crane, Jeffers, and Dylan Thomas, when occasion and need made it appropriate, did not avoid Shakespearean or even Miltonic vividness. The implications for prosody should be clear. Rhetoric can only be sustained by consummate rhythmic control; the great masters of rhetoric in English, Shakespeare and Milton, have also been the greatest masters of metric. Rhetoric is language with more sensuous surface than conceptual substance; it becomes the job of prosody, then, to keep rhetoric from flowing into pure sound or dissolving into pure image. Rhythm, the container that holds time, tells us how an idea feels; rhythm will rescue for cognition what may never receive articulate verbal expression, what rhetoric may overstate or conceal.

❧ *1. Wallace Stevens*

Stevens's rhetoric is not often amazed by experience and never ignorant; rather, it is diffident: an effort to bring, without philosophical pompousness, the indefinable to definition. Stevens's purest rhetoric, his infamous use of nonsense syllables, has irritated many; but it is precisely here that we frequently discover Stevens bringing the subtlest thought and feeling into view:

> We say: At night an Arabian in my room,
> With his damned hoobla-hoobla-hoobla-how,
> Inscribes a primitive astronomy
>
> Across the unscrawled fores the future casts
> And throws his stars around the floor. By day
> The wood-dove used to chant his hoobla-hoo
>
> And still the grossest iridescence of ocean
> Howls hoo and rises and howls hoo and falls.
> Life's nonsense pierces us with strange relation.
> > "Notes toward a Supreme Fiction"

Stevens's rhetoric, the hoobla-hoobla of "life's nonsense," forms part of his meaning, piercing us "with strange relation." But this rhetoric does not always convince, as in that conclusion. "With strange relation" is a flat yet oddly preening effort. Who could imagine any native speaker, moved by emotion and touched by rhetorical power, ever naturally saying such a thing? It is precisely when Stevens attempts to name the unnameable—not by subtle indirection, but blatantly— that he sounds most unnatural, most unbelievable. This is the flaw in Stevens's rhetoric that so plagues the work of his followers like John Ashbery. Even so, we are grateful for the beauty of the lines surrounding his summarizing failure. Elsewhere, Stevens's rhetoric may break down in simple windiness, as it does in the opening lines of "Credences of Summer:"

> Now in midsummer come and all fools slaughtered
> And spring's infuriations over and a long way
> To the first autumnal inhalations, young broods
> Are in the grass.

Though some may find the rhythms gripping, the movement compelling, we cannot forget our syntactical bafflement (is *come* noun or verb?); and what particular fools were slaughtered, and why? The rhythm affects our inner perception with a feeling of overripeness. The fullness of time becomes static, giving no sense of the continual change that penetrates all life, all reality.

Stevens had dealings with the imagists, but what he bought from them he invested at considerable profit. *Harmonium* contains a number of poems in short lines that might be labeled imagist; they concentrate on presenting a single effect of sound or sight. But the "imagist" poem in *Harmonium* adds metaphysical depth to imagist descriptive brilliance; we must pursue meaning down elusive symbolic ways. An imagist poem usually has height and width, the image and its accompanying or resultant aura of feeling:

OREAD

> Whirl up, sea—
> Whirl your pointed pines
> On our rocks,
> Hurl your green over us—
> Cover us with your pools of fir.

H.D.

H.D. renders rather than describes her feelings; we sense the violence as we see the scene.

Stevens's three-dimensioned "imagist" poem may be illustrated by the brief and tantalizing "Valley Candle" (from *Harmonium*):

> My candle burned alone in an immense *valley*.
> Beams of the huge night converged upon it,
> Until the wind blew.
> Then beams of the huge night
> Converged upon its image,
> Until the wind blew.

The poem states in highly condensed and elliptical fashion what was to become Stevens's perennial theme: the interaction of the poetic mind with the creative imagination and final reality. As we read this poem, the candle symbolizes Coleridge's imagination that "dissolves, diffuses, dissipates in order to recreate"; the poem turns on its most surprising word, "Beams," leading off line 2. The huge night is not unilluminated; rather, it burns with darker reality, with the scarcely imaginable fire of chaos. The candle—the poet's imagination—burns in isolation; it only partially illuminates, for the beams of unimagined reality threaten the flickering light. The coming of the wind marks the cessation of imaginative activity. First the candle, then its image vanish—and reality vanishes with both. The poem expresses a deep and characteristic pessimism; with the extinguishing of imagination, chaos extends its dominion and brings oblivion both to mind and its imaginative constructs. Depending on how we read the symbols, the poem explores epistemological or ontological landscapes. The only sure approach toward Stevens is through his other poems. "Valley Candle" is a sketch, a prelude in the sense that Chopin's Preludes make use of material elsewhere exploited. Stevens tells us that

> One poem proves another and the whole,
> For the clairvoyant men that need no proof:
> The lover, the believer and the poet.
> "A Primitive Like an Orb"

Poetry, like religion and love, is self-justifying. This may seem to resemble the doctrine of art for art's sake, but Stevens makes no dichotomy between poem and world, imagination and reality. For the art-for-art's-saker the poem builds a reality apart from experience; for Stevens all experience is aesthetic experience:

>   It is
>   As if the central poem became the world,
>   And the world the central poem, each one the mate
>   Of the other, as if summer was a spouse,
>   Espoused each morning.
>
>   "A Primitive Like an Orb"

Given his theme, then, "The essential poem at the centre of things," we might expect to find Stevens a most delicate and elegant master of prosody. We return to "A Primitive Like an Orb" for further enlightenment; no one explains Stevens better than Stevens himself. The essential poem, "the miraculous multiplex of lesser poems," appears as

>   A giant, on the horizon, glistening,
>
>   ———
>
>   And in bright excellence, adorned, crested
>   With every prodigal, familiar fire,
>   And unfamiliar escapades: whirroos
>   And scintillant sizzlings such as children like,
>   Vested in the serious folds of majesty,
>   Moving around and behind, a following,
>   A source of trumpeting seraphs in the eye,
>   A source of pleasant outbursts on the ear.

Obviously, for Stevens the "plain style" of poetry does not exist. Another "piece of sophisticated looniness" (to quote Theodore Roethke)[1] that we cherish for its delicious music is the "Cortege for Rosenbloom." The rhythmic theme, stated in the first stanza, derives from the two heavy stresses in the name of the departed:

>   Now, the wry Rosenbloom is dead
>   And his finical carriers tread,
>   On a hundred legs, the tread
>   Of the dead.
>   Rosenbloom is dead.

This processional music turns exotic, and the meter settles into two strong beats as the feet of "the finical carriers" rise and fall:

To a chirr of gongs
And a chitter of cries
And the heavy thrum
Of the endless tread
That they tread;

To a jangle of doom
And a jumble of words
Of the intense poem
Of the strictest prose
Of Rosenbloom.

A world of preoccupation has been discovered beneath the "scin-
tillant sizzlings" of Stevens's highly finished poetic surfaces. "Le Mono-
cle de Mon Oncle" is as successful a poem about a self-mocking
middle-aged lover as "Prufrock"; "Sunday Morning" deals as signifi-
cantly with the problems of religious belief as *The Waste Land*. We
might match tropes from "Le Monocle de Mon Oncle" and "Prufrock"
to show Stevens as Eliot's prosodic equal.[2] The thematic material of
both poems is similar:

And so I mocked her in magnificent measure.
Or was it that I mocked myself alone?
I wish that I might be a thinking stone.

———

I should have been a pair of ragged claws
Scuttling across the floors of silent seas.

———

Shall I uncrumple this much-crumpled thing?
I am a man of fortune greeting heirs;
For it has come that thus I greet the spring.
These choirs of welcome choir for me farewell.

———

Shall I part my hair behind? Do I dare to eat a peach?
I shall wear white flannel trousers, and walk upon the beach.
I have heard the mermaids singing, each to each.

I do not think that they will sing to me.

If anything, Stevens achieves greater subtlety in his exact iambics than Eliot in his more elastic metric. The most memorable lines of both poets, however, fall into quite close pentameters. Eliot's pentameter lines follow some anapestic stretching; the couplet of the ragged claws, and the stiffly iambic

> I do not think that they will sing to me

afford a marked change of pace. The prosody is also aided by the self-consciously portentous visual isolation of the lines. Stevens maintains a more homogenous texture, though he will occasionally invert feet and add hypermetrical syllables:

> And so | I mocked | her in | mag ni | fi cent mea | sure.

The prosody of "Valley Candle" is based on simple repetitions and parallelisms. "Anecdote of the Prince of Peacocks" has a delicately varied two-stress line; we quote the final strophe:

> I knew from this
> That the blue ground
> Was full of blocks
> And blocking steel.
> I knew the dread
> Of the bushy plain,
> And the beauty
> Of the moonlight
> Falling there,
> Falling
> As sleep falls
> In the innocent air.

How "free" this highly controlled verse actually is we leave to the reader's judgment; note the use of rhythmic constants such as the minor Ionic ("That the blue ground . . . Of the moonlight"), the occasional rhyme, and the diminuendo indicated by the channeling of the line from long to short to long again (through anapestic resolution).

A more formal prosodic scheme orders the rhythms of "Peter Quince at the Clavier." The title and the opening image,

> Just as my fingers on these keys
> Make music, so the selfsame sounds
> On my spirit make a music, too,

signal an explicit musical organization. Stevens comments on his own method, and on the functions of prosody as we conceive it, when he shrewdly meditates

> Music is feeling, then, not sound.

Phoneticians, please take note!

The four movements of "Peter Quince" offer contrasts in tempo, and critics have recognized affinities to the four-movement form of the classical symphony. We make no positive point-for-point identifications other than noting that the third section might be considered a scherzo, *allegro molto vivace*. The first movement is moderato, the second andante, and the last andante again. This does not correspond to the movements of classical sonata-symphony form (allegro-andante-minuet-allegro), and it reverses the scheme of the baroque sonata (slow-fast-slow-fast). However, the obvious juxtaposition of contrasting movements and the use of repeated themes justify naming the structure of "Peter Quince" a musical one.

The meter of movements 1, 3, and 4 is iambic tetrameter; Stevens gets fabulous variety in this traditional line. Two significant sources of metrical interest are the initial trochee,

> Júst as | my fíng | ers on | these kéys . . .
>
> Mú sic | is feél | ing, thén, | not soúnd . . .
>
> Hére in | this roóm, | de sír | ing yoú,
>
> Thínk ing | of yoúr | blue-shá | dowed sílk,

and the slight tension of a metrically stressed syllable nudging a non-metrically but rhetorically stressed syllable:

> the sélf | same soúnds . . .
>
> And thús | it ís | that whát | I feél . . .
>
> . . . of yoúr | blue-shá | dowed sílk.

A rising Ionic marks a shift in the poet's thought when he forgets the object of his own desire and remembers Susanna:

Of a gréen éve | ning, cléar | and wárm . . .

Alliteration emphasizes the mounting blood pressure of the lecherous elders:

> The red-eyed elders watching, felt
>
> The basses of their beings throb
> In witching chords, and their thin blood
> Pulse pizzicati of Hosanna.

Again we have the delicate crowding of metrically and rhetorically stressed syllables:

> The réd- | eyèd él | ders . . .
> and théir | thìn blóod . . .

The second movement alternates a slow two-and-one-stress line; it also introduces a tender, sensuous feminine rhyming. The last three lines of the second movement serve as an *attacca,* indicating that the third movement follows without a break:

> She turned—
> A cymbal crashed,
> And roaring horns.

Stevens's musical vocabulary underscores his intentions. A mention of horns and cymbals leads us into dance rhythms, although the meter remains four-stress iambic:

> Soon with a noise like tambourines,
> Came her attendant Byzantines.
>
> They wondered why Susanna cried
> Against the elders by her side;
>
> And as they whispered, the refrain
> Was like a willow swept by rain.

In the final movement the music returns to the meditative pace of the opening. But there are important prosodic changes. The obsessive feminine rhyming,

> So evenings die, in their green going,
> A wave, interminably flowing.
> So gardens die, their meek breath scenting
> The cowl of winter, done repenting.
> So maidens die, to the auroral
> Celebration of a maiden's choral,

contains reminiscences of the second movement; the repetitions of words and rhythms suggest Romantic, cyclical, rather than eighteenth-century sonata form. These quiet feminine endings give a "dying fall," a vanishing quality to the whole passage.

Theme and variation stand at the very center of Stevens's poetic method. It is no exaggeration to say that all his work after *Harmonium* represents variations on a single theme: a theory of poetry that would also be a theory of reality. This is, of course, a large order; it limited Stevens no more than James's obsession with innocence and evil limited him. Stevens set a high value on developing a theory of poetry. Something of his passion about aesthetic matters can be felt in these excerpts from *The Necessary Angel:*

> The theory of poetry, as a subject of study, was something with respect to which I had nothing but the most ardent ambitions. It seemed to me to be one of the great subjects of study.[3]

> Yet hypotheses relating to poetry, although they may appear to be very distant illuminations, could be the fires of fate, if rhetoric ever meant anything.[4]

Stevens believed that poetry's mode of operation lay in the recognition of resemblances. Metaphor, not imitation, formed the basis of poetic knowledge; quarreling with Aristotle, Stevens wittily observed "An imitation may be described as an identity manqué."[5]

In surveying the development of Stevens's blank verse, "Sunday Morning" stands as our point of departure. The opening lines define iambic movement without maintaining a clear metrical norm. The first and third lines have only three rhetorical stresses; the second line has eleven syllables, the fourth has a trochaic third foot.

> Complacencies of the peignoir, and late
> Coffee and oranges in a sunny chair,

> And the green freedom of a cockatoo
> Upon a rug mingle to dissipate
> The holy hush of ancient sacrifice.

Not until the fifth line does the verse settle down into regular iambic pentameter. Throughout the rest of the poem, scansion shows the usual departures from the traditional blank-verse "code": the inverted initial foot; the caesura after the fourth, fifth, or sixth syllable; the maintenance of the decasyllabic line. The trisyllabic foot, common to Websterian blank verse, is rare, and can be usually rationalized in elision:

> The sky | will be | much friend | li er then | than now.
> The trees, | like se | ra fin, | and ech | o_ing hills . . .

Still rarer is the inverted final foot; we find one example, however, in "Sunday Morning,"

> E la | tions when | the for | est blooms; | gus ty,

and another in a later poem, "A Primitive Like an Orb":

> And in | bright ex | cel lence | a dorned, | cres ted.

Numerous lines contain only four strong rhetorical stresses with the fifth metrical accent falling variously on syllables of low dynamic quality. We find the typically Shakespearean,

> Of men that perish and of summer morn . . .

> A part of labor and a part of pain,

where four-stress structure peers through the pentameter. There is little cross-rhythmical tension, however; Stevens is controlling rather than releasing feeling. The position of the light metrical stress varies; it sometimes falls on *and,*

> The bough of summer *and* the winter branch . . .

> Deer walk upon our mountains, *and* the quail . . .

and occasionally on an auxiliary or a preposition,

> Does ripe fruit never fall? Or *do* the boughs . . .
>
> Alone, shall come fulfillment *to* our dreams . . .
>
> By the consummation *of* the swallow's wings.

The last line above begins with a trisyllabic foot; this eleven-syllable line is an obvious exception to the usual elision of the extra syllable.

The music of "Sunday Morning" is not Shakespearean throughout; we hear other harmonies, Tennyson's, for example:

> Winding across wide water, without sound.
> The day is like wide water, without sound,
> Stilled for the passing of her dreaming feet.

The unbroken sentence concluding "Sunday Morning," with its energetic verbs and active syntax, suggests the last stanza of Keats's "Ode to Autumn":

> Deer walk upon our mountains, and the quail
> Whistle about us their spontaneous cries;
> Sweet berries ripen in the wilderness;
> And, in the isolation of the sky,
> At evening, casual flocks of pigeons make
> Ambiguous undulations as they sink,
> Downward to darkness, on extended wings.

We feel here that pulse of meditation which quickens the Keatsian sublime: a physical sense of thought dramatized for the eyes and ears of the reader. The deer "walk," the quail "whistle," the berries "ripen," the pigeons "sink"; these actions are bound together by the sounding rhythms of superlative blank verse aided by recurring patterns within the metrical structure. The final line, by way of valediction, shows the characteristic rhythmic constant of the whole poem: four strong rhetorical stresses, here pointed up by alliteration.

The blank verse of "The Idea of Order at Key West" is pitched higher than the verse of "Sunday Morning"; it has a surface hardness, a more emphatic drive to its rhythms. While the opening of "Sunday

Morning" is quiet and metrically evasive, "The Idea of Order" opens
with strident precision:

> She sang beyond the genius of the sea.
> The water never formed to mind or voice,
> Like a body wholly body, fluttering
> Its empty sleeves; and yet its mimic motion
> Made constant cry, caused constantly a cry,
> That was not ours although we understood,
> Inhuman, of the veritable ocean.

We find less delicacy than in "Sunday Morning" but considerably more
energy. Occasional rhymes and repetitions punctuate the line end-
ings. Perhaps nowhere in Stevens's poetry does his central theme
achieve such luminously clear expression.

The volume *Ideas of Order* (1935) contains several poems in three-
line stanzas. We notice a change in prosodic style, a shift away from
blank-verse firmness and resonance to a newer kind of transparence
and rhythmic freedom. A poem such as "Anglais Mort à Florence"
retains the foot structure of blank verse, but the grand rhetoric of "The
Idea of Order at Key West" and the Shakespearean cadences of "Sun-
day Morning" have both disappeared. In their place we find elements
of the style that receives apotheosis in *Notes toward a Supreme Fiction* and
the superb valedictory poems of *The Rock*. Individual sentences tend to
be short, the rhythms clipped, and the texture thinned out.

The line and stanza patterning of *Notes toward a Supreme Fiction*
would delight a medieval poet's sense of the power and significance of
number. Three, seven, ten, and their related sums and multiplications
figure in the poem's organization. Each large section is subdivided
into ten smaller sections; each of these smaller sections is made up of
seven three-line stanzas.

We have no difficulty scanning the verse of *Notes toward a Supreme
Fiction;* the usual "rules" work well enough. Most of the lines are five-
stressed, though less than half the lines contain ten syllables. The
rhythm of blank verse surges forward at times, then fades and dissolves
into other cadences. Stability and change are not, however, poles of
absolute dramatic contrast but elements interfused in the overriding
rhythms of the poem. The following section begins with marked metri-
cal irregularities that modulate at the seventh line into closer pen-

tameter. The rhythm actually contracts from a rhetorical flow, controlled by a figure of grammar ("To sing . . . To be crested . . . to exult," etc.) to lines controlled by precisely metrical feet:

> To sing jubilas at exact, accustomed times,
> To be crested and wear the mane of a multitude
> And so, as part, to exult with its great throat,
>
> To speak of joy and to sing of it, borne on
> The shoulders of joyous men, to feel the heart
> That is the common, the bravest fundament,
>
> This is a facile exercise. Jerome
> Begat the tubas and the fire-wind strings,
> The golden fingers picking dark-blue air:
>
> For companies of voices moving there,
> To find of sound the bleakest ancestor,
> To find of light a music issuing
>
> Whereon it falls in more than sensual mode.

The meter impresses itself upon the meaning with considerable ingenuity. The first two stanzas speak of actual human emotions: praise, the sharing of communal feelings, joy, and exultation. The second pair of stanzas turn toward feeling as it is transformed into music, into the "more than sensual mode." An emphatic antithesis is clarified by the metrical stressing of "That" and "This":

> That is I the com I mon, the brav I est fun I da ment,
>
> This is I a fa I cile ex I er cise. I Je rome . . .

Our "facile exercise" proceeds with facility in clearest pentameter:

> Be gat I the tu I bas and I the fire- I wind strings,
> The gol I den fin I gers pick I ing dark- I blue air:
> For com I pa nies I of vio I ces mov I ing there.

Feelings of the heart, however, move in quite different rhythms:

> To sing | ju bi las | at ex act, | ac cus | tomed times,
> To be cres | ted and wear | the mane | of a mul | ti tude.

Stevens never wrenches his tone to accommodate the meter. He never omits syllables to achieve a more precise beat, but allows the movement of conversation to take over whenever the argument of the poem demands it. Often the rhythm shifts in midline, from rising to falling:

> On her trip around the world, Nanzia Nunzio
> Confronted Ozymandias.

The rising iambic rhythm is occasionally confuted by an inverted final foot, a metrical mannerism of Stevens,

> The first idea was not our own. Adam . . .
>
> To speak of joy and sing of it, borne on . . .

or by reversing the highly susceptible second foot,

> The book, hot for another accessible bliss . . .
>
> The spent feeling leaving nothing of itself . . .

A syllable that would ordinarily have been omitted by an earlier poet will intrude in an otherwise regular passage:

> It might and might have been. But as it was,
> A dead shepherd brought tremendous chords from hell
>
> And bade the sheep carouse. Or so they said.
> Children in love with them brought early flowers
> And scattered them about, no two alike.

This "dead" Saintsbury would have certainly named a "perversity." But in Stevens's metrical context the extra syllable scarcely stirs a ripple.

The metrical form of "Notes toward a Supreme Fiction" dominates the important poems of Stevens's two final volumes, *The Auroras of Autumn* and *The Rock*. The three-line stanza, the open rhythms approaching blank verse, and a new clarity of texture mark the final evolution of Stevens's prosody. The stanza itself, the triad, enters more actively into rhythmic structure; it retards, connects, holds over, or looks ahead.

Stevens uses the caesura not only as a metrical comma, a breathing pause in the middle of the line, but also as an integral element in rhythmic phrasing. Interior pausing conceals the metrical pulse and heightens the normal tensions of meaning: the resolutions of syntactical expectation and the logic of grammar. In the lines below, the caesuras continually delay our full apprehension of the sense; the syntactical cadence is held off until we nearly lose the grammatical thread:

> The flowers against the wall
> Are white, a little dried, a kind of mark
>
> Reminding, trying to remind, of a white
> That was different, something else, last year
> Or before, not the white of an aging afternoon.

Each caesural pause affects the dynamics of the phrasing; the repeated hesitations build up in a minor crescendo, a steadily rising curve of intensity. Stevens phrases his lines as a musician might phrase a melody.

The stylistic development evident in these two final volumes approaches that ultimate poetry beyond poetry envisioned by Eliot.[6] The prosody has dissolved into meaning; technique has become both thought and expression. We may exclaim, as Thomas Mann's Wendell Kretschmar exclaimed over the second movement of Beethoven's Sonata op. 111, "here—the appearance—of art is thrown off—at last—art always throws off the appearance of art."[7]

ɚ *II. Robert Frost*

Frost followed Robinson in adapting the measure of blank verse to the rhythms of common New England speech, and thereby played a major role ushering into twentieth-century poetry a significant cast of American characters. Here is an example from the dramatic dialogue, "West-Running Brook":

> "Fred, where is north?"
>   "North? North is there, my love.
> The brook runs west."
>   "West-running Brook then call it."

The speakers divide up a nearly strict blank-verse line. Frost allows the metrical pulse to shade the feeling and meaning of three identical words:

> . . . is nórth?" |
>
> | "North? North | is thére.

Rhetorical stress falls nearly equally on the three *norths,* but since the second *north* falls between the metrically strong *norths,* its intensity is weakened. Meaning requires a lower level of stress: the second *north* has some emotive but no semantic value; it is Fred's vocalized pause while remembering his directions. The meter ingeniously adjusts and modifies both concept and feeling.

Later in "West-Running Brook" we find a line with six contiguous rhetorical stresses:

> And it is tíme, stréngth, tòne, líght, lífe and lóve.

Words of greater conceptual value fall beneath the ictus; "life" and "love" must be stressed slightly more than "strength" and "tone." It may be possible to read the six nouns with absolutely level stress. But prevailing iambic movement and the slight variations in vowel length force greater emphasis on the fourth and fifth feet.

Frost may have had a Miltonic rhythm in his head ("Rocks, Caves, Lakes, Fens, Bogs. Dens and Shades of Death") that suggested the context for the line above:

> And it is time, strength, tone, light and love—
> And even substance lapsing unsubstantial;
> The universal cataract of death
> That spends to nothingness—and unresisted,
> Save by some strange resistance in itself,
> Not just a swerving, but a throwing back,
> As if regret were in it and were sacred.

The learned Latinate punning and inverted syntax of

> And even substance lapsing unsubstantial

echoes and parodies Milton: a fine example of rhythmic feeling preceding and stimulating an idea.

Like Robinson, Frost introduces many eleven-syllable lines:

> It was to me—in an annunciation . . .

> Long, long before we were from any creature . . .

> Get back to the beginning of beginnings.

The hypermetrical syllable is generally unaccented; however, Saints-bury would have decried as deliberate metrical mischief the poem's last line,

> To day | will be | the day | of what | we both said,

and spluttered that "both" was a perversity. Even if he were correct, we might hope that Saintsbury, in a fit of revelatory passion, would cast out his theories altogether on seeing the face and hearing the voice of this great poem. It is impossible to know for certain what Saintsbury would have done, but in context, and if we see that the line is hen-decasyllabic, then it moves smoothly enough; the extra syllable allows the line to hang as a partial question in the air:

>   "Today will be the day
> You said so."
>   "No, today will be the day
> You said the brook was called West-running Brook."

> "Today will be the day of what we both said."

The slight bump in the rhythm slows the line down; we must speak the last words deliberately, hesitating, pondering, as if reaching carefully for every word.

Frost builds his prosody close to common speech as he builds his poetry close to humanity's recurrent experience. His rhythms issue from the meter in a way that seems without artifice; yet every line is a skillful modification of the metrical norm:

> And then—the watcher at his pulse took fright.
> No one believed. They listened at his heart.
> Little—less—nothing!—and that ended it.
> No more to build on there. And they, since they

Were not the one dead, turned to their affairs.
                                        "Out, Out—"

The crushing and humiliating fact that life goes on despite human tragedy is the vital feeling in the rhythmical hesitations of the last lines:

No more | to build | on there. | And they, | since they
Were not | the one | dead, || turned | to their | affairs.

The caesura, a dead stop, coming in the middle of the foot, the spondaic foot itself with its two heavy stresses, are powerful evocations of feeling. The syntactical units are agonizingly short—each is a blow to head and body. We have rhythms symbolizing vital import; we feel the boy's death at basic levels. It is the prosody which images the nervous agony and the blank despair, the terrible concern and the even more terrible indifference.

What Frost called "sentence sounds" in his verse line provide a framework for his extensive use of colloquial expression.

"Home," he mocked gently.
            "Yes, what else but home?
It all depends on what you mean by home.
Of course he's nothing to us, any more
Than was the hound that came a stranger to us
Out of the woods, worn out upon the trail."

"Home is the place where, when you have to go there,
They have to take you in."
                        "Death of the Hired Man"

Again we see the blank-verse line harnessed to conversation, the trochaic first foot packed with emotive freight and relieved by the caesura falling in the middle of the third foot—"Home," he | mocked gent | ly. "Yes, | what else but home?"—then the ictus smoothing out in monosyllabic nuggets that, if not Truth itself, form its gritty exhalation. In this light the impact of Frost's pithy wisdom comes from his phrasing, his invention of lines that dangerously teeter on violations of the metrical pattern, teasing the reader with disaster, then pulling back from the edge just in time to leave us amazed, the click of the lid of Yeats's well-made box echoing in our ears.

"Home is | the place | where, when | you have | to go there,

They have | to take | you in."

Is it far-fetched to speculate that Frost's wide appeal has something to do with this illusion of metrical shape-shifting? No lines by other poets so consistently lend themselves to the fallacy of spoken emphasis, in which the speaker-reader imposes a rhythmical interpretation on the metrical pattern.

> He is said to have been the last Red Man
> In Acton. And the Miller is said to have laughed—
> If you like to call such a sound a laugh.
> But he gave no one else a laugher's license.
> For he turned suddenly grave as if to say,
> "Whose business—but why talk round the barn?—
> When it's just that I hold with getting a thing done with.
> You can't get back and see it as he saw it.
> It's too long a story to go into now.
> You'd have to have been there and lived it.
> Then you wouldn't have looked on it as just a matter
> Of who began it between the two races . . ."
>
> "The Vanishing Red"

This opening stanza provides a remarkable opportunity for creative rhythmical scanning, which misses altogether the dominant metrical pattern. Many might scan the first lines:

He is said | to have been | the last | Red Man

In Ac | ton. And the Mill | er is said | to have laughed—

If you like | to call | such a sound | a laugh.

Metrically, this is senseless. Rather, Frost loosens the blank-verse line, accommodating the casual speech of his narrator. The first line opens with two trochaic feet, line 2 concludes with two anapests, and line 3 opens with three inversions:

He is | said to | have been | the last | Red Man

In Ac | ton. And | the Mill | er is said | to have laughed—

If you | like to | call such | a sound | a laugh.

But he | gave no | one else | a laugh | er's license.

But for shrewd variations appropriate to meaning, the blank verse is quite regular—disguised but regular. Lines 7 and 8 are also problematic, one seemingly pedestrian tetrameter, and one of thirteen syllables that's purely prose. In this view the lines scan:

Whose bus | iness—but | why talk | round the barn?—

When it's just | that I hold | with get | ting a thing | done with.—

In fact, they scan:

Whose bus | i ness— | but why | talk round | the barn?—

When it's just | that I hold | with get ting a | thing | done with.

Line 7's variations include the anapest (further disguised by the caesura) in the second foot, and the use of elision in the fourth. Line 8's include the first two anapestic feet, and the hypercatelectic extra syllable at line's end. Line 8, with its extra syllables and variations, stretches the meter about as far as it can go; not surprisingly, the rest of the stanza settles down, though not entirely. Line 9 also carries an extra syllable at the end, and line 11 depends on elision for its integrity within the metrical pattern:

You'd | have to | have been | there and | lived it.

This is the craft of *seeming* natural. Frost worked it to perfection in any meter he turned his hand to, refining the poetry of "natural speech" in his time. His metrics, on the surface so simple, in fact give new meaning to the word *subtle*. Even in the less than promising meters, as in the anapest-dominated pattern of his late, eerie masterpiece, "The Draft Horse," Frost performs a feat of astonishing, concise magic:

With a lantern that wouldn't burn
In too frail a buggy we drove
Behind too heavy a horse
Through a pitch-dark limitless grove.

And a man came out of the trees
And took our horse by the head
And reaching back to his ribs
Deliberately stabbed him dead.

The ponderous beast went down
With a crack of a broken shaft,
And the night drew through the trees
In one long invidious draft.

The most unquestioning pair
That ever accepted fate
And the least disposed to ascribe
Any more than we had to to hate,

We assumed that the man himself
Or someone he had to obey
Wanted us to get down
And walk the rest of the way.

In a meter one might associate with running doggerel, Frost intro-
duces a hushed, tenuous journey—

With a lan | tern that would | n't burn
In too frail | a bug | gy we drove
Be hind | too hea | vy a horse
Through a pitch | -dark lim | it less grove.

The balky lantern and "frail" buggy, the "heavy," sluggish horse and
"limitless" darkness of the grove impose on the traditionally light me-
ter ominous weight. The gloomy nexus arrives at its physical resolution
in the man stepping out of the trees in stanza 2. Frost describes the
shocking brutality of his act in the most economical fashion. The
placement of anapestic feet—in the first position in line 1, in the first
and third positions in lines 2, 3, and 5, in the last position of lines 6
and 7, in the second position of line 8, and so on—compliments the
meaning by speeding up and slowing down the action. What happens
in the poem is enhanced by meter that works *by working against* what is
described. The elision yoking the third and fourth syllables beginning
line 8 also evokes the breathless finality of the sin committed by the

man from the woods. The poem's resolution in its final three stanzas
deftly evolves from the manipulation of anapests, with Frost moving
their placement in the lines about like a champion checkers player
negotiating a series of intricate jumps—

> The pón der ous beást | went dówn
> With a cráck | of a bró | ken sháft.
> And the níght | dréw through | the treés
> In one lóng | in víd | i ous dráft.
>
> The móst | un qúes | tion ing páir
> That é | ver ac cépt | ed fáte
> And the leást | dis pósed | to as críbe
> An y móre | than we hád | to to háte,
>
> We as súmed | that the mán him sélf
> Or sóme | one he hád | to o béy
> Wán ted | us tó | get dówn
> And wálk | the rést | of the wáy.

"The Draft Horse" is an example of unlikely meter and bizarre content
meshing in a cooperation of opposites. It is indicative of Frost's bold-
ness and metrical range. His lines offer a surface smoothness—and
occasional rudeness—masking exquisite skill.

☙ III. *Robinson Jeffers*

Jeffers's life and work present the most dramatic paradox in modern
American poetry. As a young man, he moved with his wife to what was
then the remote Monterey peninsula in Northern California. There
he built a stone house and tower out of granite boulders he rolled up
from the seashore; they lived frugally on a small inheritance, raised
twin sons, and planted more than a thousand trees on and around
their property. Jeffers, encouraged by his wife, worked every morning
on poems, creating what must finally be recognized as one of the most
original oeuvres of our age.

This proud and solitary life, which ended in 1962, was lived out deep in the grain and flux of a dramatic landscape. That life's uncompromising asceticism seems to us today a little unreal, something many wish for but find impossible to achieve. Its very consistency runs counter to the critical storms that seemed always to be swirling around Jeffers's poems and philosophy. His first two books, privately printed in limited editions, reached no very large audience; but a copy of the second of these, *Tamar,* found its way to Mark Van Doren, who reviewed the collection, argued on behalf of the poetry's freshness and power, and pointedly wondered why no major New York publisher had taken this poet on. That fact was quickly corrected as a major trade edition of *Tamar and Other Poems* appeared. This new edition, widely and positively reviewed, made Jeffers famous. In a few years he would appear on the cover of *Time* as a great modern poet. As Jeffers's new books methodically appeared, critical attention was always intense and generally favorable among that generation of twentieth-century American critics, but the situation changed as the country drew closer to World War II, a war the poet opposed. By the late 1930s a generation of critics, most notably Yvor Winters, rejected Jeffers, dismissing his technique as crude, his philosophy as overbearing and fraudulent. Postwar American critics, poets, and readers inherited this negative assessment and, for the most part, embraced it, failing to carry out their own revaluation of the work itself. That task has fallen to writers, most in their forties as 1990 arrived, and partially through their efforts Jeffers has enjoyed something of a rebirth.

Jeffers is one of our first great environmentalist poets. His doctrine of inhumanism, frequently misinterpreted as a bitter, antihuman vision, is in fact a doctrine of humility and acceptance. Jeffers sees the eventual destruction of civilization and the obliteration of humankind as *inevitable,* not as *good.* His unnerving perspective acknowledges the primacy of sea, sky, rock, and tree, and the small part humans play in the cosmic drama.

Putting his much debated philosophy aside, for our purposes, we stress Jeffers's versatility of style, which is expressed in an equally wide range of prosodic skills. Though known best for his long narratives in long lines, in which his training in the classical languages, use of Whitman's pattern of recurrence, and mix-and-match variations of metrical and prose patterns similar to those practiced by Pound are evident, Jeffers is also capable of writing exquisite lyrics in traditional forms. Only when his penchant for didacticism overtakes him do his lines lapse into a prose paste. This excerpt from *Cawdor* gives us some idea of the long line's use in extended narrative. In this passage the death and afterdeath of a caged eagle becomes a meditative celebration of corporeal release and spiritual perfection and freedom.

> While George went to the house
> For his revolver, Michael climbed up the hill
> Weeping; but when he came with death in his hand
> She'd not go away, but watched. At the one shot
> The great dark bird leaped at the roof of the cage
> In silence and struck the wood; it fell, then suddenly
> Looked small and soft, muffled in its folded wings.
> The nerves of men after they die dream dimly
> And dwindle into their peace; they are not passionate, . . .
> The unsocial birds are a greater race;
> Cold-eyed, and their blood burns. What leaped up to death,
> The extension of one storm-dark wing filling its world,
> Was more than the soft garment that fell. Something had
> flown away. Oh cage-hoarded desire,
> Like the blade of a breaking wave reaped by the wind,
> or flame rising from fire, or cloud-coiled lightning
> Suddenly unfurled in the cave of heaven.

Especially in Jeffers's longer poems, we find a nervous, expansive shift from meter to meter, from stanzaic form to prose paragraph and back again—and all of it often occurring in the same poem. The passage above begins with a lean narrative discourse of strong stresses. The dominant iambic pattern undercuts the high drama of the eagle's execution. Even so, the first seven and a half lines are dense with the variations of trisyllabic substitution; the deft Ionic (At the one shot) at the moment the deed is accomplished arrests the line in time as if it were heavily end-stopped, then releases it to the shock of the bird's dying act and the resumption of the predominant blank-verse pattern. This pattern continues to the transition occurring in the fourth foot of line 8 and fulfilled by the clipped assertion (and four stresses) in line 10 ("The unsocial birds are a greater race"). At this point the lines expand from strong stress to quantity, a progression that seems brazenly appropriate as the poet follows the eagle's spirit after death. Jeffers's accumulative anapestic-trochaic, Ionic measure emphatically fuels the engine of content, driving us on in stops and starts, skirting (and sometimes crossing over) the borders of prose, as we come to full awareness (though not always altogether willingly) of the shadings and sense of the poet's difficult thought. This finds direct expression in the passage below. All of Jeffers's long poems contain segments where the author halts the narrative to address his cast of characters, or the reader, or both. These asides can be irritating, but not here:

> I that am stationed, and cold at heart; incapable of burning,
> My blood like standing sea-water lapped in a stone pool,
>   my desire to the rock, how can I speak of you.
> Mine will go down to the deep rock.

The direct speech to the eagle, or the eagle's spirit, serves as a rest stop where the rush of the preceding action concludes and the narrative gathers force to expand into the next charged section. Appropriately, the lines in Jeffers's speech spread out in his familiar, odd quantities, as if he doubled the blank-verse line, then relaxed it without letting it slip away into prose. The interplay between quantity and strong stress continues over this section's last sixty-one lines.

> This rose,
> Possessing the air over its emptied prison . . .
> Burned itself into meteor freedom and spired
> Higher still, and saw the mountain-dividing
> Canyon of its activity (that was to Cawdor
> Almost his world) like an old crack in a wall.

At the moment the eagle's spirit soars from its body, beginning its ascent, the movement through time returns to blank verse launched by forceful trochees at the head of lines. Again, anapestic ("Possessing the air") and Ionic ("like an old crack") substitution are common. The

eagle's spirit rises higher and higher above the earth as all the terms of
its earthly confinement become progressively smaller in its sight. The
mountains become mere specks, the ocean itself "lay on the shore like
the great shield of the moon come down," and as the diminishing
scale of the world below comes into final focus, the verse line once
again expands to contain the eagle's rush in that discovery:

> It saw from the height and space of unbreathable air
> Where meteors make green fire and die, the ocean dropping
>   westward to the girdle of the pearls of dawn
> And the hinder edge of the night sliding toward Asia.

Just as swiftly, as the eagle's awareness becomes complete, the line
constricts once more to a blank-verse norm with substitutions of fours
and sixes; these carry the bird-spirit into the sun:

> Pouring itself on fulfillment the eagle's passion
> Left life behind and flew at the sun its father.
> The great unreal talons took peace for prey
> Exultantly, their death beyond death; stopped upward,
>   and struck
> Peace like a white fawn in a dell of fire.

Jeffers's double-pentameter line, broken by compressed passages of
prose, shapes his signature long poems to the end of his career. But
late in his work expression coheres into pared-down yet packed clus-
ters of gatherings and heaves forward. It is as if language actually
moved with the movement of the tides. In "The Inhumanist," part 2 of
"The Love and the Hate," an old man, a caretaker of the ranch we have
seen devastated by insanity and patricide in part 1, meditates on the
world's sickness, a world weary of war yet drunk on it, too. The poem
opens with five lines of prose that set the scene and introduce the
caretaker ("Old men and gray hawks need solitude, / Here it is deep
and wide.") From there the poem divides into fifty-two sections (a
consciously imposed symmetry with the weeks of the year) comprised
mostly of the caretaker holding a one-sided conversation with God, or
with Western civilization's *idea* of God. The double pentameter forms
the bedrock of most of these passages:

> Peace creeps out of war, war out of peace; the stars
>   rise and they set; the clouds go north

And again they go south.—Why does God hunt in circles?
   Has he lost something? Is it possible—himself?
In the darkness between the stars did he lose himself
   and become godless, and seeks—himself?

The lines are enhanced by interior parallelism ("Peace creeps out of war, war out of peace / the stars / rise and they set; the clouds go north / And again they go south") and the Dickinsonian use of dashes (imposing a double caesura when they come) imparting heightened pauses, emphasis. The speculative does God seek himself? inevitably leads to the next question, in section 2:

"Does God exist?—No doubt of that," the old man says.
   "The cells of my old camel of a body,
Because they feel each other and are fitted together,—
   through nerves and blood feel each other,—all the little animals
Are the one man: there is not an atom in all the universes
But feels every other atom; gravitation, electromagnetism,
   light, heat, and the other
Flamings, the nerves in the night's black flesh, flow them
   together; the stars, the winds and the people: one energy,
One existence, one music, one organism, one life, one God:
   star-fire and rock-strength, the sea's cold flow
And man's dark soul."

The list making, the accumulation of evidence amid anapestic and spondaic substitution, the carefully spaced unstressed line endings, the boldly shortened third line bringing us to full rest after the minor Ionic of the first foot, and the last line's suspension and conclusion leading off the next section may be lost on the careless or indifferent reader who cannot recognize the flowering of a traditional prosody into one of highly original syntax. We must go back to Whitman, or move laterally to Eliot, to find appropriate parallels.

As Jeffers's verse line blossoms, it carries the poem's concerns along with it. Dramatic monologue is an effective but limited use of narrative. In "The Inhumanist," Jeffers faced an early decision—confine the poem to the caretaker's speculations, his talking *at* God, or open the poem up to other voices and their points of view. Wisely, he chose the latter course. Later sections introduce various characters in attitudes of displacement, in the process of escape or pursuit;

deluded, demonic, exiles all. In finding speech patterns to accommodate his apocalyptic vision, Jeffers accomplishes what the greatest poets of all historical moments manage to do—he creates anew the verse line and the perspectives of poetry; at the same time, he confirms the importance and power of *story* in verse, story told in measured, versatile patterns of speech.

❧ IV. Hart Crane

T. S. Eliot's prosody could be both an inspiration and an obstacle to younger writers. A poet, coming under its shadow, could write his heart out, as did Hart Crane. The tone and texture of Crane's verse are notably uneven; we are frequently jarred by the crudity of his rhythms, his inability to discover the appropriate metrical form for his feelings. Much that is rhythmically bad in Crane's poetry has its origin in Eliot's unassimilated influence: Crane never learned to master the delicate balance between "fixity and flux" that sets Eliot apart from the large numbers of his imitators. Crane did discover a metrical idiom congenial to his talent, but not before he endured considerable stress.

Here is Crane's version of Eliotic ennui and urban despair:

> Behind
> My father's cannery works I used to see
> Rail-squatters ranged in nomad raillery,
> The ancient men—wifeless or runaway
> Hobo-trekkers that forever search
> An empire wilderness of freight and rails.
> Each seemed a child, like me, on a loose perch,
> Holding to childhood like some termless play.
> John, Jake or Charley, hopping the low freight
> —Memphis to Tallahassee—riding the rods,
> Blind fists of nothing, humpty-dumpty clods.
>
> "The River"

And here is the passage Crane was, consciously or otherwise, using as his model:

> A rat crept softly through the vegetation
> Dragging its slimy belly on the bank

> While I was fishing in the dull canal
> On a winter evening round behind the gashouse
> Musing upon the king my brother's wreck
> And on the king my father's death before him.
>
> *The Waste Land*

Crane maintains a steady iambic beat; the lines are clinched with resonant rhymes. Crane's language intends to express something of *Waste Land*–ish hopelessness and horror, of the desolate landscapes behind the gashouse and the cannery works, but the couplets almost bounce with good-humored vitality. We wonder if Crane's intention might not be parody here: as if he were deliberately trying to show there is life and energy behind the gashouse yet!

"The Bridge" gives other evidence of Crane's struggle against the Eliotic mode. Occasionally Crane gets close to the spirit of Eliot's technical discoveries, but his discomfort with freer rhythms leads him into awkward rhyming and odd locutions:

> So memory that strikes a rhyme out of a box
> Or splits a random smell of flowers through glass—
> Is it the whip stripped from the lilac tree
> One day in spring my father took to me,
> Or is it the Sabbatical, unconscious smile
> My mother almost brought me once from church
> And once only, as I recall—?
>
> "Van Winkle"

The third line is beautifully sprung by the trochaic third foot; the next line, with its doggerel meter and rhyme, wrecks the passage.

Crane knew what he was up against, playing Eliot's gambits. In letters to Allen Tate and Gorham Munson, he assesses his situation:

> I have been facing [Eliot] for four years—and while I haven't discovered a weak spot yet in his armour, I flatter myself a little lately that I have discovered a safe tangent to strike which, if I can possibly explain the position,—goes through him toward a different goal. You see it is such a fearful temptation to imitate him that at times I have been almost distracted. . . . In his own realm Eliot presents us with an absolute impasse, yet oddly enough he can

be utilized to lead us to, intelligently point to, other positions and "pastures new." Having absorbed him enough we can trust our-selves as never before, in the air or on the sea.[8]

However, I take Eliot as a point of departure toward an almost complete reverse of direction. His pessimism is amply justified in his own case. But I would apply as much of his erudition and tech-niques as I can absorb and assemble toward a more positive, or (if [I] must put it so in a skeptical age) ecstatic goal. I should not think of this if a kind of rhythm and ecstasy were not (at odd moments, and rare!) a very real thing to me.[9]

Crane quarrels with Eliot's temperament; he could not *feel* what Eliot felt but suggests that Eliot's techniques might be used to express his own more exuberant, more violent nature. Unfortunately, Eliot's metrical techniques, his subtle and limpid rhythms, were hardly suited to Crane's emotional makeup and even less suited to Crane's subjects. And Crane did not have Eliot's ear for conversation, the gift for ren-dering contemporary speech. The overheard conversations and inter-polated monologues in "The Bridge" are fashionable pastiche effects and now sound dated. The distance between Crane and verse-as-speech was considerable; note the unevenness of tone and uncertain rhythm in this passage:

> "I ran a donkey engine down there on the Canal
> in Panama—got tired of that—
> then Yucatan selling kitchenware—beads—
> have you seen Popocatepetl—birdless mouth
> with ashes sifting down—?
>   and then the coast again."
>
>   "Cutty Sark"

Crane does not maintain convincing speech cadence; the last line shifts suddenly into formal hexameter, breaking cleanly at the sixth syllable:

> with ásh | es síft | ing dówn—? ||
> and thén | the cóast | a gáin . . .

The final lines of "Cape Hatteras" explode down the page in fine imagist disorder; it looks like authentic visual prosody:

> Yes, Walt,
> Afoot again, and onward without halt,—
> Not soon, nor suddenly,—No, never to let go
> My hand
>
> in yours,
>
> Walt Whitman—
>
> so—.

The fermatas for the eye function aurally, but the lines scan as regular iambics. We have the curious case of a perfectly conventional syllable-stress meter masquerading as the wildest free verse. Crane's prosodic posing conceals a pedestrian rhythm and an embarrassingly maudlin sentiment.

The example of Crane underlines a continuing assertion of this book: that prosody has neither decorative nor semantic functions apart from the work it does as a conveyor of feeling. As long as Crane used, or tried to use, Eliot's rhythms, he was expressing feelings inimical to his own temperament. He could not adapt Eliot's loosened metric to what he had to say. His view of the world did not include Eliot's particular horror and despair. Crane's gift, like Whitman's, was ceremonious and rhetorical; his true poetic métier was the apostrophe, the classic form of lyric celebration. His best works are set pieces: "Proem: To Brooklyn Bridge," the "Voyages," and the magnificent conclusion to "The River."

In these poems we observe a sureness of prosodic technique; the rhythms neither falter nor prove embarrassing to the concepts. Crane settles on a traditional pentameter that lends itself to the cadences of invocation. The form may seem limiting; it restricts Crane to only a few octaves of feeling. But Crane's development as a poet, up to the time he leapt from the SS *Orizaba,* was perfectly congruent with the meter in which he accomplished his best work. Actually, he had absorbed from Eliot and others more technique than his sensibility and experience could possibly transmute into first-rate poetry. Or, to put it differently, he possessed metrical knowledge that his emerging powers as a poet could not put to use.

Crane's true metrical idiom was the unashamedly rhetorical line of the Elizabethans. If Eliot at a crucial point in his career found the relaxed blank verse of Jacobean dramatists suited to his moods, so

Crane discovered in Marlowe and Jonson rhythms consonant with his
exuberance and awe. Hart Crane celebrates the Brooklyn Bridge:

> O harp and altar, of the fury fused,
> (How could mere toil align the choiring strings!)
> Terrific threshold of the prophet's pledge,
> Prayer of pariah, and the lover's cry,—
>
> Again the traffic lights that skim thy swift
> Unfractioned idiom, immaculate sigh of stars,
> Beading thy path—condense eternity:
> And we have seen night lifted in thine arms.
>
> Under thy shadow by the piers I waited;
> Only in darkness is thy shadow clear.
> The City's fiery parcels all undone,
> Already snow submerges an iron year . . .
>
> O Sleepless as the river under thee,
> Vaulting the sea, the prairies' dreaming sod,
> Unto us lowliest sometime sweep, descend
> And of the curveship lend a myth to God.
>
> > "Proem: To Brooklyn Bridge"

Earlier we suggested that the success of a prosody might be mea-
sured by what a poet can get away with. Crane's rhythm minimizes his
uncertain, almost haphazard syntactical progression. Perhaps, by
definition, the apostrophe requires no explicit grammar; the under-
stood subject of every sentence is the Bridge, and every verb links the
poet to his love. But without the binding meter, the omission of verbs
and uncertain use of reference would be destructively apparent.

Crane's "mighty line" also overrides his flawed diction and conceals
his queer metaphorical mixtures; carried along by the excited move-
ment, we are not disposed to wonder what "unfractioned idiom"
means, what precisely is intended by the image "Vaulting the sea," or
whether a neologism such as "curveship" is defensible. Similarly,
caught up in Crane's rhythms, we are apt to overlook obvious errors in
the choice of words; "wrapt" in the fifth line below (from "Voyages II")
has grotesque connotations:

> And yet this great wink of eternity,
> Of rimless floods, unfettered leewardings,

> Samite sheeted and processioned where
> Her undinal vast belly moonward bends,
> Laughing the wrapt inflections of our love.

Crane meant *rapt*—his misspelling may be a case of homonymic confusion. Again, the sounding rhythms conceal an ill-contrived syntax: every line is a shifted construction; images drift and float off, cut from their grammatical moorings. Crane's derangement of language is the result of his Dionysiac methods of composition, the raging of his personal demon, and his commitment to symbolist practice. But the flaring heat of Crane's rhythm, the absolute energy of his genius, fuses the second stanza of "Voyages II":

> Take this Sea, whose diapason knells
> On scrolls of silver snowy sentences,
> The sceptered terror of whose sessions rends
> As her demeanors motions well or ill,
> All but the pieties of lovers' hands.

In three lines we find compacted grammatical ambiguity (is "knells" verb or noun?), a wild synaesthesia ("diapason" is *seen* on scrolls of snowy sentences), and Shakespearean cliché ("sceptred terror").

These two stanzas appear to live on their prosody alone; the emotional force and solemn dignity of their rhythms seem, on first impact, independent of what the language is saying. But the metrical craft surprises with its sudden relevance; eternity's wink is felt as the spasmodic tremor of an inverted third foot:

> And yét | this gréat | wínk of | e tér | ni tý . . .

We note other prosodic details. With few exceptions the lines are heavily end-stopped. Crane unconsciously feels for rhymes: "bends" in the first stanza is echoed by "rends" and "hands" in the second stanza; "knells" is echoed by "ill." The last two stanzas modulate into new clarity; aided now by syntactical closeness, a grammatically precise handling of imperatives, the metrical pressure forces the poet into prophetic lucidity as he foretells his own death by water:

Mark how her turning shoulders wind the hours,
And hasten while her penniless rich palms
Pass superscription of bent foam and wave,—
Hasten, while they are true,—sleep, death, desire,
Close round one instant in one floating flower.

Binds us in time, O Seasons clear, and awe.
O minstrel galleons of Carib fire,
Bequeath us to no earthly shore until
Is answered in the vortex of our grave
The seal's wide spindrift gaze toward paradise.

Perhaps Crane's greatest sustained passage is the concluding section of "The River." Syntax and meter are exactly suited here to Crane's feelings of relentless movement and religious awe:

Down, down—born pioneers in time's despite,
Grimed tributaries to an ancient flow—
They win no frontier by their wayward plight,
But drift in stillness, as from Jordan's brow.

You will not hear it as the sea; even stone
Is not more hushed by gravity . . . But slow,
As loth to take more tribute—sliding prone
Like one whose eyes were buried long ago

The River, spreading, flows—and spends your dream.
What are you, lost within this tideless spell? . . .

O quarrying passion, undertowed sunlight!
The basalt surface drags a jungle grace
Ochreous and lynx-barred in lengthening might;
Patience! and you shall reach the biding place!

Over De Soto's bones the freighted floors
Throb past the City storied of three thrones.
Down two more turns the Mississippi pours
(Anon tall ironsides up from salt lagoons)

And flows within itself, heaps itself free.
All fades but one thin skyline 'round . . . Ahead

No embrace opens but the stinging sea;
The River lifts itself from its long bed,

Poised wholly on its dream, a mustard glow
Tortured with history, its one will—flow!
—The Passion spreads in wide tongues, choked and slow,
Meeting the Gulf, hosannas silently below.

If, as Eliot points out, Marlowe "commenced the dissociative process which drew [blank verse] farther and farther away from the rhythms of rhymed verse,"[10] it was Crane who worked blank verse back into the rhythms of rhymed verse, and then attempted to revive rhymed verse as a major form. In these "heroic quatrains" from "The River" Crane discovers the prosodic form most congenial to his genius. His failures in freer rhythms and unrhymed verse point to the unformed, highly uneven quality of his genius—he had nowhere attained full powers before his death—and to a striking conflict of Zeitgeist and sensibility.

IX

Auden and After

Auden's work set new fashions in prosody. Nearly half the poems in his first book, *Poems* (1930), are in regular stanzaic forms. Hopkins, whose work was published too late to have had any significant effect on Pound and Eliot, is prosodically very much in evidence. It is largely through Auden and Dylan Thomas that Hopkins's techniques became common currency during the 1930s and 1940s. Auden also made good use of some of Wilfred Owen's experiments in off-rhyme and assonance. Other of Auden's interests, especially in Anglo-Saxon poetry, have borne important fruit. Some critics of the 1950s even saw Auden's efforts as a much needed correction of course after the experiments of Pound and Eliot. The discerning of trends is especially dangerous, and it is not essentially true that with Auden, for example, twentieth-century poetry suddenly turned back to traditional metric. Auden lived well into the era in which prosodic style veered sharply away from unmetered and loosely metered verse. This trend held for the poets of the late 1940s and 1950s who practiced an almost religious devotion to intricate stanzas and close formal arrangements. In two representative first volumes, W. S. Merwin's *A Mask for Janus* (1952) and Anthony Hecht's *A Summoning of Stones* (1954), we find several sonnets, a rare double sonnet, a couple of sestinas, a half-rondel, and one poem of seven stanzas built on two rhymes and a refrain.

Then a reaction to the reaction unquestionably set in. We find in Theodore Roethke's *Words for the Wind* (1958) a wealth of poems written in traditional meters, but also the magnificent "Elegy for Jane," composed in unmetered, Whitmanesque lines of varied length. Robert Lowell's first major collection, *Lord Weary's Castle* (1946), written entirely in rhymed syllable-stress meters, was followed by *Life Studies* (1959), whose verse is sharply stressed but rarely metrical. Certainly most of the poetry of the 1960s and 1970s turned away from the technical influence of Auden. In this period a generation of American writers, many of them students or teachers, or both, from creative-writing programs, did not so much reject traditional forms; rather they moved through their apprenticeship estranged from the knowledge and hands-on practice of such forms. A proliferation of nonmetrical prosodies both energized and confused assessments of poetry's landscape. Clearly, we had moved into a period of relaxed meters and loose rhythms, of measures so relaxed and loose that distinctions between poetry and prose became blurry. The neosurrealist poems of Robert Bly and James Wright and followers and the fierce confessional poems of Sylvia Plath come close to identifying a new period style. But no dominating figure, such as Pound or Auden, exerted a major influence, urging prosodic discoveries on a new generation of poets. By the mid-1980s (a decade that already appears to be more a span of reaction and redirection than a flowering of the type of poetry in the years that immediately preceded it) a new generation of poets revived interest in metrical prosody and narrative techniques, recognizing, in the process, Auden's seminal contributions and place in poetry.

❧ 1. W. H. Auden

Auden would trust implicitly a critic who could say "yes" to this query:

> "Do you like, and by like I really mean like, not approve of on principle:
> Complicated verse forms of great technical difficulty, such as Englyns, Drott-Kvaetts, Sestinas, even if their content is trivial?"[1]

Auden may be indulging in some good-natured critic-baiting. Only students of Old Norse are apt to have developed an affection for *drott-kvaett* ("court measure"), the intricate stanza of Skaldic poetry. But the query is not facetious. The most ingenious explicator of texts will neglect to name the meter and stanza of a poem from which he has extracted fourteen levels of meaning. To most critics prosody is simply not "meaning"; metrics and versification are deemed contemptible studies. Poets are afflicted with similar ignorance. Auden, in his

"Daydream College for Bards," requires the study of Greek, Hebrew, rhetoric, comparative philology, and prosody.

Auden's work reflects his fascination with prosodic techniques. He used the sestina, the villanelle, the canzon; he invented or adapted many complicated stanzas; he is a master of assonance, rhyme, para-rhyme, and refrain. He wrote songs and sonnets with the fluency of an Elizabethan; he revived the ballad. To many this makes him a poet's poet, or worse, a prosodist's poet! Admittedly, Auden's poetry presents a prosodist's feast, not unlike that offered a musical analyst by the ingenuity and wealth of Bach's fugues and canons.

Our first example is the title poem from *Look, Stranger* (1936), a fine illustration of Auden's lyric manner:

> Look, stranger at this island now
> The leaping light for your delight discovers,
> Stand stable here
> And silent be,
> That through the channels of the ear
> May wander like a river
> The swaying sound of the sea.
>
> Here at the small field's ending pause
> Where the chalk wall falls to the foam, and its tall ledges
> Oppose the pluck
> And knock of the tide,
> And the shingle scrambles after the suck-
> ing surf, and the gull lodges
> A moment on its sheer side.
>
> Far off like floating seeds the ships
> Diverge on urgent voluntary errands;
> And the full view
> Indeed may enter
> And move in memory as now these clouds do,
> That pass the harbour mirror
> And all the summer through the water saunter.

The wealth of prosodic detail, including interior rhymes and a variety of metrical feet, does not impede its iambic music. The first line, with its initial major Ionic, is balanced by the next line, with its quick iambs and inner rhyme. The rhyming deserves special notice. The mixture of conventional rhymes and consonantal half-rhyme (sometimes called pararhyme) derives from Wilfred Owen. The jamming together of strong stresses, the programmatic alliteration, and the mannerism of splitting a rhyme word between two lines are familiar features of Hopkins's idiom.

In *Another Time* (1940) Auden moves away from his early masters and writes a number of his most characteristic pieces. A new style is apparent; we find none of the articleless mannerism and Old English primitivism of

> Save him from hostile capture,
> From sudden tiger's spring at corner;
> Protect his house
> His anxious house where days are counted
> From thunderbolt protect . . .
>
>   II

but a more personal, more unadorned speech. Auden emigrated to America in 1939; his new style, with its eschewal of the deliberately literary and its sloughing off of obvious influences, has the appearance of a symbolic gesture to his adopted country. The prosody shows diminished contrivance and a greater operating efficiency. The first three lines of *Musée des Beaux Arts* are decasyllabic, but only roughly iambic:

> A bóut | súf fer | ing théy | were né | ver wróng,
> The Óld | Más ters: | how wéll | they ún | der stóod
> Its hú | man po sí | tion; | how it tákes pláce.

The unsettling trochee in the second foot of the first two lines and the anomalous third line pull the rhythm away from blank verse. Succeeding lines amble into prose:

> While someone else is eating or opening a window or just
>   walking dully along;
> How, when the aged are reverently, passionately waiting
> For the miraculous birth, there always must be
> Children who did not specially want it to happen, skating.

Rhyme serves to punctuate, to either separate or link sections of the poem. The final lines fall in approximate dactyls, suggesting, perhaps, Icarus's spiraling descent. A ship, watching

> Some thing a | maz ing, a | boy fal ling | out of the | sky,
> Had | some where to | get to and | sailed calm ly | on.

The metric of *The Unknown Citizen* urges along the poem's ironic implication. Bland officialese, the language of the Social Worker's Report, is undercut by mincing anapests; the effect is like a sneer:

> He was found by the Bureau of Statistics to be . . .
>
> And all the reports on his conduct agree . . .
>
> Except for the War till the day he retired
> He worked in a factory and never got fired,
> But satisfied his employers, Fudge Motors, Inc.

Auden changes the line when the Public Opinion Researchers give their report:

> When there was peace, he was for peace; when there was
>   war, he went.
> He was married and added five children to the population,
> Which our Eugenist says was the right number for a
>   parent of his generation,
> And our teachers report that he never interfered with
>   their education.

Auden crams the line with more syllables than the meter can comfortably contain. The sequence of rhyme suggests calypso or Ogden Nash; the lines hurry, trying fruitlessly to avoid metrical disaster, toward the deliberately clumsy triple rhymes. The final couplet swings into double iambics: the tripping meter of Gilbert's patter songs ("If you're anxious for to shine, in the high aesthetic line"):

> Was he free? Was he happy? The question is absurd:
> Had anything been wrong, we should certainly have heard.

How well the silly lilt of the meter demolishes the glib certainty and smug authority of the final statement!

Another Time contains the two superb elegies on Yeats and Freud. (We analyze "In Memory of Sigmund Freud" in chapter 2.) "In Memory of W. B. Yeats" falls into three contrasted sections: the first in Eliotic unmetered verse; the second in regular blank verse; the third (the section to which the poem owes its longevity among readers), a dirge in heavily accented trochaic stanzas. Syntactical repetition, the use of refrain, the elaboration of metaphor by grammatical symmetry direct the rhythm of the first section; trochaic tetrameters of the last section move with the measured tread of a *marcia funebre* or the Celtic coronach:

> Earth, receive an honoured guest;
> William Yeats is laid to rest:
> Let the Irish vessel lie
> Emptied of its poetry.

Auden's *Collected Poetry* (1976) merits the accolade Eliot bestowed on Pound's *Selected Poems:* "This book would be, were it nothing else, a textbook of modern versification." Auden's range of stanzaic forms is tremendous; we are tempted to arrange and classify, to note ingenuities and acclaim the sheer virtuosity of technique. Within the stanzas the meters may be free or strict; they may follow traditional syllable-stress patterns; they may move according to syllabic or strong-stress principles. Auden gives the lie to the notion that the more intricate forms may only be used for trivial themes. One of Auden's gifts to his own generation is that a difficult metric and a complex stanza need not signify merely Petrarchan elaboration; the modern villanelle may be a poem of serious wit, like Auden's "Time Will Say Nothing but I Told You So," a powerful and terrifying incantation, like Dylan Thomas's "Do Not Go Gentle into That Good Night," or a somber lament on the expense of spirit, like William Empson's "Missing Dates."

Auden goes further than either Pound or Eliot toward solving the problems of the English sestina. An early example of this difficult Provençal form, "Hearing of Harvests Rotting in the Valleys," follows the traditional paradigm; Auden even meets the ancient requirement that each end word be a noun of two syllables:[2]

Hearing of harvests rotting in the valleys,
Seeing at end of street the barren mountains,
Round corners coming suddenly on water,
Knowing them shipwrecked who were launched for islands,
We honour founders of these starving cities,
Whose honour is the image of our sorrow.

The trochaic form of the end word gives flexibility to the prevailing iambic meter; the line is blank verse but (rare for English) hendecasyllabic, a common Latin form and the traditional line of Italian poetry. A later sequence of four sestinas, "Kairos and Logos," does not use the traditional order of end words—where the last word of the sixth line is picked up by the first line of the succeeding stanza; rather, Auden devises an original sequence, 123456, 315264, 536142, and so on. This arrangement mutes the insistence of the end words and allows greater syntactical freedom. In another sestina, from "The Sea and the Mirror," Auden experiments with still a different order of end words.[3] Auden chooses these end words with great care. He generally uses either neutral and tractable abstractions, death, love, time, world; or simple concrete nouns, child, home, garden, forest. He thus avoids the clatter and bang of Pound's "Altaforte" with its "crimson," "clash," and "opposing"; and the straitjacketed somnolence of Eliot's modified sestina in "The Dry Salvages" with its "wailing" and "bailing" and "motionless" and "erosionless."

We turn to Auden's longer poems. No single prosodic mode carries "The Sea and the Mirror" and "For the Time Being"; each is a suite of lyrics with interspersed free verse and prose, "a medley composed of meters of all kinds."[4]

These poems are cast in dramatic form, and the prosodic modes adjust themselves to both characters and chorus. The narrator in "For the Time Being" speaks matter-of-fact unmetered verse:

If, on account of the political situation,
There are quite a number of homes without roofs, and men
Lying about in the countryside neither drunk nor asleep,
If all sailings have been cancelled till further notice,
If it's unwise now to say much in letters, and if,
Under the subnormal temperatures prevailing,
The two sexes are at present the weak and the strong,
That is not at all unusual for this time of year.

The rhythm is syntactical; Auden delays the resolution of the conditional clause until the eighth line and builds tension through the persistently repeated *if.* The Chorus follows with a tail-chasing stanza of five lines:

> Alone, alone, about a dreadful wood
> Of conscious evil runs a lost mankind,
> Dreading to find its Father lest it find
> The Goodness it has dreaded is not good:
> Alone, alone, about a dreadful wood.

(This is the stanza of Baudelaire's "Lesbos.") The great variety of stanzaic forms in "For the Time Being" recalls Romantic closet drama with its elaborate lyrical interludes and continued suggestion of musical setting. Of course, Auden has music in mind; "For the Time Being" is subtitled "A Christmas Oratorio."

Auden's volumes beginning with *Nones* (1951) contain an abundance of merely occasional pieces. We have the hilarious "Under Which Lyre," the best spoof of academia yet written. We must all keep well the Hermetic Decalogue:

> Thou shalt not do as the dean pleases,
> Thou shalt not write thy doctor's thesis
>   On education,
> Thou shalt not worship projects nor
> Shalt thou or thine bow down before
>   Administration.
>
> Thou shalt not answer questionnaires
> Or quizzes upon World Affairs,
>   Nor with compliance
> Take any test. Thou shalt not sit
> With statisticians nor commit
>   A social science.

These lines place Auden among the great comic rhymers, Byron, Gilbert, and Ogden Nash—to whom they are obviously indebted. The stanza is borrowed from Chaucer's *Sir Thopas,* itself a burlesque of the tail-rime stanza of fourteenth-century metrical romance.

Throughout the later poetry we find, prosodically, a general loosening of the line; the rhythms tend to run slack—effortlessly, to be sure—but their very relaxation has become a mannerism. Two pieces in prose, "Vespers" *(The Shield of Achilles)* and "Dichtung and Wahrheit" *(Homage to Clio)*, are symptomatic of Auden's desire to break free of prosodic regulation and abandon obvious device. Like Eliot in the *Quartets,* he wants to sublimate technical skill and release the pure concept, the naked emotion.

But Auden does his best work under the supervision of stanzaic form and precise metrical cadence. The title poem from *The Shield of Achilles* is one of his most powerful performances: a clear and crushing prophecy of life in the cheerless utopian world. Instead of scenes of Arcadian joy, Thetis sees in the handicraft of Hephaestos

> A million eyes, a million boots in line,
> Without expression, waiting for a sign.

Thetis's Arcadian expectations are set in three-stress lines, eight lines to the stanza:

> She looked over his shoulder
>   For athletes at their games,
> Men and women in a dance
>   Moving their sweet limbs
> Quick, quick, to music,
>   But there on the shining shield
> His hands had set no dancing-floor
> But a weed-choked field.

The utopian reality follows in iambic pentameter, arranged in the rime-royal stanza:

> A ragged urchin, aimless and alone,
>   Loitered about that vacancy; a bird
> Flew up to safety from his well-aimed stone:
>   That girls are raped, that two boys knife a third,
>   Were axioms to him, who'd never heard
> Of any world where promises were kept
> Or one could weep because another wept.

The contrast between Arcadian grace and utopian misery is admirably served by the alternation of the eight- and seven-line stanzas. Consonant with the poem's theme and subject, the rhythms move with hard precision in the scenes of utopian desolation and with greater fluidity and variety in the scenes of Arcadian abundance and freedom. Three of the four eight-line stanzas conclude with the same pattern of stress,

> And a sky like lead . . .

> But a weed-choked field . . .

> Who would not live long . . .

forming a punctuating rhythm constant to each section and, finally, to the entire poem.

At his death in 1973, Auden left a body of work second to none in influence and technical accomplishment. Though his poems have inspired two generations of writers of free verse, he may also deserve considerable credit for sparking the current revival of form in poetry. Few poets, of any time, were ever so agile.

ᨠ *II. Louis MacNeice and Patrick Kavanagh*

The reputation of the three leading members of the "Auden Group," Stephen Spender, C. Day-Lewis, and Louis MacNeice, faded in the postwar period. Reasons are not hard to find. The hegemony of the New Criticism, with its rigid ontological bureaucracy, was not sympathetic to any poetry fiercely committed to "subject"; and the poetry of the 1930s was crying for political action. Guilt-stricken liberals are apt to be embarrassed by poems like Spender's, "Oh Young Men Oh Young Comrades," and feel such effusions belong more to the history of lost causes than to poetry.

The best work, from the prosodist's point of view, that came from the group has little to do with Popular Front communism or the defense of the Spanish Republic. Which is to say that whatever survives as good poetry has lasted because the poet exercised due technical care and wrote with appropriate sensibility and concern for language. MacNeice possessed a beautiful ear, was capable of innovation, and is today seriously overlooked. We give the two final stanzas of the prosodic tour-de-force, "The Sunlight on the Garden":

> The sky was good for flying
> Defying the church bells
> And every evil iron
> Siren and what it tells:
> The earth compels,
> We are dying Egypt, dying
>
> And not expecting pardon,
> Hardened in heart anew,
> But glad to have sat under
> Thunder and rain with you,
> And grateful too
> For sunlight on the garden.

The head rhymes, *flying-defying, iron-siren,* and so on, produce a peculiarly sweet and astringent melody.

A fine classical scholar, MacNeice experimented with pseudoquantitative meters. His version of *Solvitur Acris Hiems* (Horace, ode 1, 4) approaches and departs from Horace's metrical scheme, illustrating the tantalizing difficulties in adapting quantitative meter to the incorrigible stresses of English:

> Win ter to | Spring: ∧ the | west wind | melts the | frozen
>   rancour,
>   The wind | lass drags | to sea | the thir | sty hull;
> Byre is no | lon ger | wel come to | beast or | fire to |
>   plough man
>   The field | re moves | the frost | cap from | his skull.

MacNeice attempts to preserve the general rhythmic outline of the Latin: a falling line (dactylo-trochaic) followed by the rising iambic. There is noticeable conflict between stress and quantity; if we scan by stresses alone, MacNeice's first line rises in a syllable-stress hexameter:

> Win ter | to Spring: | the west | wind melts | the fro | zen
>   ran | cour.

But in some details MacNeice comes surprisingly close to the Latin. The contrast between the longer and shorter half of the first and third lines, the preservation of the spondee in the third foot of the first line and the second foot of the third line, the pleasing alternation of falling and rising rhythm—all are happy inspirations from Horace's original.

MacNeice's sapphics, in the poem "June Thunder," make no pretence at exact adherence to the paradigm. Three lines set in falling rhythm are followed by the shorter fourth line:

> Blackness at half-past eight, the night's precursor,
> Clouds like falling masonry and lightning's lavish
> Annunciation, the sword of the mad archangel
> Flashed from the scabbard.
>
> If only now you would come and dare the crystal
> Rampart of rain and the bottomless moat of thunder,
> If only now you would come I should be happy
> Now if now only.

One line corresponds to the lesser sapphic:

Clouds like | falling | masonry_and | lightning's | lavish . . .

And the fourth lines are acceptable Adonics:

Flashed from the | scab ard . . .

Now if now | only . . .

MacNeice infuses his sapphics with those qualities of yearning and wonder that characterize the great examples of the form.

Patrick Kavanagh's poetry provides the sharpest Irish voice of dissent in the twentieth century. His primary foes were not political; rather, they came from the second wave of those promoting the Irish Literary Movement, and from those supporting the Roman Catholic Church. Born in Inniskeen, County Monaghan, Kavanagh knew firsthand the harsh poverty and hopelessness of rural life. To the end, he attacked other writers who claimed to spring from that life yet romanticized it in art. Earning a marginal living as a newspaper columnist and movie critic, Kavanagh started his own magazine, *Kavanagh's Weekly,* endured serious illness that dogged him through more than a decade at the end of his life, yet managed to produce a body of work that is second, perhaps, in Ireland only to Yeats in its versatile execution and breadth of vision. Unlike many an embittered poet, Kavanagh possessed a remarkable facility for comedy (see his *Adventures in the Bohemian Jungle*). But he was equally adept in serious narratives, songs, and poems for diverse voices. His early sonnet, "Peasant," expresses his constant identification with the struggling people and circumstances of his beginnings:

> I am the representative of those
> Clay-faced sucklers of spade-handles,
> Bleak peasants for whom Apollo blows
> Aesthetic winds in nine-day laboured scandals.

The poem "My People" is a dialogue, after the fashion of Yeats, between a stranger and a poet concerning differing perceptions of the essential character of such rural people:

Stranger:
> What kind your people are
> I would wish to know:
> Great shouldered men like rolling stock,
> Great in despair,
> Simple in prayer,
> And their hard hands tear
> The soil on the rock
> Where the plough cannot go?

Poet:
> 'Tis not so.
> Faint-hearted folk my people are,
> To Poverty's house they have never invited
> The giant Pride,
> But await the world where wrongs are righted.
> They till their fields and scrape among the stones
> Because they cannot be schoolmasters—
> They work because judge Want condemns the drones.

> Dear stranger, duty is a joke
> Among my peasant folk.

The nervous, heavy accenting of the stranger's constricted lines effectively fit the proper expression to the character. The poet apes the stranger's uneasiness in the inversion of line 2 ("Faint-hearted folk my people are"), and again in the closing couplet; otherwise, the poet's lines are longer, more relaxed. This is appropriate in that the two meet on the poet's turf, discussing things the poet knows best.

"The Great Hunger," a long narrative, chronicles the rural life of one Patrick Maguire, a man who, at his death, "will hardly remember that life happened to him," a man who grudgingly takes his place in the universal procession that "passed down a mesmerized street." In matriarchal Ireland, Maguire tends the fields and livestock according to the instructions of his domineering mother. As a young man he dreams of marriage and money yet is forever checked by church and parent in his desire to realize his sexual, romantic, and worldly ambitions. Like his spinster sister he will live and die, a stunted possibility, in the same place.

> That was how his life happened.
> No mad hooves galloping in the sky,
> But the weak, washy way of true tragedy—
> A sick horse nosing around the meadow for a clean place to die.

The poem's fourteen sections run the gamut of prosodic organization. Some sections move in long lines bordering prose; others are clipped in length and syntax, while still others return to tight metrics and rhyme. As a whole, the poem is a model of pacing and manipulation of a single, obsessive theme.

A more haunting, tender aspect of Kavanagh's poetry can be found in the classic lyric "Raglan Road." Written to the tune "The Dawning of the Day," the poem laments lost love and the catalyst-singer's shame at his lack of foresight, his inability to alter the encounter's outcome:

> On Raglan Road of an autumn day I met her first and knew
> That her dark hair would weave a snare that I might one day rue;
> I saw the danger, yet I walked along the enchanted way,

And I sáid, let gríef be a fállen léaf at the dáwning óf the dáy.

The echoing couplets and regular iambic movement through the seven-stress lines evoke to perfection the speaker's sorrowful contemplation of lost love. Far removed from the ironic criticism of the ballads and dialogue poems, "Raglan Road" is song itself, a simple, memorable manifestation of the unity of music and poetry:

> On a quiet street where old ghosts meet I see her walking now
> Away from me so hurriedly my reason must allow
> That I had wooed not as I should a creature made of clay—
> When the angel woos the clay he'd lose his wings at the dawn
> of day.

ᐳ III. *Dylan Thomas*

Dylan Thomas had no personal intimacy with Auden's Oxford Movement, but he shared its ancestry. Thomas read Hopkins and Wilfred Owen; he experimented with a great variety of prosodic shapes and forms and devised some of the most intricate stanzas to be found in poetry. The effect of Auden was chiefly technical; Thomas's poetry, from the very first, was unpolitical and unpreachy: aggressively unconcerned with "ideas" and revolutionary only in the sense that it was temperamentally in agreement with all revolution.

The nature of Thomas's poetry demanded severe prosodic regulation. A typical Thomas poem does not move by careful grammatical articulation but is carried headlong by highly formal rhythmic patterns. Rhythm in a Thomas poem is a sounding rhythm—rarely the hard-to-hear music of inspired syntax. We are hardly aware that the opening stanza of "Poem in October" proceeds along a series of shifted constructions; the images are separated by a very acute sense of metrical timing. Typography, syllable count, and a texture of interior rhymes and alliteration allay the feeling of incompleteness occasioned by the lack of exact grammatical relationships.

We see the extreme of Thomas's poetic method in the ten sonnets from *Twenty-Five Poems* (1936). We attempt no exegesis of these poems; none is probably possible. But a comparison between Sonnet 4 and George Herbert's "Prayer" offers a clue to the kind of poetic structure Thomas had in mind and how well he succeeds in handling associative progression:

PRAYER

Prayer the Churches banquet, Angels age,
  Gods breath in man returning to his birth,
The soul in paraphrase, heart in pilgrimage,
  The Christian plummet sounding heav'n and earth;

Engine against th'Almightie, sinners towre,
  Reversed thunder, Christ-side-piercing spear,
The six-daies world transposing in an houre,
  A kinde of tune, which all things heare and fear;

Softnesse, and peace, and joy, and love, and blisse,
  Exalted Manna, gladnesse of the best,
  Heaven in ordinarie, man well drest,
The milkie way, the bird of Paradise,

  Church-bells beyond the starres heard, the souls bloud,
  The land of spices; something understood.

SONNET 4

What is the metre of the dictionary?
The size of genesis? The short spark's gender?
Shade without shape? The shape of Pharaoh's echo?
(My shape of age nagging the wounded whisper).
Which sixth of wind blew out the burning gentry?
(Questions are hunchbacks to the poker marrow).
What of a bamboo man among your acres?
Corset the boneyards for a crooked lad?
Button your bodice on a hump of splinters,
My camel's eyes will needle through the shroud.
Love's reflection of the mushroom features,
Stills snapped by night in the bread-sided field,
Once close-up smiling in the wall of pictures,
Arc-lamped thrown back upon the cutting flood.

Herbert's poem accumulates power with each successive brilliant
phrase; image and metaphor are spaced by rhythmic pauses, and syn-
tactical completeness is suspended until the end of the poem. The
grammatical structure is appositive; the body of the poem follows the
suppressed copula *is*. However, the images and abstractions do not
ride free; even the striking and often-quoted "Church-bells beyond

the starres" makes its full effect only in context. Herbert provides a severe logic of context, a syntax of clearly defined categories: the terms of each appositive phrase belong to theology, music, biblical reference, and the well-understood language of religious discourse.

We discover no clear linkages among Thomas's gnomic questions. According to one exegete, the child Dylan is asking his mother "embarrassing questions about sex and obstetrics."[5] Maybe; but more likely Thomas was freely associating on

> Goe, and catche a falling starre,
>   Get with child a mandrake roote,
> Tell me, where all past yeares are,
>   Or who cleft the Divels foot

without bothering to drop the referential thread and bind up the seeming irrelevancies into a meaningful bundle. The sonnet form, by itself, does not supply sufficient connective power to compensate for Thomas's abjuration of logical syntax. Nor is iambic verse strongly rhythmical enough to space out Thomas's images; there are no significant pauses loaded with surging emotional content.

To represent Thomas by one of his earlier, image-clotted sonnets does him an injury. His best work lies in those spacious stanzas where the long-breathed rhythms can rise and fall, move up to a climax, and dwindle to silence. The stanza of "Poem in October" is a beautiful prosodic mechanism:

> It was my thirtieth year to heaven
> Woke to my hearing from harbour and neighbour wood
>   And the mussel pooled and the heron
>   Priested shore
>   The morning beckon
> With water praying and call of seagull and rook
> And the knock of sailing boats on the net webbed wall
>   Myself to set foot
>   That second
> In the sleeping town and set forth.

Thomas counts syllables (in analogous lines of succeeding stanzas), but unlike Marianne Moore, whose anecdotal rhythm has close affinities with prose, he weights each line with strong stresses. His model here is Hopkins's "The Wreck of the Deutschland"; like Hopkins he often crowds his stresses together:

> And the knock of sailing boats on the *net webbed wall* . . .

> Beyond the border and under the *lark full cloud* . . .

> And the *twice told fields* of infancy.

Although Thomas truculently denied any knowledge of Welsh and its highly formal metrical systems,[6] his lines chime with internal consonantal correspondence, or *cynghanedd,* a prescribed feature of Welsh versification:

> Woke to my hearing from harbour and neighbour wood . . .

The correspondence in this line forms *cynghanedd croes:* a pattern of alliterated syllables in symmetrical arrangement *(w . . . h:h . . . w).*[7] *Fern Hill* abounds in such permutations:

> Above the lilting house and happy as the grass was green . . .

> And once below a time I lordly had the trees and leaves . . .

> And green and golden I was huntsman and herdsman . . .

> And honoured among foxes and pheasants by the gay house . . .

Another feature of Welsh versification is the rich use of internal rhyme and assonance. Thomas often rhymes from the middle of one line to the middle of the next, or from middle to end. The rhyming here is approximate:

> Now as I was young and *easy* under the apple boughs
> About the lilting house and *happy* as the grass was green,
> The night above the dingle *starry* . . .

"The Conversation of Prayers" systematically rhymes end and middles in a crisscross pattern:[8]

> The conversation of *prayers* about to be *said*
> By the child going to *bed* and the man on the *stairs*
> Who climbs to his dying *love* in her high *room,*
> The one not caring to *whom* in his sleep he will *move*
> And the other full of *tears* that she will be *dead.*

The rhyme scheme actually mirrors the theme of the poem, which expounds the old Protestant idea of "reversibility of grace."[9] The prayers of the child and the man cross in night; the child, praying for quiet rest,

> Shall drown in a grief as deep as his made grave.

The man, "Who climbs to his dying love in her high room,"

> Tonight shall find no dying but alive and warm

> In the fire of his care his love in the high room.

Through the mysterious efficacy of prayer, the boy assumes the burden of the man's grief; through prayer their situations suffer a spiritual reversal. As the poem develops, certain lines and half-lines are repeated, but their positions are shifted:

> By the child going to bed and the man on the stairs . . .

> From the man on the stairs and the child by his bed . . .

This may be an example of "imitative form," but we can scarcely deny its effectiveness.

Similarly, in one of Thomas's greatest poems, "Do Not Go Gentle into That Good Night," the formal demands of the villanelle enhance the meaning. Thomas makes the most of his form: we can think of no other villanelle in the language that seems so little contrived. The refrain lines of most villanelles bear scant relationship to the poetic argument; their function is usually decorative. But Thomas manages his syntax cannily; the repetition of the refrain completes the grammatical sense of each tercet:

Do not go gentle into that good night,
Old age should burn and rave at close of day;
Rage, rage against the dying of the light.

Though wise men at their end know dark is right,
Because their words had forked no lightning they
Do not go gentle into that good night.

Good men, the last wave by, crying how bright
Their frail deeds might have danced in a green bay,
Rage, rage against the dying of the light.

The lines are, without exception, decasyllabic; Thomas varies the rhythm with contiguous heavy stressing, an occasional trochee, or an Ionic:

Ráge, ráge | agáinst | the dý | ing óf | the líght . . .

Though wíse | men at | their énd | know dárk | is ríght . . .

And yóu, | my fá | ther, thére | on the sád | height.

The meter of one splendid line makes a crucial semantic choice for the reader:

Curse, bléss, | me nów | with yóur | fierce teárs, | I práy.

If we resist the temptation to read the first and fourth feet as emphatic accentual spondees, we understand that blessing outweighs the cursing and the ferocity.

Toward the end of his life, especially in the poems of *In Country Sleep,* Thomas's prosody sometimes hardens into a set of predictable mannerisms. At times the rhythms become more emphatic but less subtle and various:

Flash, and the plumes crack,
And a black cap of jack-
Daws Sir John's just hill dons, and again the gulled birds hare
To the hawk on fire, the halter height, over Towy's fins,
In a whack of wind.

> "Over Sir John's Hill"

We hear the violence of Hopkins's strong-stressing and dislocated grammar; the jar of cross-currents and the crunch of rhymes and consonants may generate more noise than feeling.

These last poems often appear to have been written for declamation; their metrical idiom shaped by Thomas's oracular, incantatory style of reading aloud. His magnificently sonorous voice imposed similar rhythms on anything he read aloud. As a result, the last poems are static, rich in bombast and ecstatic rant, impressive as runes, charms, or chants. In his generation, Thomas's ear is unsurpassed, his poetry utterly original.

૨ IV. *Theodore Roethke*

A high order of technical accomplishment distinguishes the poetry of two American poets who emerged in the early 1940s: Theodore Roethke and Robert Lowell. Roethke enjoyed a steadily growing postwar reputation; Lowell belonged to the generation of American poets that includes John Berryman, Randall Jarrell, Elizabeth Bishop, J. V. Cunningham, Howard Nemerov, and Richard Wilbur.

The earlier poems of Roethke show the sustaining influence of Auden. This stinging light verse, from *Open House* (1941), with its deceptively easy doggerel meter, has the unmistakable Auden touch:

ACADEMIC

The stethoscope tells what everyone fears:
You're likely to go on living for years,
With a nurse-maid waddle and a shop-girl simper,
And the style of your prose growing limper and limper.

We note the wobbly anapests (mixed with an occasional iamb) and zany unstressed rhyming of Auden:

The poet reciting to Lady Diana
While the footmen whisper "Have a banana,"
The judge enforcing the obsolete law,
The banker making the loan for the war,

The expert designing the long-range gun
To exterminate everyone under the sun,
Would like to get out but could only mutter;—
"What can I do? It's my bread and butter."

Look, Stranger!

The steady trimeter of Roethke's "Night Journey" also suggests Auden's handling of traditional meter; if anything, these lines have a purity of language and firmness of rhythm Auden rarely achieves:

> Beyond the mountain pass
> Mist deepens on the pane;
> We rush into a rain
> That rattles double glass.
> Wheels shake the roadbed stone,
> The pistons jerk and shove,
> I stay up half the night
> To see the land I love.

In a brief prose excursion, "Some Remarks on Rhythm,"[10] Roethke allows us a theoretical glimpse into his prosodic methods. The essay begins with the modest question, "What do I like?" and continues with carefully detailed prosodic analyses of nursery rhymes, his own poems, and poems by Blake, Janet Lewis, D. H. Lawrence, and others. The analyses are extraordinarily fine, as we might expect from a poet with Roethke's rhythmic sensitivity. His first example, from Mother Goose, is a mysterious precursor of *symboliste* significances:

> Hinx, minx, the old witch winks.
> The fat begins to fry,
> There's nobody home but Jumping Joan,
> And Father and Mother, and I.

Roethke remarks:

> Now what makes that catchy . . . For one thing, the rhythm, Five stresses out of a possible six in the first line. Though maybe "old" doesn't take quite as strong a stress as the others. . . . Notice the second, "The fat begins to fry," is absolutely regular metrically. It's all iambs, a thing that often occurs when previous lines are sprung or heavily counterpointed. The author doesn't want to get too far from his base, from his ground beat. The third line varies again with an anapest and variations in the "O" and "U" sound.[11]

From *Hinx, Minx* and other nursery rhymes, Roethke generalizes "that while our genius in the language may be essentially iambic, particularly in the formal lyric, much of memorable or passionate speech is strongly stressed, irregular, even sprung, if you will."[12] Of course Roethke's nursery rhyme examples, written when English verse was moving from strong-stress to syllable-stress meters, tend to confirm his generalization.

It is only a short hop from Roethke's speculations to his practice—a hop backward, since it is obvious his theories are based on what he has done in his own work. The love poem "Words for the Wind" opens with hinx, minx rhythms:

> Love, love, a lily's my care,
> She's sweeter than a tree.
> Loving, I use the air
> Most lovingly: I breathe;
> Mad in the wind I wear
> Myself as I should be,
> All's even with the odd,
> My brother the vine is glad.

The second line, regularly iambic, occurs after a heavily stressed opening line. Other lines vary with trochaic and anapestic substitutions. Later in the poem, Roethke moves further from his iambic base:

> The sun declares the earth;
> The stones leap in the stream;
> On a wide plain, beyond
> The far stretch of a dream,
> A field breaks like the sea;
> The wind's white with her name,
> And I walk with the wind.

The measure now sounds familiar: the irregularly metered three-stress line we find in Yeats's mature poems. Roethke acknowledges his ancestor, in some lines from his "Four for Sir John Davies":

> I take this cadence from a man named Yeats;
> I take it, and I give it back again:
> For other tunes and other wanton beats
> Have tossed my heart and fiddled through my brain.

While the counterpointed iambic line remains a mainstay of Roethke's prosody, he has listened closely to "other tunes and wanton beats." He has himself parsed the music of his moving "Elegy for Jane"—certainly one of his best performances in unmetered verse. We quote the first strophe:

> I remember the neckcurls, limp and damp as tendrils;
> And her quick look, a sidelong pickerel smile;
> And how, once startled into talk, the light syllables
>   leaped for her,
> And she balanced in the delight of her thought,
> A wren, happy, tail into the wind,
> Her song trembling the twigs and small branches.
> The shade sang with her;
> The leaves, their whispers turned to kissing;
> And the mold sang in the bleached valleys under the rose.

Roethke's analysis of these lines explains how he maintains restraint and balance without the control of regular meter. He comments on the "Elegy":

> let me indicate one or two technical effects in my little piece. For one thing, the enumeration, the favorite device of the more irregular poem. We see it again and again in Whitman and Lawrence. "I remember," then the listing, the appositions, and the absolute construction. "Her song trembling," etc. Then the last lines in the stanza lengthen out. . . . There is a successive shortening of the line length, an effect I have become inordinately fond of, I'm afraid. This little piece indicates in a way some of the strategies for the poet writing without the support of a formal pattern—he can vary his line length, modulate, he can stretch out the line, he can shorten.[13]

Enumeration and varying the line length—these dominate the prosody of those wild, free-associating poems collected in *Praise to the End* (1951), and in his last volume, especially, *The Far Field* (1964). "The successive shortening of line length" does indeed become almost a signature. Aggressively, diminishingly gnomic, the poet attempts to wake up the Mother Goose in us all:

See what the sweet harp says.
Should a song break a sleep?
The round home of a root,—
Is that the place to go?
I'm a tune dying
On harsh stone.
An Eye says,
Come.

I keep dreaming of bees.
This flesh has airy bones.
Going is knowing.
I see; I seek;
I'm near.

Be true,
Skin.

"O, Thou Opening, O"

It would be a misnomer to call this free verse: to paraphrase Eliot, no verse could be free that so successfully captures such awareness exploding from underground. Or to bring Roethke to bear on himself again:

> We must permit poetry to extend consciousness as far, as deeply, as particularly as it can, to recapture, in Stanley Kunitz' phrase, "what it has lost to some extent to prose." We must realize, I think, that the writer in freer forms must have an even greater fidelity to his subject matter than the poet who has the support of form. He must keep his eye on the object, and his rhythm must move as a mind moves, must be imaginatively right, or he is lost.[14]

"Rhythm must move as a mind moves." This is especially pertinent when the poet's mind turns inward, when he greets his "thingy spirit" and deliberately abandons the logic of usual relationships:

> Reason? That dreary shed, that hutch for grubby schoolboys!
> The hedgewren's song says something else.
> I care for a cat's cry and the hugs, live as water.
> I've traced these words in sand with a vestigial tail;

Now the gills are beginning to cry.
Such a sweet noise: I can't sleep for it.
Bless me and the maze I'm in!
Hello, thingy spirit.

"I Cry, Love! Love!"

The irrelevancy here is not like Auden's often kitschy surrealism; Roethke writes the phylogeny of the subconscious. The rhythms are imaginatively right. As in Whitman, each line comprises the prosodic unit; each line draws exactly enough breath to sustain it. Regular meter would destroy the sense of improvisation, the sense that the movements of the poem trace an ontogony that repeats racial history.

"Meditations of an Old Woman"—the five-part poem concluding *Words for the Wind*—has been noted critically as a response to *Four Quartets*.[15] Roethke was certainly thinking of Eliot; we find in the "Meditations" many echoing passages, many lines that pick up Eliot's words for refutation or amplification. A comparison of two passages shows what Roethke owes Eliot; the first is from "The Dry Salvages," the second from the "First Meditation":

When the train starts, and the passengers are settled
To fruit, periodicals and business letters
(And those who saw them off have left the platform)
Their faces relax from grief into relief,
To the sleepy rhythm of a hundred hours.
Fare forward, travellers! not escaping from the past
Into different lives, or into any future;
You are not the same people who left that station
Or who will arrive at any terminus.

All journeys, I think, are the same:
The movement is forward, after a few wavers,
And for a while we are all alone,
Busy, obvious with ourselves,
The drunken soldier, the old lady with her peppermints;
And we ride, we ride, taking the curves
Somewhat closer, the trucks coming
Down from behind the last ranges,
Their black shapes breaking past;
And the air claps between us,

> Blasting the frosted windows,
> And I seem to go backward,
> Backward in time.

The bases of the prosody are the same: we discover enumeration, a gradual narrowing of line length and rhythmic period, and the repeated use of "verbal forms that keep the action going."[16] Roethke's rhythm is tauter, charged with more specifics in portrayal. Eliot sprawls, his line runs slacker, and his self-conscious use of clichés subverts verbal excitement. Prosodically, Roethke improves upon his original.

Most of the "Meditations" are written in unmetered verse. However, Roethke frequently turns to a lyrical, unrhymed stanza of three beats,

> What lover keeps his song?
> I sigh before I sing.
> I love because I am
> A rapt thing with a name,

or to a highly personal blank verse:

> By swoops of bird, by leaps of fish I live.
> My shadow steadies in a shifting stream;
> I live in air; the long light is my home;
> I dare caress the stones, the field my friend;
> A light wind rises: I become the wind.

This short-breathed line, characterized by the nervous end-stopping, is an identifying feature of Roethke's style. It is especially effective in those exclamatory passages of sudden association and rapt discovery— passages that resemble the speech of a verbally gifted and extraordinarily sensitive five-year-old:

> How sweetly I abide. Am I a bird?
> Soft, soft, the snow's not falling. What's a seed?
> A face floats in the ferns. Do maimed gods walk?

Of course, the last question could have been asked only by a sophisticated five-year-old who had read *The Golden Bough!*

The best parts of the "Meditations" approach the transcendence and ecstasy of *Four Quartets*. Roethke affirms the natural life, a world of the sentient body as well as a world of spiritual exaltation. When Eliot tells us,

> Sin is Behovely, but
> All shall be well, and
> All manner of thing shall be well.

Roethke answers, with some acidity,

> It is difficult to say all things are well,
> When the worst is about to arrive;
> It is fatal to woo yourself,
> However graceful the posture.

For Eliot, all things will be well in the new world; but Roethke prefers "Instead of a devil with horns . . . a serpent with scales." For Eliot, ends are beginnings and the road up is the road down; Roethke—or his persona in the poem—cries:

> I'm released from the dreary dance of opposites.

Paradoxically, Eliot's influence is also Roethke's release; the final strophe of "What Can I Tell My Bones" (the fifth and last meditation) is written in "free" meter that Roethke characterizes in nearly Eliotic terms: "I agree that free verse is a denial in terms. There is, invariably, the ghost of some other form, often blank verse, behind what is written, or the more elaborate rise and fall of the rhythmical prose sentence."[17] More than "the ghost" of blank verse haunts this passage:

> The sun! The sun! And all we can become!
> And the time ripe for running to the moon!
> In the long fields, I leave my father's eye;
> And shake the secrets from my deepest bones;
> My spirit rises with the rising wind;
> I'm thick with leaves and tender as a dove,
> I take the liberties a short life permits—

> I seek my own meekness;
> I recover my tenderness by long looking.
> By midnight I love everything alive.
> Who took the darkness from the air?
> I'm wet with another life.
> Yea, I have gone and stayed.
>
> What came to me vaguely is now clear,
> As if released by a spirit,
> Or agency outside me.
> Unprayed-for,
> And final.

Like Eliot, Roethke had great gifts for modulation, for loosening the meter without audible creaks and bumps. The first six lines are stable blank verse; the change in movement comes with the seventh line:

> I take the liberties a short life permits.

The line is sprung by an extra monosyllabic foot, "life"; the sprung line serves as a rhythmic junction for the freer lines that follow. And we note again the long morendo as the line length shortens. Such prosodic manipulation is exemplary "imitative form." Release and resignation, an end to searching, and the resolution of spirit with nature find their expressive container in the slowly diminishing rhythm.

❧ v. *Robert Lowell, John Berryman, Sylvia Plath, Weldon Kees, Elizabeth Bishop*

Robert Lowell's initial volumes, *Land of Unlikeness* (1944), *Lord Weary's Castle* (1946), and *The Mills of the Kavanaughs* (1951), stride in a "Goliath's armor of brazen metric."[18] His later poems walk relatively unarmed. The change in Lowell's prosody, from a strict convention of carefully worked stanzas and rhyming couplets to a mode of nearly naked speech, did not come easily. Lowell admitted, "I never dared write [free verse] until I was almost forty. If it doesn't work, if the rhythm isn't right and the experience isn't right, you have nothing, I think." The crux is *experience:* Lowell affirms, "I'm sure the rhythm is the person himself."[19]

The person behind the drama and violence, the *Schrei*, of *Land of Unlikeness* is obscurely realized. Lowell's muscular Catholicism exercises itself in dense, harsh language; the prosody, as Allen Tate points out in his brief introduction, seems *willed* on the language. The result is often a poetry of religious exhibitionism; not always, as Tate suggests, a poetry of strong religious struggle that attempts to recover Christian symbolism for a world gone rotten with material progress. Struggle, as well as a complex, even burlesqued symbolism, is present; but the defects and distortions of these first poems emerge as much out of confusion and bad taste as out of Lowell's religious agonies.

In "Christ for Sale" Lowell attempts the recovery of that seventeenth-century "integrated sensibility" and presents the doctrine of the Redemption in language and images that willfully disgust:

> In Greenwich Village, Christ the Drunkard brews
> Gall, or spiked bone-vat, siphons His bilged blood
> Into weak brain-pans and unseasons wood:
> His auctioneers are four hog-fatted Jews.
> In furs and bundlings of vitality,
> Our ladies, ho, swill down the ichor in this Dye.
>
> Drying upon the crooked nails of time,
> Dirty Saint Francis, where is Jesus' blood,
> Salvation's only Fountainhood and Flood?
> These drippings of the Lamb are Heaven's crime.
> Queens, Brooklyn and Manhattan, come and buy:
> Gomorrah, had you known the wormwood in this Dye!
>
> Us still our Savior's mangled mouth may kiss
> Although beauticians plaster us with mud:
> Dog of the veins, your nose is stopped with blood;
> Women are thirsty, let them lap up this:
> The luncher's stop to spit into Christ's eye.
> O Lamb of God, your loitering carrion will die.

Neither the forced language and the imagery of emesis nor the strident rhythms do much to clarify the poet's blasphemies. (We understand, of course, that Lowell is blasphemous in the modern sense: in the way that Baudelaire and Joyce are Catholic blasphemers and hence deeply, though paradoxically, religious.) The second line is sprung by strong stressing:

> Gáll, or spíked bóne-vát, síphons His bílged blóod.

The emotional intention, white-hot anger, is lost in the incoherent splutter of consonants.

Lowell omitted "Christ for Sale," along with ten other poems from *Land of Unlikeness*, in his actual debut volume *Lord Weary's Castle*.[20] Those poems reprinted from the earlier book were revised, a few heavily. Many of the revisions entail only the change of a single line or a single word, but all the changes offer prosodic improvements. Thus the final couplet of "Children of Light"

> And light is where the ancient blood of Cain
> Is burning, burning the unburied grain.

becomes in *Lord Weary's Castle*

> And the light is where the landless blood of Cain
> Is burning, burning the unburied grain.

"Landless" alliterates with "light"; it also removes the unpleasantly nasal "an-" and its unfortunate rhyme with "Cain." The change of a single word strengthens the opening of "The Crucifix":

> How dry Time screaks in its fat axle-grease,
> As sure November strikes us through the ice.
> *Land of Unlikeness*

> How dry time screaks in its fat axle-grease,
> As spare November strikes us through the ice.
> *Lord Weary's Castle*

Extensive revisions improve the rest of the poem; lines 5 through 8 are both verbally and metrically strengthened:

> It's time: the worldly angels strip to tease
> And wring out bread and butter from their eyes,

To wipe away the past's idolatries;
Tomorrow's seaways lurch through Sodom's knees.

Land of Unlikeness

It's time: the old unmastered lion roars
And ramps like a mad dog outside the doors,
Snapping at gobbets in my thumbless hand.
The seaways lurch through Sodom's knees of sand
Tomorrow.

Lord Weary's Castle

The striking feature of the metric of *Lord Weary's Castle* is its overwhelming physicality. Lines clang and grind; the movement stops dead and resumes with a shudder; stress jams against stress until lines break under the tension:

With flat glass eyes pushed at him on a stick . . .
"Between the Porch and the Altar"

It is an exciting workout for both ear and eye to read "The Quaker Graveyard in Nantucket"—as exciting as to read "Lycidas": a poem it resembles thematically and prosodically.[21] Note the even roll of the enjambed lines after the full stop of the first descriptive fragment:

A brackish reach of shoal off Madaket,—
The sea was still breaking violently and night
Had steamed into our North Atlantic Fleet,
When the drowned sailor clutched the drag-net. Light
Flashed from his matted head and marble feet,
He grappled at the net
With the coiled, hurdling muscles of his thighs.

Note Lowell's penchant for the double foot of two light and two heavy stresses; these lines are from the second strophe of "The Quaker Graveyard":

Sea-gulls blink their heavy lids
Seaward. The wind's wings beat upon the stones,
Cousin, and scream for you and the claws rush

> At the sea's throat and wring it in the slush
> Of this Old Quaker graveyard where the bones
> Cry out in the long night for the hurt beast
> Bobbing by Ahab's whaleboats in the East.

This Ionic rhythm is obsessive: "and the claws rush . . . at the sea's throat . . . in the long night for the hurt beast." The movement of the gracefully expressive slow line

> Cry out in the long night for the hurt beast

shows a tremendous advance in feeling and technique over the strained awkwardness of

> Us still our Saviour's mangled mouth may kiss.

Lowell's thematic rhythms and the repetition of metrically similar lines give "The Quaker Graveyard" a powerful stylistic consistency; Moby Dick rises and menaces us in constant Ionics:

> The bones cry for the blood of the white whale.

The occasional alternation of a short line (usually trimeter) with the prevailing pentameters adds another "rhythmic constant." Lowell owes this metrical suggestion to Milton; a comparison of lines from "Lycidas" and the first strophe of "The Quaker Graveyard" shows the extent of Lowell's debt and how expertly he has adapted Milton's rhythm to his own use:

> Begin then, Sisters of the sacred well,
> That from beneath the seat of Jove doth spring,
> Begin, and somewhat loudly sweep the string.
> Hence with denial vain, and coy excuse;
> So may some gentle Muse
> With lucky words favor my destin'd urn,
> And as he passes turn,
> And bid fair peace be to my sable shroud.

> The corpse was bloodless, a botch of reds and whites,
> Its open, staring eyes

Were lustreless dead-lights
Or cabin-windows on a stranded hulk
Heavy with sand. We weight the body, close
Its eyes and heave it seaward whence it came.

Acting as his own critic, Lowell remarks, "this is a poem by someone who's read Milton very carefully, and yet it's not very Miltonic."[22]

Lowell's awareness of English metrical tradition crops up everywhere in *Lord Weary's Castle.* The nine-line stanzas of "The Ghost" and "Mr. Edwards and the Spider," while not corresponding exactly to a specific pattern in the *Songs and Sonnets,* are unmistakably Donne-like. The stanza of "The Drunken Fisherman" comes from Marvell's "The Garden":

> Wallowing in this bloody sty,
> I cast for fish that please my eye
> (Truly Jehovah's bow suspends
> No pots of gold to weight its ends);
> Only the blood-mouthed rainbow trout
> Rose to my bait. They flopped about
> My canvas creel until the moth
> Corrupted its unstable cloth.

The run-on couplet, "with its rhymes buried," of "Between the Porch and the Altar" and "After the Surprising Conversions" "is very much like the couplet Browning uses in "My Last Duchess," in *Sordello.*"[23] Lowell also inherits from Browning the unbeautiful mannerism of beginning a new sentence with the last foot of the line:

> Time runs, the windshield runs with stars. The past
> Is cities from a train, until at last
> Its escalating and black-windowed blocks
> Recoil against a Gothic church. The clocks
> Are tolling. I am dying. The shocked stones
> Are falling like a ton of bricks and bones.
> > "Between the Porch and the Altar"

The two finest poems of Lowell's third book, *The Mills of the Kava-naughs,* are hammered into the close-fitting armor of the run-on couplet. But Lowell is now a master of the form; the two poems "Falling Asleep Over the Aeneid" and "Mother Marie Therese" are little hampered by the requirements of rhyme and meter. Lowell achieves a controlled freedom where "any sort of compression or expansion is possible."[24]

> But my dishonor makes him drink. Of course
> I'll tell the court the truth for his divorce . . .
>
>   One
> Must have a friend to enter there, but none
> Is friendless in this crowd, and the nuns smile.
> I stand aside and marvel; for a while
> The winter sun is pleasant.

"Of course"/"divorce," "One"/"none," and "smile"/"for a while" are neutral rhymes of convenience that betray Lowell's struggle to get on with the poem.

We already see in "Thanksgiving's Over," the last poem in *The Mills of the Kavanaughs,* some of the prosodic flexibility and close personal rhythm of Lowell's later work. "Thanksgiving's Over" is phantasmagoric, fevered; Michael, the narrator, dreams of his mad wife who committed suicide. She speaks to him in his dream:

> *But Michael, I was well;*
> My mind was well;
> I wanted to be loved—to thaw, to change,
> To April! Now our mountains, seventeen
> Bald Brothers, green
> Below the timberline, must change
> Their skullcaps for the green of Sherwood Forest;
> Mount Leather-Jacket leads the season. Outlaws,
> We enter a world of children, perched on gaunt
> Crows-nests in hemlocks over flat-iron torrents;
> And freely serve our term
> In prison. I will serve you, Love. Affirm
> The promise, move the mountains, while they lean,
> As dry as dust for want
> Of trusting.

Lowell does not quite break the meter here; the footwork is recognizably iambic, although the lines are highly irregular in length and run over with absolute freedom. The later poems in *Life Studies* (1959) and beyond fragment, and at times completely discard, the dominant iambic meter. We hear the thick rhythms of Lowell's speaking voice unaffected by the exigencies of precise line length and exactly patterned stresses.

A willful, self-conscious craftsman, Lowell explains how he effected a major change in his prosodic style. In an interview Lowell tells us,

> I began to have a certain disrespect for the tight forms. If you could make it easier by adding syllables, why not? And then when I was writing *Life Studies,* a good number of the poems were started in very strict meter, and I found that, more than the rhymes, the regular beat was what I didn't want. I have a long poem in there about my father, called Commander Lowell, which actually is largely in couplets, but I originally wrote perfectly strict four-foot couplets. Well, with that form it's hard not to have echoes of Marvell. The regularity just seemed to ruin the honesty of sentiment, and became rhetorical; it said, "I'm a poem"—though it was a great help when I was revising having this original skeleton. I could keep the couplets where I wanted them and drop them where I didn't; there'd be a form to come back to.[25]

Heartbreaking in their "honesty of sentiment" are the lines addressed to Lowell's infant daughter in "Home after Three Months Away." The metric, moving "between fixity and flux," is strict enough to keep the emotions in order, supple enough to prevent artificiality:

> Three months, three months!
> Is Richard now himself again?
> Dimpled with exaltation,
> my daughter holds her levee in the tub.
> Our noses rub,
> each of us pats a stringy lock of hair—
> they tell me nothing's gone.
> Though I am forty-one,
> not forty now, the time I put away
> was child's-play. After thirteen weeks

> my child still dabs her cheeks
> to start me shaving. When
> we dress her in her sky-blue corduroy,
> she changes to a boy,
> and floats my shaving brush
> and washcloth in the flush . . .
>
> Dearest, I cannot loiter here
> in lather like a polar bear.

These lines are not unmetered; the meter is concealed by running over the lines, breaking the syntax with numerous heavy pauses and occasional heavy-handed rhyme, and abruptly shifting the tempo:

> my daughter holds her levee in the tub.
> Our noses rub . . .
>
> we dress her in her sky-blue corduroy,
> she changes to a boy.

Perhaps the most shattering poem in *Life Studies* is the last one in the volume, "Skunk Hour." The idiom is so personal that it is difficult to separate technical means from Lowell's anguish. Rhythm touches raw nerves moved by hysteria held barely in check by minimal prosodic means: the six-line stanza and the rhyme:

> One dark night,
> my Tudor Ford climbed the hill's skull;
> I watched for love-cars. Lights turned down,
> they lay together, hull to hull,
> where the graveyard shelves on the town . . .
> My mind's not right.
>
> A car radio bleats,
> "Love, O careless Love. . . ." I hear
> my ill-spirit sob in each blood cell,
> as if my hand were at its throat . . .
> I myself am hell;
> nobody's here—

only skunks, that search
in the moonlight for a bite to eat.
They march on their soles up Main Street:
white stripes, moonstruck eyes' red fire
under the chalk-dry and spar spire
of the Trinitarian Church.

Lowell crowds together, in an unmetered line, as many as six strong stresses:

my ill-spirit sob in each blood cell . . .

white stripes, moonstruck eyes' red fire . . .

The effect is explosive, or claustrophobic, depending on your point of view—a rendering of emotion stopping just short of spluttering incoherence, or a clotted effusiveness that does not. The strained rhythm marks the limits to which agonized personal experience can be pushed. Lowell himself has expressed doubts about this kind of confessional poetry:

> I don't think that a personal history can go on forever, unless you're Walt Whitman and have a way with you. I feel I've done enough personal poetry. That doesn't mean I won't do more of it, but I don't want to do more now. . . . other things being equal it's better to get your emotions out in a Macbeth than in a confession.[26]

Some of Lowell's later work sought greater objectivity in subjects partially removed from the suffering intimacies of *Life Studies*. In *Imitations* (1961) Lowell turns to translation, perhaps to distance himself from personal pain. Yet he imposes such extreme subjectivity on his chosen subjects that his "translations" often only remotely resemble the original poems.

The uncomfortable transition this book represents finds resolution in *For the Union Dead* (1964). Once again, Lowell makes—and composes from—his unique pact with the personal and history. In these poems he shows greater confidence and control in breaking down his forms. And, for Lowell, the language is clear, almost spare. Three stanzas from "The Drinker" illustrate the poet's method:

The man is killing time—there's nothing else.

No help now from the fifth of Bourbon

chucked helter-skelter into the river,

even its cork sucked under . . .

Once she was close to him
as water to the dead metal.

He looks at her engagements inked on her calendar.
A list of indictments.
At the numbers in her thumbed black telephone book.
A quiver full of arrows.

The first stanza is regularly stressed, with the first line iambic pentameter. As the stanza progresses, each line drops a unit until the fourth line contains only three stresses. Lowell employs end rhyme in lines 3 and 4. This is the poem's opening stanza (of ten). Beginning with the poem's second stanza, Lowell discards rhyme; in stanza 5 (above), he boils the quatrain down to an unrhymed couplet, and in stanza 6 (also above) he elongates line 1 (six stresses), and violently compacts lines 2 (two stresses) and 4 (three stresses). Overall, this sort of concision is fairly regular, in its odd way, and elevates the book to one of Lowell's best efforts.

In a later volume, *Notebooks: 1967–68* (1969), Lowell veers into at least the semblance of stricter form. In "Afterthought," he describes his intentions:

the poems in this book are written as one poem, jagged in pattern, but not a conglomeration or sequence of related material. It is not a chronicle or almanac; many events turn up, many others of equal or greater reality do not. This is not my diary, my confession, not a puritan's too literal pornographic honesty. . . . My meter, fourteen line unrhymed blank verse sections, is fairly strict at first and elsewhere, but often corrupts in single lines to the freedom of prose.[27]

The loose sonnet form allows Lowell's vocabulary and diction to dwell, not always to the best effect. As Lowell says, subjects range from familiar poems about ancestors ("Charles Russell Lowell: 1835–1864") to poems about historic moments or figures ("Che Guevara"; "The

March"). The first of four sonnets under the title *Harvard* is representative:

> Beauty-sleep for the writer, and the beauty,
> both fighting off muscular cramps, the same fatigue.
> Lying in bed, letting the bright, white morning
> rise to mid-heaven through a gag of snow,
> through high school, through college, through the
>   last vacation—
> I've slept so late here, snow has stubbled my throat;
> students in their hundreds rise from the beehive,
> swarm-mates; they have clocks and instincts, make
> classes. In the high sky, a parochial school,
> the top floors looking like the Place des Vosges—
> a silk stocking, blown thin as smog, coils in a twig-fork,
> dangling a wire coathanger, rapier-bright—
> a long shot for a hard cold day . . . wind lifting
> the stocking like the lecherous, lost leg.

This lacks the punch of much of Lowell's earlier work. Here the poet manipulates his pentameter as if he were pushing out the insides of an envelope. We note the twelve syllables of line 5, and the agitated enlistment of hyphenated words ("swarm-mates," "twig-fork," "rapier-bright") to both speed up lines and heighten description. Throughout this book, Lowell often does achieve a more relaxed distance from his most dreaded, challenging subject—himself.

A majority of his later poems, however, including those splintered pieces in his last volume, *Day by Day* (1977), return to grind in the confessional mill. The structures of individual lines, poems, and books themselves become increasingly fragmented. As Lowell's understanding of his own vulnerabilities grew, his prosodic concerns became increasingly relaxed. The unfettered depression of the life of the Poet, always a major concern of Lowell's circle, became at last *the* key impetus behind the writing of poems. This influence persists to the present day.

Perhaps none of the poets aptly identified with Lowell's influence was so staggered by personality, so fascinated with the self, as John Berryman. Berryman's life and death may be best described as *frenetic*. His verse, especially in his ongoing *Dream Songs*, an explosive, passionate expression of that life and rehearsal for death, can similarly be understood. But in an equally important touchstone in our poetry, Berryman's book-length narrative drama *Homage to Mistress Bradstreet* (1956), the poet often exercises a restraint that becomes increasingly rare as his career develops.

Doubtless the parameters of the *Homage* helped, bound as it was by historical fact and a set cast of characters. Briefly, the modern poet evokes, not just the honored memory, but the *essence* of the seventeenth-century poet who shipped to America as a girl in 1630. The later poet's aim is nothing less than to achieve the perfect union between man and woman, artist and artist, a union that is sexual yet transcends sexuality (or at least those aspects of mortality inevitably associated with sexual experience) and germinates from an exquisite sense of sympathy. Thus the poem fluctuates between almost pastoral descriptions of Bradstreet's life and times and a dialogue, spanning centuries, between the two poets:

> The winters close, Springs open, no child stirs
> under my withering heart, O seasoned heart
> God grudged his aid.
> All things else soil like a shirt.
> Simon is much away. My executive stales.
> The town came through for the cartway by the pales,
> but my patience is short.
> I revolt from, I am like, these savage foresters.

The poem consists of fifty-seven numbered, eight-line stanzas, of which the one above is indicative of the whole. Line lengths vary, shifting constantly from the pentameter norm to create the nervous syntax so characteristic of the later Berryman of *The Dream Songs*. This and the frequently surprising placement of off-rhymes reveal the influence of Hopkins, especially, but Berryman's own style does assertively emerge.

In *The Dream Songs* Berryman spins off Pound's example to present his version of a poem in progress. His stanza of choice for the poem shrinks from the eight lines above to six lines, with each numbered song consisting of three stanzas. The intense dialogue of *Homage to Mistress Bradstreet* expands as a device in *The Dream Songs* to include the voices of a multifaceted self-in-torment. Characters include *I, Henry,* and others expressing themselves in minstrel show dialect, the language of vaudeville, jazz, self-recrimination, and analysis.

A STIMULANT FOR AN OLD BEAST

Acacia, burnt myrrh, velvet, pricky stings.
—I'm not so young but not so very old,
said screwed-up lovely 23.
A final sense of being right out in the cold,
unkissed.
(—My psychiatrist can lick your psychiatrist). Women
       get under things.

All these old criminals sooner or later
have had it. I've been reading old journals.
Gottwald and Co., out of business now.
Thick chests quit. Double agent, Joe.
She holds her breath like a seal
and is whiter and smoother.

Rilke was a *jerk.*
I admit his griefs & music
& titled spelled all-disappointed ladies.
A threshold worse than the circles
where the vile settle & lurk,
Rilke's. As I said,—.

Berryman's level of diction spans territory from the exalted (line 1) to the mundane (line 9), from the delicate (line 11) to the ponderous (lines 16 and 17). Expectations established by the first line's strong stresses are immediately surprised by the basic pentameter of line 2. The poet's wit, as in the *Homage,* is made manifest in irregularly placed, off-rhymes ("unkissed," "psychiatrist"). The compositional goal is to maintain a constant excited state of surprise, of discovery. Hence the second stanza is shadowed by commerce, and the third by literature. Berryman obsessively pursues the perfect depiction of the modern American mind in all its sanctioned and condemned schizophrenia. His dogged adherence to this agenda, despite numerous sentimental and self-pitying lapses, and his superior technical skill elevate his body of work to a position of pivotal importance in our understanding of American poetry in the second half of this century.

Though much younger than other poets discussed in this section, Sylvia Plath, by virtue of her brief, brilliant body of work and dramatic exit from life (she committed suicide in 1963), demands inclusion in any examination of the first postwar generation of modern poets. Plath's celebrated volume *Ariel* (1965) redefined the confessional mode, introducing a repressed feminist at the end of her rope into what had been a modern masculine poetry of angst. Even after taking into account the occasional spasms of Whitmanesque joy in the last poems, Plath wrote as if life for her were a drama in which the prospects for happiness were permanently banned. Marshaling nervous groupings, parallel constructions, and sporadic rhyme, Plath's prosody seems always on the verge of flying apart. Her poem "Lady Lazarus" perhaps best personifies the horror and terrible honesty of an artist headed straight into the heart of oblivion. Composed in twenty-eight tercets, "Lady Lazarus" is a predatory, chanting meditation on suicide.

> The nose, the eye pits, the full set of teeth?
> The sour breath
> Will vanish in a day.
>
> Soon, soon the flesh
> The grave cave ate will be
> At home on me
>
> And I a smiling woman.
> I am only thirty.
> And like the cat I have nine times to die.
>
> This is Number Three.

The impassive listing of body parts, the ominous pause of repetition consumed by alliterative stresses, and the surprising turn, grounded in the specificity of the personal, beginning "And I a smiling woman," codify a pattern of wished-for annihilation that is both the curse of, and release from, a blasted life. What survives is the spirit made powerful, and dangerous:

> Out of the ash
> I rise with my red hair
> And I eat men like air.

More than thirty years after her death, it is still difficult to separate the narrow yet considerable achievement of Plath's best poems from the particulars of her sad life. Like her friend and contemporary, Anne Sexton (who survived Plath by eleven years, then ended her life in a similar fashion), Plath's artistry, at its best, and her emotional honesty sprung open possibilities that writers who followed her continue to explore to this day.

Easily the most mysterious member of what we have labeled the Lowell generation, Weldon Kees was also its most versatile artist. Successful as a poet, painter, jazz pianist and composer, fiction writer, radio writer and performer, and filmmaker, Kees personified American rootlessness and restlessness, moving from his native Beatrice, Nebraska, to Denver, to Manhattan, and finally to San Francisco in the twenty years following his graduation from college. On July 18, 1955, his abandoned car was found at an on-ramp to the Golden Gate Bridge. Kees had confided in friends that he was contemplating suicide or a disappearance into Mexico where he might begin a new life. Despite some unconfirmed sightings (a journalist may have met Kees in a Mexican bar; Kees's mother thought she saw her son on a ferry in the East), Kees has not been heard from since his disappearance; no body was ever recovered from the waters of San Francisco Bay.

An additional resonant mystery permeates Kees's considerable reputation, especially among poets. His small body of work, made up of three volumes published in his lifetime, was not gathered into a widely accessible volume until the edition edited by Donald Justice and published by the University of Nebraska Press (1960). This volume, along with the critical attention of younger poets more than a decade later, succeeded in assuring Kees's inclusion in many of the major anthologies and thereby introducing a larger audience to his poetry. These readers discovered a poetry of bitter essences and elegant execution. Like many moderns, Kees's persona represents the intelligent, disappointed, and deeply damaged individual stepping back from a failed civilization. At times satirical, always enduring, the typical Kees poem ruthlessly and quietly observes the terms and props of our collective disappointment. Even his prosodic achievement builds quietly, subtly. In his introduction to the *Collected Poems,* Justice explained:

> To originality in style and technique his poetry would seem to lay little claim. Yet since the whole style of his poetry lies in its very

unobtrusiveness, it is a crucial part of his individual tone. It is a style which answers to what seems to me the classical definition of a good *prose* style: natural words in natural order.[28]

Justice and others have noted Kees's grounding in traditional forms, and his habit of relaxing them, as in "Farrago," a variation on the villanelle.

> The housings fall so low they graze the ground
> And hide our human legs. False legs hang down
> Outside. Dance in a horse's hide for a punctured god.
>
> We killed and roasted one. And now he haunts the air,
> Invisible, creates our world again, lights the bright star
> And hurls the thunderbolt. His body and his blood
>
> Hurry the harvest. Through the tall grain,
> Toward nightfall, these cold tears of his come down like rain,
> Spotting and darkening.—I sit in a bar
>
> On Tenth Street, writing down these lies
> In the worst winter of my life. A damp snow
> Falls against the pane. When everything dies,
>
> The days all end alike, the sound
> Of breaking goes on faintly all around,
> Outside and inside. Where I go,
>
> The housings fall so low they graze the ground
> And hide our human legs. False legs fall down
> Outside. Dance in a horse's hide. Dance in the snow.

The opening lines move along a recognizable pentameter curve, which is swiftly distorted in line 3 by the addition of extra stress. Kees sustains the hexameter through lines 4 and 6, intending that it hold up the awkward fifth line, then compresses the movement (and tension) through the dactylic, trochaic, and Ionic substitutions of line 7. The introduction of the speaker "I" in line 9 signals a further constriction of pace, alternating between four and five stresses per line, as if breathing itself were becoming harder. This quickening is enhanced by the straight rhymes of stanzas 3 through 5 (bracketed by the off-rhymes of stanzas 1, 2, and 6). Relief comes in the expanded stresses of stanza 6 as the individual returns to an identification with the community, the whole. In tone and theme, Kees often reminds us of another superior poet of his generation, Randall Jarrell. In reading both poets, one learns something about reading poetry. Returning to Justice's introduction:

> The poetry of Kees makes its deepest impression when read as a body of work rather than a collection of isolated moments of brilliance. This may account in part for the neglect from which it has suffered. Though a number of the poems are brilliant and many are moving, no single poem perhaps is flawless. . . . Moreover, the taste at work is throughout of a kind which forbids the glittering surfaces of a more fashionable poetry. But there is a cumulative power to the work as a whole to which even the weaker poems contribute. Kees is original in one of the few ways that matter: he speaks to us in a voice or, rather, in a particular tone of voice which we have never heard before.[29]

Elizabeth Bishop's poetry can read like a tonic to the excesses (emotional pyrotechnics) of the confessional writers. Inherently reticent, intensely private, Bishop wrote poems that expose and examine by indirection her observations, wit, and emotions. Deceptively cool—even distant—in their surfaces, they contain the heart's fire, the soul's unadorned discourse. "The Man-Moth" (the title comes from a newspaper misprint for *mammoth*) provides an example of polished wit that also transcends the good humor of its inspiration. Applying the qualities of the moth to a human, Bishop succeeds in coupling disparate experiences:

He thinks the moon is a small hole at the top of the sky,

proving the sky quite useless for protection.

He trembles, but must investigate as high as he can climb.

The poem's normative six stresses (with occasional, pivotal resolutions in fives and sevens) fall subtly through a series of bright substitutions. In the lines above, we note Bishop's fondness for the Ionic foot by its use in line 1's third position; we also observe the anapests that follow, filling out and threatening to overcome the measure, the inverted trochaic foot opening line 2 and the extra syllable at line's end, then the drawn-out seven stresses of line 3. Perhaps no line so ably displays Bishop's prosodic dexterity as one that occurs in the poem's fourth stanza. The man-moth, having failed to ascend through the moon's small hole, returns "to the pale subways of cement he calls his home." With difficulty he boards a subway train; he "seats himself facing the wrong way—"

and the train starts at once at its full, terrible speed.

The train's jarring launch, its physical journey, is perfectly conveyed by the initial Ionic, a construction Bishop boldly repeats in the line's third foot, creating even greater emphasis by positioning a caesura between the two stresses, then releasing the pent up tension through the concluding anapest.

In much of her poetry Bishop is constantly breaking away from metrical norms:

> A new volcano has erupted,
>
> the papers say, and last week I was reading
>
> where some ship saw an island being born:
>
> At first a breath of steam, ten miles away;
>
> And then a black fleck—basalt, probably—
>
> rose in the mate's binoculars
>
> And caught on the horizon like a fly.
>
> They named it. But my poor old island's still
>
> Un-rediscovered, un-renamable.
>
> None of the books has ever got it right.
>
> "Crusoe in England"

But for lines 1 and 6, this stanza opens the poem with supple pentameter made all the more intriguing by end and interior rhymes ("say,"
"away," "fly"), and variations such as the inverted opening foot of line
10.

In succeeding stanzas the pentameter base is thoroughly disrupted
(though its echo persists, rounding off the rough edges of the
substitutions):

> and if I had become a giant,
>
> I couldn't bear to think what size
>
> the goats and turtles were,
>
> or the gulls, or the over-lapping rollers
>
> —a glittering hexagon of rollers
>
> closing and closing in, but never quite,
>
> glittering and glittering, though the sky
>
> was mostly overcast.

The lines become compacted, as if with the charged multiplicity of
contemplation itself, and rely increasingly on repetition and parallelism for organization. Bishop's versatility, whether in metrical or nonmetrical verse, constantly startles with its clean, concise striking of
essential chords. Her work as a whole adds distinction to the writers
with whom she is most often associated, and it continues to exert ever
greater influence on the younger generation of poets just now coming
into their own.

✎ VI. *Advanced Discretion: Larkin, Wilbur, and Company*

An alternative to the confessional branch discussed above existed before confessional poetry achieved such prominence; this alternative
poetry continued to thrive, though quietly, in the work of poets such as
Philip Larkin, Richard Wilbur, Anthony Hecht, John Hollander, James
Merrill, Frederick Morgan, and others. It slights the accomplishments
of these artists to lump them together, but in our poetry's late-Modern
development they do share, to considerable though varying degrees,
similarities of temperament and design. Lowell himself defined the

difference as that between the *raw* and the *cooked,* with himself and his followers writing the kind of verse that could be described as *raw.* Put another way, the Confessional poets saw themselves as more radical for their willingness to break away from traditional, formal structures to present theme and subject without adornment. Their Apollonian counterparts, the Others, found themselves tagged with labels of conservatism and restraint. As is usually the case, reality falls somewhere between these simplistic, extreme poles. We have seen that all great poetry exercises considerable restraint—even in expansiveness (we remind readers of the examples of Whitman and Jeffers). Larkin, Wilbur, and like minds chose to utilize, and often reinvent or modify, the materials of traditional forms. Therefore, their prosody is more immediately recognizable, though no less exciting and original. Their preoccupation with personal struggles, especially in the cases of Larkin, Hecht, and Merrill, mirrors similar concerns in their Confessional peers (though the portrayals of the former are more tautly drawn, more often shaded by wit). Thus Anthony Hecht launches a terrific poem about guilt, tricks of historical placement, horror, and rage with the unexpected:

> Tonight my children hunch
> Toward their Western, and are glad
> As, with a Sunday punch,
>
> The Good casts out the Bad.
>> "It Out-Herods Herod, Pray You, Avoid It"

This is a long way from the poem's conclusion. The children asleep at last, and the father "Who could not, at one time, / Have saved them from the gas," prays for their well-being.

Frederick Morgan, who did not publish his first book until he was fifty, covers similar terrain, giving voice to a complex individual speaking honestly and directly to his fellow creatures. As his work has matured, he has increasingly returned to formal structures in his philosophical meditations, and lyrics celebrating love. His interest in mysticism and Eastern thought are often apparent, as in the poem "After Shen Zhou":

> A single chime of jade across the waters
>
> as along this rocky shore the moment expands

and somewhere within it is hidden a dwelling apart
to which only the absolute ones make good their escape.

The Way seems not to exist (so the master taught)
and yet it is there—and springtime returns once more,
ageless and unreclaimed, to the inner lands.
What purity! The peach trees are in blossom,
birds chirp and stir, and there by the narrow stream
two white-robed figures wait to greet my crossing . . .

Shall I not make my move at last, and join them?

Vigorous substitution within the established pentameter both re-
fers back to the influence of free-verse prosody and points ahead to
the prosodic concerns of the generation we discuss in our epilogue.

Though all of the poets above have produced important work, the
poems of Larkin and Wilbur, perhaps, stand out as most representa-
tive. For many years Philip Larkin's personal modesty and reticence so
defined him for readers of poetry that his originality and facility were
often overlooked. That is no longer true. From a decade preceding his
death to the present, he has come to be regarded as possibly the finest
English poet of the twentieth century. Philip Larkin grew up in Coven-
try, attended Oxford, and in 1955 became curator of the University
library at Hull, where he remained for the last thirty years of his life.
Looking back on his childhood Larkin remembered: "I wrote
ceaselessly . . . : now verse, which I sewed up into little books, now
prose, a thousand words a night after homework."[30] The librarian's
meticulousness is apparent here, as is the poet's familiar sense of
exquisite privacy. In his introduction to the *Collected Poems*, Anthony
Thwaite notes the very early influence on Larkin of Keats, then briefly
Eliot, then Auden in the early 1940s, and finally Yeats and Watkins.[31]
"Wedding-Wind" (1946) shows how well Larkin assimilated his influ-
ences. The poem itchily reacts against a pentameter inevitability, mak-
ing good use of sporadic end and interior rhyme. The packed repeti-
tion, especially opening the poem, establishes an Eliotic mood of
heavy emphasis and circular inevitability. Then the rhythm and star-

tling honesty of the mature Larkin burst forth with the surprising first foot and shortened fourth foot of line 5:

> The wind blew all my wedding-day,
> And my wedding-night was the night of the high wind;
> And a stable door was banging, again and again,
> That he must go and shut it, leaving me
> Stupid in candlelight, hearing rain,
> Seeing my face in the twisted candlestick,
> Yet seeing nothing. When he came back
> He said the horses were restless, and I was sad
> That any man or beast that night should lack
> The happiness I had.

In "Compline," a poem traced to 1950, Larkin's metrical nervousness settles down into the crisp, disarming delivery that is his signature:

> Behind the radio's altarlight
> The hurried talk to God goes on:
> *Thy Kingdom come, Thy will be done,*
> *Produce our lives beyond this night,*
> *Open our eyes again to sun.*
>
> Unhindered in the dingy wards
> Lives flicker out, one here, one there,
> To send some weeping down the stair
> With love unused, in unsaid words:
> For this I would have quenched the prayer,
>
> But for the thought that nature spawns
> A million eggs to make one fish.
> Better that endless notes beseech
> As many nights, as many dawns,
> If finally God grants the wish.

The effortless tetrameter accommodates Larkin's serious wit. Two disparate images are immediately yoked together (radio, altarlight); the poet's perception of the anxiety and speed that grip (and blur) the pace of modern life is made clear in line 2, where prayer becomes the more casual, familiar "talk"; even that talk is rushed. Then the Lord's Prayer itself, positioned intact in line 3, surprisingly turns from the traditional, humble request for sustenance and forgiveness to a desperate plea for physical protection. The second stanza exudes bitterness as the poet, observing the squalor and futility of so much human life, imagines having the power to stifle the prayer—or talk—itself. But the poem's conclusion smoothly sheds its harshness all in the swing of two lines: "But for the thought that nature spawns / A million eggs to make one fish." It is as if the poet concludes that the cosmic evidence is so vast that to consider it too closely (or only parts of it, for we cannot possibly take in the whole) is to limit our existence on earth, to cheat ourselves out of much of life's significance. It is remarkable that Larkin, in fifteen lines, can travel the distance from intense anxiety, through bitterness, to the sweetness of his conclusion.

This poetry (along with Dickinson's) is an example of the tremendous variety in the verse of the miniaturists. "Days," from 1953, chooses a relaxed arrangement that perfectly sets up the emphasis of the closing scene:

> What are days for?
> Days are where we live.
> They come, they wake us
> Time and time over.
> They are to be happy in:
> Where can we live but days?
>
> Ah, solving that question
> Brings the priest and the doctor
> In their long coats
> Running over the fields.

Though hardly indicative of Larkin's normal mode, the poem shows us how surprising he could be, and how influential he *would* be, indirectly or otherwise.

Of the American traditionalists, Richard Wilbur, an offspring of Stevens and Moore, commands the most attention. Like them, Wilbur sees the writing of verse as a way to celebrate the unexpected, veiled essence of experience while also probing the mysteries of the natural world. In his first book, *The Beautiful Changes and Other Poems* (1947), a

meditation on a potato expands from simple description ("An under-
ground grower, blind and a common brown") of its physical state to a
consideration of all of harrowing human history ("Therein the taste of
first stones, the hands of dead slaves, / waters men drank in the
earliest frightful woods"). But despite all hardship, "We shall survive,"
as will the potato, "Awkward and milky and beautiful only to hunger."
Wilbur injects this theme with more active yearning in "Conjuration,"
a poem from his second collection, *Ceremony and Other Poems* (1950).
Composed in four six-line stanzas, the poem acknowledges the sorry
mess experience can make of dreams—"as dreams / Drain into morn-
ing shine, and the cheat is ended." As we find elsewhere in Wilbur,
what is dark or hidden, the mystery, fuels the fire of our inner lives. But
in harsh daylight the broken images of dreams confront us in stark
relief, and we can only wish to return to the darkness: O tides, /
Return a truer blue, make one / The sky's blue speech, and what the
sea confides.

This expression of the classic yearning that lies at the core of ro-
manticism is not without its liabilities, even in the hands of so capable
a practitioner as Wilbur:

> The sea's receding fingers terribly tell
> Of strangest things together grown . . .
>
> Hang among single stars, and twin
> My double deep.

An alliterative infatuation betrays the poet and reader, as does the
ponderous inversion in the second line; also, sense itself recedes in
obscurity ("and twin / My double deep").

A more mature, confident expression is found in "A Grasshopper,"
from Wilbur's *Advice to a Prophet and Other Poems* (1961). Working in his
more comfortable compressed quatrains, Wilbur perfectly conveys
that holy moment of utter silence when all the world and its creatures
hold their breath:

> A quiet spread
> Over the neighbor ground;
> No flower swayed its head
> For yards around;

The wind shrank
Away with a swallowed hiss;
Caught in a widening, blank
Parenthesis,

Cry upon cry
Faltered and faded out.

The diction is appropriate, the movement inspired as the poem's concluding stanzas help us to see and hear the world awakening at the grasshopper's signal:

Crickets resumed their chimes,
And all things wakened, keeping
Their several times.

In gay release
The whole field did what it did,
Peaceful now that its peace
Lay busily hid.

In the wit of these last lines is the essence, perhaps, of Wilbur's best poetry.

There is a method in equestrian training, centered riding, that stresses achieving, and riding from, a firm, contemplative union of mind and body between horse and human. Wilbur repeatedly strives to evoke that quiet, assured, and awakening moment between an individual and the world. Even a poem like "Piccola Commedia" (*The Mind-Reader: New Poems* 1976), which possesses all the trappings of narrative, remains curiously still in its perfect quatrains. The poet recalls his own Kansas hitchhiking experience of "thirty-odd years ago." The narrator finds himself on the porch at a tourist cabin with two women. Having invited him up to escape the heat, they give him a drink, "an Orange Crush and gin." The drink and the heat trigger his carnal imagination:

Laughter. A combine whined
On past, and dry grass bent

> In the backwash; liquor went
> Like an ice-pick into my mind.

> Beneath her skirt I spied
> Two sea-cows on a floe.

The woman instructs him to go inside, where

> A pink girl, curled in a chair,
> Looked up with an ingénue stare.
> *Screenland* lay on the floor.

> Amazed by her starlet's pout
> And the way her eyebrows arched,
> I felt both drowned and parched.
> Desire leapt up like a trout.

> "Hello," she said, and her gum
> Gave a calculating crack.

And that's where the action stops. A man, Ed, whose appearance is rather obviously prepared for in earlier lines (one of the women says "And I'll take no lip from Ed, / Him with his damn cigars") gets out of bed, lights up, and silently walks through the room, ignoring the narrator and the girl. In recollection the narrator is both reticent ("This is something I've never told") and uncertain ("And some of it I forget"). The memory of characters and incidents becomes hazy, but sensation survives:

> But the heat! I can feel it yet,
> And that conniving cold.

This confidence in riding the wave of sensation and its accompanying nervousness with regard to getting straight the details of experience surface throughout Wilbur's oeuvre. Even a recent poem like "The Ride" *(New Poems 1987)* evokes a lone figure at a crossroads of perception. The poem's horse and rider united in a journey "Through the horror of snow" and its measure invite favorable comparison to Frost's "The Draft Horse," which we analyzed earlier. Wilbur's poem extends itself for two additional quatrains; its iambic regularity ("I rode with magic ease . . . On into what was not") admits fewer substitutions than are found in the Frost poem. The poem's conclusions differ markedly, too. While Frost's poem ends with the narrator's interpretation of the significance of the stranger's act, and an unsettling acceptance of the encounter's future consequences, be what they may, Wilbur's poem ends with a question and a yearning to return to the world of sensations and dreams:

> How shall I now get back
> To the inn-yard where he stands,
> Burdened with every lack,
> And waken the stable-hands
>
> To give him, before I think
> That there was no horse at all,
> Some hay, some water to drink,
> A blanket and a stall?

ɝ *vii. Robert Creeley, Robert Bly, Adrienne Rich, Denise Levertov*

While the prosody of Larkin, Wilbur, and others springs from traditional sources, other writers rally round the example, in verse and criticism, of Charles Olson. Olson's essay "Projective Verse," which appeared in 1950, and his epic, *The Maximus Poems,* show the influence of Pound and Williams; they promote "composition by field," or open form. Fundamental to the composition of this type of poetry is the importance of *ear,* as opposed to *eye.* Olson also argued for objective perception of the world as opposed to a human, ego-centered extension of recognition and naming. Olson's ideas and the poetry he wrote and inspired others to write have many advocates, especially in the academy, where highly subjective, almost reactionary interpretations of literature are in vogue (so many scholars today prefer literature that asks the reader to supply the *sense,* to fill in the blanks of connections and meanings). Robert Duncan's generation produced some important poems, but the most original work coming from Olson's influence may be found in the volumes of Robert Creeley, who, more than most, takes to heart Pound's observation that "Prosody is the articulation of the total sound of a poem."

In shape, at least, Creeley's short-lined, casually brief poems would seem to be the antithesis of Olson's epic extravagance. But he shares with Olson and others mentioned the belief that the poem is a series of immediate perceptions unfettered by tradition or time.

A COUNTERPOINT

Let me be my own fool
of my own making, the sum of it

is equivocal.
One says of the drunken farmer:

leave him lay off it. And this is
the explanation.

"A Counterpoint" becomes more than a casual, odd aside when one studies the taut complexity of its making. One notes the balance of the pleas that make up lines 1 and 5, the syllabic equality of the shorter lines 3 and 6. The poem is also stitched together with Creeley's characteristic echoing vowels (m*e*, b*e; own, own*) and strategic, shrewdly executed enjambment (see the turns from lines 2 to 3, and from lines 5 to 6). The poem is indicative of Creeley's minimalist method. Undeniably, it is an engaging one. Creeley's observations and insights are fresh, honest, and repeatedly expressed in surprising ways. Though he would appear to be a staunch antiformalist, he is not above using rhyme (and using it very well) in poems such as "The Warning" and "A Wicker Basket." His breezy sense of humor drives poems like "Naughty Boy" and "Ballad of the Despairing Husband," and his love poems may be the most delicate and beautiful of their time.

THE WAY

My love's manners in bed
are not to be discussed by me,
as mine by her
I would not credit comment upon gracefully.

But I ride by that margin of the lake in
the wood, the castle;
and have a small boy's notion of doing good.

Oh well, I will say here,
knowing each man,

> let you find a good wife too,
> and love her as hard as you can.

Unfortunately, discussions of Robert Bly's poetry are obstructed by the celebrity resulting from his founding role in the men's movement. But it was not always so difficult to observe Bly's methods and achievements. As editor of the influential *Fifties* (later the *Sixties,* and *Seventies*), as a translator of Spanish and Scandinavian poetry, as an antiwar activist in verse and in deed, and as one of the more popular draws on the poetry-reading circuit that thrived in the 1960s, Robert Bly's influence transcended schools and allegiances. He is perhaps best known as the principle advocate and practitioner of the Deep Image. This extension of imagism begins in description and ends, at its best, in a revelation of the individual's hidden psyche:

THE GREAT SOCIETY

Dentists continue to water their lawns even in the rain;
Hands developed with terrible labor by apes
Hang from the sleeves of evangelists;
There are murdered kings in the light-bulbs outside
    movie theaters;
The coffins of the poor are hibernating in piles of new tires.

The janitor sits troubled by the boiler,
And the hotel keeper shuffles the cards of insanity.
The President dreams of invading Cuba.
Bushes are growing over the outdoor grills,
Vines over the yachts and the leather seats.

The city broods over ash cans and darkening mortar.
On the far shore, at Coney Island, dark children
Play on the chilling beach: a spring of black seaweed,
Shells, a skyful of birds,
While the mayor sits with his head in his hands.

The poem's prosody is the accumulation of images and the exploitation of an abundance of end-stopped lines. The effectiveness of such lines is baffling, because the method does not work for most poets. It works for Bly because he shrewdly evokes the echoes of rhymes, because each end-stopped line contains equal value in terms of surprising content (as if each line were a poem in its own right). The poet's intention is to convey the reader through an ever more disturbing, descriptive list to the revelation of all the threatening terror bubbling under the surface as the children play. For more than a decade in the 1960s and 1970s, this poetry dominated the mainstream discussion and practice of American verse. It served to resurrect the image as an essential element in the poem, and it created the most socially conscious, public poetry of our time. Virtually every mainstream poet attempted poems in this vein, as the pages of the period's important magazines, such as Bly's own publication (*The Fifties, The Sixties,* etc.), and *Kayak,* demonstrate. *Kayak*'s editor, George Hitchcock, also wrote poems of this type, including noteworthy late efforts to convey the Deep Image in traditional form:

SOLITAIRE

All that winter you were gone
the skylarks went on crutches
I woke up every dawn
to crows quarreling in ditches

I'd been there before I knew
that landscape of demented kings
I'd seen the courtiers in blue
masks and idiot posturings

when you're nailed to a scar
you don't care for fine words
the juggler at the bazaar
or the chap who eats swords

the world's deceptive—too many
crafty smiling bones
eyes masquerading in money
and loquacious spoons

so I say goodbye to the foxtrot
and to badminton in the park
I shuffle the deck and deal out
snowflakes in the dark.

Despite limitations perceived by some observers, this type of verse undeniably increased the audience for poetry and expanded the field of possibilities for practitioners to come.

The same assertion can be made for the poetry and criticism of Adrienne Rich. Recognition of Rich's eminence has come only after numerous spasms of hot debate. But from our vantage point of the mid-1990s, we can now see that her personal, poetic transformation may have been the most startling of any poet of the last half-century. Her first volume, *A Change of World*, selected by W. H. Auden for the Yale Younger Poets Prize for 1951, was a collection of formal poems suggesting the influence of Frost, Stevens, and Auden himself. Though highly accomplished, the poems gave little evidence of Rich's potential for innovation, her eventual break with tradition. In an important essay written twenty years later, Rich reconsidered these poems: "I'm startled because beneath the conscious craft are glimpses of the split I even then experienced between the girl who wrote poems, who defined herself in writing poems, and the girl who was to define herself by her relationships with men. . . . In those years formalism was part of the strategy—like asbestos gloves, it allowed me to handle materials I couldn't pick up bare-handed."[32] The poet's dissatisfaction also extends to the poems of her second book, *The Diamond Cutters and Other Poems* (1955); though the poems are excellent Frostian narratives of domesticity, Rich sees them as "mere exercises for poems I hadn't written."

So much for apprenticeship. With *Snapshots of a Daughter-in-Law* (1963), Rich righted her course, becoming over the next thirty years our most important feminist poet, and one of the movement's most perceptive essayists. Her mature vision regards *craft* as a barrier between the individual and experience, between women and the life of freedom that tradition refuses them. These violent free-verse poems attack our inherited views of history, time, even literature itself. By the 1970s, Rich's long, aggressive poems expanded in attempts to represent the struggles of oppressed women of color, and by extension all women suffering economic oppression. Never a mere polemicist, Rich in her later poems has fluctuated widely between provocative meditation and scorching anger. This fascinating high-wire act might best be observed in one volume in *Diving into the Wreck* (1973), which received the National Book Award the following year. Though the title poem is well crafted and symbolically explores the unconscious, other poems celebrate feminist anger and attack male violence.

Throughout the last two decades, reading Rich has proved a far from comfortable experience, especially for men. Always challenging, she confronts not only stereotypes of male dominance and more malignant forms of male oppression, she also forces us to examine anew our moral conduct. This last challenge transcends the crucial world of the feminist movement, extending the discussion to the wider world of universal experience. In her sequence "Contradictions: Tracking Poems" (from *Your Native Land, Your Life,* 1986), Rich meditates on history and process, coming repeatedly to the necessity to transcend dogma:

> *He slammed his hand across my face   and I*
> *let him do that until   I stopped letting him do it*
> *so I'm in for life.*
>
> *. . . he kept saying I was crazy, he'd lock me up*
> *until I went to Women's Lib and they*
> *told me he'd been abusing me as much*
> *as if he'd hit me: emotional abuse.*
> *They told me how to answer back.   That I could*
> *answer back.   But my brother-in-law's a shrink*
> *with the State.   I have to watch my step.*
> *If I stay just within bounds they can't come and get me.*
> *Women's Lib taught me the words to say*
> *to remind myself and him I'm a person with rights*
> *like anyone.   But answering back's no answer.*

Set in italics to distinguish the character's confession from the observations of the narrator, the segment's prosody is skeletal at its most complex. The space after line 3 imposes a stanzaic appearance on the page; the fourteen lines echo the form of the sonnet; the additional spaces inserted in lines 1, 2, 7, 8, 9, 10, and 14 establish a visual balance, while at the same time a spare parallelism creates a similar aural, echoing balance. This is very much the prosody of typography, prosody of the printed page and the reading platform. Such concreteness is appropriate when one considers that Rich believes poetry, pain, truth, and solutions come from the body, not from history, culture, and the patterns of tradition.

This compositional pattern allows for great flexibility. As the longer meditations found in Rich's *An Atlas of the Difficult World* (1991) demonstrate, it is the poet's mature expression at last—unadorned, political and passionate, and personal. As Harriet Davidson observed, "Her perspective is simultaneously inside a history and culture and outside of it; she wants to change prevailing histories and representations while she is constantly critiquing even her language of change. Her vision is always a split one, inside and outside at once, the assimilated Jew, the Southerner/Northerner, the wife/lesbian."[33]

Denise Levertov's first book, *The Double Image* (1946), is mostly written in traditional patterns. After that, her poems relax into less formal constructions that invite comparison to the mature poetry of Creeley and Robert Duncan, contemporaries Levertov greatly admires. But one discovers in Levertov's best work, as in the poems of many writers of her generation, the shadows of traditional, guiding forms. These shadows are well suited to Levertov's subjects, which are consistently presented as intriguing puzzles of the domestic and the spiritual. In her essay "Levertov and the Poetry of Politics," Sandra Gilbert elaborates:

> For Levertov, the ancient female tasks of keeping and cleaning, sewing and baking, loving and rearing, often become jobs as sacred as the apparently humdrum task of spinning the prayer wheel in the archaic temple—which is not to say that she is the "Dear Heloise" of poetry but rather that she is a sort of Rilke of domesticity, turning her talent for what the German poet called *einsehen* ("in seeing") toward those supposedly mundane but really central occupations which bring order out of the chaos of dailiness. Whether gathering rebellious laundry or stirring holy grains, she means to invest her housework (and her spouse's) with meaning, and she is often awestruck by its implications.[34]

Levertov's "free" prosody consists largely of repetition—of words, phrases, and line units. In "The Dog of Art" repeated words and their echoes ("dog," "sharp," "bright") create a wraparound effect that proves to be a capable alternative to conventional stanzas and rhyme.

> That dog with daisies for eyes
> who flashes forth

> flame of his very self at every bark
> is the Dog of Art.
> Worked in wool, his blind eyes
> look inward to caverns and jewels
> which they see perfectly,
> and his wife
> measures forth the treasure
> in music sharp and loud,
> sharp and bright,
> bright flaming barks,
> and growling smoky soft, the Dog
> of Art turns to the world
> the quietness of his eyes.

The two stresses of lines 2, 4, 8, and 11 harness the longer lines, restricting their tendency to open up the poem and dissipate its compact tension. When Levertov's poems succeed, they do so because she manages to negotiate such prosodic reconciliations between expansive and private uses of language and examinations of life.

⅜ VIII. *New York Poets and the Beats: Frank O'Hara, Allen Ginsberg, John Ashbery*

Yet another kind of poetry emerged in the 1950s, a poetry inspired by urban life and influenced by modern and pop art. Originally surfacing in New York, it quickly appeared in major cities throughout the country, announcing itself in opposition to the prevailing literary winds. This was a poetry that sought to break down literary and social barriers; in some ways it predicted the coming of the Beats, as well as the Language poets decades later.

Frank O'Hara published six volumes of poems between 1952 and 1965, when he was run over by a dune buggy on Fire Island. A prominent member of this new school of poetry with James Schuyler, John Ashbery, Kenneth Koch, and others, O'Hara debunked the notion that we must enter the House of Poetry with hands clasped and heads bowed in supplication. He insisted that poetry was an amusement, though not suited to everyone. In an afterword to his *Collected Poems* (1971) he wrote, "if they don't need poetry bully for them. I like the movies, too." Following the example of Whitman, Crane, and Williams (the only American poets he thought better than the movies), O'Hara eschewed abstraction and philosophy in the writing of his poems. An art critic, he claimed to have been inspired by painters like Willem de Kooning and Jackson Pollock, but many of his straightforward descriptions, especially of Manhattan, seem to have more in common with the world of pop art. The best of O'Hara's poetry is refreshingly direct, ingratiating, and witty. The couplets of "Poem" pound with the insistence of enjambment and three emphatic beats per line:

> At night Chinamen jump
> on Asia with a thump
>
> while in our willful way
> we, in secret, play . . .
>
> Chinese rhythms beat
> through us in our heat . . .
>
> we couple in the grace
> of that mysterious race.

More typical of O'Hara's method is his well-known "The Day Lady Died," an homage to Billie Holiday:

> It is 12:20 in New York a Friday
> three days after Bastille day, yes
> it is 1959 and I go get a shoeshine . . .
>
> I walk up the muggy street beginning to sun
> and have a hamburger and a malted and buy
> an ugly *New World Writing* to see what the poets
> in Ghana are doing these days.

Certainly the prosody of these opening stanzas must be described in terms of units of breath packed with details of specificity and the mundane. It is O'Hara's balancing of these details that imposes shape on the poem's material. Subject, tone, and pacing are manipulated so that we do not realize the poem's full emotional impact until the closing stanza:

and I am sweating a lot by now and thinking of
leaning on the john door in the 5 Spot
while she whispered a song along the keyboard
to Mal Waldron and everyone and I stopped breathing.

Much of O'Hara seems simple, yet that is deceptive. There is no denying the energy and excitement of his best work.

Allen Ginsberg, born in Newark, New Jersey, enrolled at Columbia University at the age of seventeen. There he met Jack Kerouac, Lucien Carr, John Clellon Holmes, and other young people bent on discovering and experiencing an American equivalent of Bohemia. By the mid-1950s everyone would know them as the leaders of the Beat movement. The Beats aimed for the raw center of life. They admired outsiders, rebels, those who broke the law. They appropriated expressions from urban African-American culture, promoted the genius of jazz, and experimented with drugs. In every way they intended to stand out—and separate from—the norms of the Eisenhower 1950s. An unusual number of the Beats had ambitions to be writers. Ginsberg was one of these, and in pursuit of this goal he outdistanced all of his peers.

He began as a writer of verses that woodenly imitated Wyatt and Donne. Under the influence of early mentors William Burroughs, William Carlos Williams, and, later, Kenneth Rexroth, Ginsberg learned to follow the examples of Williams, Whitman, and William Blake, loosening and elongating his line, reducing abstractions, and admitting any and all subjects into his verse. After Columbia suspended him, Ginsberg eventually traveled to San Francisco where Lawrence Ferlinghetti published "Howl" in his Pocket Poets Series. On October 13, 1955, Ginsberg read the poem at Gallery Six, formerly a car repair shop. No reading or poem has ever had such an immediate impact on the literary landscape.

"Howl" is arguably the most important American poem of the second half of the twentieth century. A chronicle of the darker side of the 1950s, the poem attempts to emulate in its prosody the poet's feverish emotional state:

I saw the best minds of my generation destroyed by madness,
    starving hysterical naked,

dragging themselves through the negro streets at dawn
  looking for an angry fix,
angelheaded hipsters burning for the ancient heavenly
    connection to the starry dynamo in the machinery
  of night,
who poverty and tatters and hollow-eyed and high
    sat up smoking in the supernatural darkness of
  cold-water flats floating across the tops of cities
  contemplating jazz,
who bared their brains to Heaven under the El and saw
  Mohammedan angels staggering on tenement
  roofs illuminated,
who passed through universities with radiant cool eyes
  hallucinating Arkansas and Blake-light tragedy
  among the scholars of war,
who were expelled from the academies for crazy &
  publishing obscene odes on the windows of the
  skull,
who cowered in unshaven rooms in underwear, burning
  their money in wastebaskets and listening to
  the Terror through the wall,
who got busted in their public beards returning through
  Laredo with a belt of marijuana for New York,
who ate fire in paint hotels or drank turpentine in
  Paradise Alley, death, or purgatoried their
  torsos night after night
with dreams, with drugs, with waking nightmares,
  alcohol and cock and endless balls.

The long lines alternately pound and race on, often barely pausing
for breath. Prepositional phrases and lists are piled on, yet harnessed
by the repetitive pronoun, which sets up a haunting, reassuring ca-
dence. Alliteration ("angel*h*eaded hipsters," "heavenly"; "dreams,"
"drugs") within lines, and liberal use of parallelism throughout the
poem, also prevents the language from flying off, dissolving into un-
structured prose. "Howl," in fact, is an inspired adaptation of Whit-
man's prosody, though its tenor, reflecting the time in which it was
written, lacks Whitman's optimism. Yet it opened doors to waves of
experimental writing (a spirit that is with us to this day) and attracted
an audience that had previously turned a deaf ear to poetry.

For the next ten years Ginsberg's remarkable fame grew as he traveled widely, lectured on college campuses, and continued to write his new poetry. "Kaddish" (1961), his long elegy for his mother, is an excellent example and successor to "Howl." But by the mid-1970s, Ginsberg seemed almost to lose interest in poetry. His manic travel schedule seemed only to intensify; his new poems read more and more like self-parodies of his earlier, powerful work. In the 1980s Ginsberg accepted an academic chair. The Outsider had voluntarily joined the Insiders for keeps.

John Ashbery, born in 1927 in Rochester, New York, graduated from Harvard in 1949. He attended graduate school at Columbia University, then went to Paris as a Fulbright Scholar in 1955. While in France he wrote art criticism for the *New York Herald Tribune*. Ashbery remained in France for ten years, writing criticism, plays, and poetry. In 1956 W. H. Auden selected *Some Trees* for the Yale Series of Younger Poets. Linked with the New York poets, Ashbery eventually became that movement's most celebrated, influential member. This is somewhat puzzling because Ashbery's poems usually prove to be impenetrable. Perhaps the academy's infatuation with *the difficult* accounts for their popularity. Ashbery's poems, more than those of his peers, can lend themselves to endless analysis because one can never quite be sure what he is talking about.

From his mentors, Auden and Stevens, Ashbery begins with a love of music, yet early on he jettisons any real commitment to making sense. His is an indirect communication, a shrouded persuasion. Indulging a fondness for unusual, surreal imagery, Ashbery hopes to approximate in verse the actual world of dreams. Thus the connections of our waking lives consistently fall away:

> The boy took out his own forehead.
> His girlfriend's head was a green bag
> Of narcissus stems. "Ok you win
> But meet me anyway at Cohen's Drug Store
>
> In 22 minutes." What a marvel is ancient man!
> Under the tulip roots he has figured out a way
>   to be a religious animal
> And would be a mathematician. But where in
>   unsuitable heaven

> Can he get the heat that will make him grow?
>   "How Much Longer Will I Be Able
>   to Inhale the Divine Sepulcher . . ."

Syntax generates the rhythm of this prosody, balancing surreal images, accommodating abundant substitutions that may see as many as ten stresses suddenly crammed into a line (as in line 6 above). The breaking of the material into quatrains seems an afterthought, an effort, perhaps, to provide some distance between the lines and prose itself. In later, longer work Ashbery will shake off even this restraint. Pieces like "Description of a Masque" are made up of pages and pages of paragraphs. Other poems, like "A Wave," ostensibly arranged in stanzas of irregular length, could just as easily be reshuffled and presented as paragraphs:

> One idea is enough to organize a life and project it
> Into unusual but viable forms, but many ideas merely
> Lead one thither into a morass of their own good intentions.
> Think how many the average person has during the course
>   of a day, or night,
> So that they become a luminous backdrop to ever-repeated
> Gestures, having no life of their own, but only echoing
> The suspicions of their possessor. It's fun to scratch
>   around
> And maybe come up with something.

The heavily enjambed language jerks back and forth between thoughtful rhetoric and conversational asides. It may be that we have never seen a prosody so thoroughly taking shape out of the poet's habits of thought. If Ashbery's gift is essentially a small, lyric one—and we believe that it is—then he often succeeds in camouflaging the fact with audacious manipulation of syntax and mannered, rhetorical flourishes. We have said that the poetry strongly appeals to many scholars; it is also a seductive model for younger poets who are tentative with subjects and uncertain about what they may really have to say.

❧ IX. *Louis Simpson, Philip Levine, Donald Hall, Maxine Kumin*

Something of a split vision lies behind the life and considerable output of Louis Simpson. The life's particulars are fascinating in and of themselves. Born in Jamaica (1923) to an influential lawyer and Russian mother, Simpson came to America at age seventeen. He studied at Columbia University both before and after World War II. During the war he served with the 101st Airborne Division in France, Belgium, Holland, and Germany. Eventually, he returned to Paris for a time, attending university there. On his return to the States, Simpson worked in publishing in New York, then pursued an academic career (though not as a teacher of writing) in Berkeley and New York. Simpson published his first book of poetry, *The Arrivistes: Poems 1940–1949,* while still in Paris. It is very much a book of beginnings—early impressions of America, of the war and the reconstructed life after it, of the poet's role in that life. Whitman's influence touches the writing here:

> Far from your crumpled mountains, plains that vultures ponder,
> White gulches wounded to pythons from gunshot of thunder:
>> What should I sing in a city of stone,
>> Drawing the bow across skull, across bone?
>
>>>>> "Jamaica"

Yet even within traditional structures Simpson achieves an early originality in the expression of personal experience that transcends the personal.

> Trees in the old days used to stand
> And shape a shady lane
> Where lovers wandered hand in hand
> Who came from Carentan.
>
> This was the shining green canal
> Where we came two by two
> Walking at combat-interval.
> Such trees we never knew.
>
>>>> "Carentan O Carentan"

The perfectly executed four-three alternating pattern, the alliterative gloss, and deftly placed trochaic substitutions evoke the pastoral elegance of the scene. Not until line 7 do we realize that this promising love poem is entirely something else. Later, the narrator wounded by sniper fire, the poem veers from its sublime, impersonal cadence to one of reassurance and fatal resignation.

> Everything's all right, Mother,
> Everyone gets the same
> At one time or another.
> It's all in the game.

The poem's third tonal shift occurs with the plaintive questioning and summing up of the final four quatrains:

> Tell me, Master-Sergeant,
> The way to turn and shoot.
> But the Sergeant's silent
> That taught me how to do it.
>
> O Captain, show us quickly
> Our place upon the map.
> But the Captain's sickly
> And taking a long nap.
>
> Lieutenant, what's my duty,
> My place in the platoon?
> He too's a sleeping beauty,
> Charmed by that strange tune.
>
> Carentan O Carentan
> Before we met with you
> We never yet had lost a man
> Or known what death could do.

We note the trochaic unity and swiftness of "But the Sergeant's silent," the inspired rhyme ("shoot"/"do it"), the appropriate finality of the sentiment. We are also reminded of the resonance an unbearable situation can release when its expression is contained in a tightly controlled, formal structure. "Carentan O Carentan" and Simpson's long pentameter piece, "The Runner" (from *A Dream of Governors*, 1959), represent both Simpson's formal verse at its best and the finest poetry we have about World War II.

After establishing himself as a writer of formal lyric, Simpson changed the direction of his verse (as did others of his generation), abandoning traditional patterns for freer forms. This decision coincided with an understanding of his subjects. Simpson speaks of this revelation in his autobiography:

> They married and lived in houses; they had children, drove cars, went to work, shopped in supermarkets, and watched TV. Poetry hardly ever spoke of this . . . it did not speak of such lives except with irony and contempt. But I was one of those people . . . the only thing that made me different was being a writer. I wanted to speak of the life I had and tell stories about the men and women I knew. The stories would be in verse, for this was what I enjoyed . . . the rhythm of the line. . . . There was no precedent for the kind of poetry I wanted to write. Some years ago I had broken with rhyme and meter and learned to write in free form. Now I discarded the traditional ornaments of language, especially metaphors. I wanted to render the thing itself exactly as it happened. I discovered what writers of novels and short stories knew: if you had a point of view everything seemed to fall into place and move. Therefore the hard work had to be done on myself, understanding what I felt and what I wanted to say. Then I could tell a story and it could be believed.[35]

The story Simpson tells, beginning with the Pulitzer Prize–winning *At the End of the Open Road* (1963), is the American experience unadorned. At times sardonic, always direct whether writing about life in the suburbs or his Jewish and colonial heritage, Simpson has created a style like nobody else's. The deceptive simplicity of "Vandergast and the Girl," "A Friend of the Family," "The Psyche of Riverside Drive," "Sway," "Unfinished Life," "Armidale," the ten-part "The Previous Tenant," and many other poems rival the difficult simplicity of Hemingway's signature prose. In the lives of Simpson's characters there is also the faint echo of Robinson's people, though Simpson's are more believable. In "The Previous Tenant" the narrator moves into new digs. Deciding what to do with some of his predecessor's belongings, the landlord tells the new tenant the story of the old one, a doctor whose infidelity wrecks his marriage. Through most of the poem the narrator, himself a writer, imagines the exchanges and dramas, the minute particulars of the earlier tenant's life. A degree of identification is inevitable, and it comes most memorably when the narrator discovers, and takes notes on, a packet of letters from the woman notoriously involved with the doctor. At last the doctor appears with a friend to pick up his things. The segment is understated, restrained:

> They drove away.
> She waved. He looked straight ahead.
> It appeared he was back on the track
> once more, after his derailment.
> With a woman of the right kind at his side
> to give him a nudge. "Say thanks!"

To speak of the prosody of such writing is to speak of pared-down lines that consistently say the right, accurate thing. It is the prosody of perfectly manipulated grammar and pacing. There is nothing else quite like it in our verse.

In noting Philip Levine's use of the conditional tense throughout his poetry, Mark Jarman defines its charm: "it blankets reality with possibilities. For this to work one must share Levine's conviction, tempered by his inimitable humor, that to say nothing is, in fact, to say something, to deny is the only way to affirm."[36] A second aspect of Levine's style is the expression of anger. The tapping of the repeated pronoun drum-beats these cadences into memory:

> The houses are angry because they're watched.
> A soldier wants to talk with God
> but his mouth fills with lost tags.
>
> The clouds have seen it all, in the dark
> they pass over the graves of the forgotten
> and they don't cry or whisper.
>
> They should be punished every morning,
> they should be bitten and boiled like spoons.
>
> > "Clouds"

We can imagine Levine saying the same thing about words themselves, for he has crafted poems much in the way one might force a viscous fluid through a strainer—all that coagulates and obscures finds itself blocked out, jammed, left behind. What emerges in the new medium, poetry, is the reordering of reality itself. In the early poems of his first book, *Not This Pig* (1963), the reordering often occurs in surreal syllabics:

> It's wonderful how I jog
> on four honed-down ivory toes
> my massive buttocks slipping
> like oiled parts with each light step.
>
> > "Animals Are Passing from Our Lives"

Later, as in the poems of *They Feed The Lion* (1972), the surrealism becomes more brazen, more open, in defiant challenge to authority. Forged to a great extent by his early factory years in Detroit, Levine writes often about the downtrodden, dispossessed, underpaid, ignored laborers who make things work. As his elastic line becomes freer, at times longer and at times more spare, he discovers the sympathetic possibilities of narrative, to which he has turned with greater frequency in more recent work. One perceives the method in the title poem of *Sweet Will* (1985):

> The man who stood beside me
> 34 years ago this night fell
> on to the concrete, oily floor
> of Detroit Transmission, and we
> stepped carefully over him until
> he wakened and went back to his press.

> It was Friday night, and the others
> told me that every Friday he drank
> more than he could hold and fell
> and he wasn't any dumber for it
> so just let him get up at his
> own sweet will or he'll hit you.

> "At his own sweet will," was just
> what the old black man said to me,
> and he smiled the smile of one
> who is still surprised that dawn
> graying the cracked and broken windows
> could start us all singing in the cold.

We note the fine-tuned, balanced grammar, the repetition and spo-radic, internal rhymes, the echoing, syllabic pattern of earlier work. Levine's influential and seductive style builds up from this simple framework. Though we may detect more artifice here than, say, in Louis Simpson's verse, the result is often the same—an open, acces-sible verse created from the elements of actual life.

Donald Hall also makes the long journey from formal poems to free verse. Even more than his contemporaries, he has gone back and forth with ever-increasing skill. It seems odd, yet somehow true, to say that in a generation that includes Ginsberg, Hall may be the most restless maker of verses. Hall's early training pointed toward a high-level, mainstream academic career. Though a graduate of Harvard and Ox-ford, editor with Robert Pack and Louis Simpson of the influential anthology *New Poets of England and America* (1957), and a professor for many years at the University of Michigan, Hall eventually quit teaching to return to his ancestral farmhouse in New Hampshire and devote his time to writing. His academic experience, and his subsequent experi-ence outside the academy, gives him unusual authority as a critic of poetry. Hall is a generous though exacting reviewer, an author of plays, stories, and books for children, an editor of widely adopted composi-tion and literature textbooks, and a writer of countless articles on subjects ranging from New England country life to baseball. His first book of poems, *Exiles and Marriages* (1955), was awarded the Lamont Prize. The book introduces readers to Hall's wit (as in "The Lone Ranger") and his interest in formal patterns. "Elegy for Wesley Wells" honors generations past, the rich legacy of the dead.

> The farmer dead, his horse will run to fat,
> Go stiff and lame and whinny from his stall.
> His dogs will whimper through the webby barn,
> Where spiders close his tools in a pale gauze
> And wait for flies. The nervous woodchuck now
> Will waddle plumply through the garden weeds,
> Eating wild peas as if he owned the land,
> And the fat hedgehog pick the apple trees.
> When next October's frosts harden the ground
> And fasten in the year's catastrophe,
> The farm will come undone—
> The farmer dead, and deep in his ploughed earth.

The polished pentameter supports the full weight of the narrator's grief; the shortened line ("The farm will come undone"), in its brevity, stresses the closure of the event that triggers the poem.

This careful, high style sustains the poems of Hall's first two books, but with *A Roof of Tiger Lilies* (1964) Hall's verses relax. With the publication of *The Yellow Room* (1971), the poetry shows the influence of surrealism and the deep image. Many of Hall's peers found this path an end in itself; for Hall, as for Simpson, it proved a diversion on his way to a greater originality. In *Kicking the Leaves* (1978) and *The Happy Man* (1986) that originality blossoms. Louis Simpson has said of these poems: "They are about the changing seasons of human life, the movement from youth to old age and death, the passing of life from one generation to another. They are infused with pity for the living and one might almost say envy of the dead. This is where Hall's peculiar courage comes in . . . Hall presents his heart's affections as if they were holy, and makes them seem so."[37]

> This year the poems came back, when the leaves fell.
> Kicking the leaves, I heard the leaves tell stories,
> remembering, and therefore looking ahead, and building
> the house of dying . . .
>
> Now I leap and fall, exultant, recovering
> from death, on account of death, in accord with the dead.
>
> *Kicking the Leaves*

These measures contain the exuberance and reverence of Whitman at his expansive best. The method gains in power and confidence in the book-length *The One Day* (1988), the new poems in *Old and New Poems* (1990), and *The Museum of Clear Ideas* (1993).

The poems of this last book perhaps best illustrate the great range Hall has mastered in form and content. "Baseball," for instance, is a long meditation divided into nine segments, or *innings;* each inning consists of nine stanzas, with each stanza made up of nine nine-syllable lines. This architectural madness impresses us, finally, as remarkably sane and appropriate. Elsewhere in this collection we discover a brilliant sequence modeled after Horace's first book of odes, and Hall makes inspiring use of syllabic stanzas. The form itself encourages the poet to assume the many shapes of a life. In what could constitute a performance that sums up all of modern life and poetry, Hall appears as husband, lover, betrayer, boozer, patient, academic, rustic, rabble-rouser, statesman, mystic—poet.

> We explore grief's borders, boundaries of mourning
> and lamentation, wild cries and unending tears,
> when the unexpected and unacceptable
> death happens. . . .

> The whole village weeps. Where shall we take our pleasures
> for validation? Houses and farms and hamlets
> mourn her absence . . .

> Or say: All tears
> weep for the weeper.
> The tissue that dries
> our eyes is a clear
> understanding that this
> disappearance we
> complain of will drop
> oblivion's lid
> over us soon enough.

Maxine Kumin's work was often overlooked among the poems of her generation. But as she and her peers approach their seventies, we are impressed by the number of her poems that rank among the best of the period. We are also impressed by the hard-earned wisdom—for lack of a better term—that emanates from the body of her work. Like Louis Simpson and her fellow New Hampshirite, Donald Hall, Kumin's poems have gotten stronger as she has grown older. No doubt most poets, given the option early in life, would choose to follow this Yeatsian model of endurance, and it is unsettling, in reviewing poets' careers, to discover how few actually do. Kumin, Simpson, and Hall are among the lucky few.

Raised in Philadelphia, Maxine Kumin has written eleven books of poetry, numerous books for children, four novels, a book of short stories, a collection of essays and interviews, and a highly regarded memoir, *In Deep: Country Essays* (1988), which is a valuable, illuminating companion to the body of her poetry. The Consultant in Poetry to the Library of Congress in 1981–82, Kumin received the Pulitzer Prize for *New and Selected Poems,* and the Poets' Prize for 1994.

Kumin's early poems focused on questions of identity, especially as defined by relationships within an intense, dynamic family. In a brief comment preceding a selection of her poems in a recent anthology of formal poetry written by women, Kumin has this to say about writing in form:

> The joy of working in form is, for me, the paradoxical freedom form bestows to say the hard truths. Constraints of rhyme and/or meter liberate the poet to confront difficult or painful or elegiac material, often elevating the language to heights unattainable in free verse, to say nothing of the extra music form admits.[38]

These "hard truths" were in evidence from the start. In early volumes she demonstrated superior skill in composing sonnets, and an almost playful quality in poems that seem to spring, in their forms, from nursery rhymes:

> Tight as beans
> in a casserole,
> greenbacks sit
> in the sugar bowl
> in the walk-in pantry
> on the tallest shelf.
> No one pokes there
> but herself.
> No one counts
> rock candy strings
> where basil tickles
> and peppercorn stings.
> The blackbottom skillet
> sizzles and sings:
> *motherwit hands*
> *and honeybun head,*
> *wife in the pantry,*
> *man in bed.*

> "Hearth"

Anapests and trochees so successfully alternate in this swift dimeter that the music created might almost be the subject of the poem itself.

The domestic division implied by the italicized refrain notwithstanding, the rhythm works as if tuned to the insights of children as they grope for explanations of the awesome world they inherit.

Another early poem, "Grace," offers an elder's perspective, through an appeal to the Divine, on how one must live:

> Hens have their gravel; gravel sticks
> The way it should stick, in the craw.
> And stone on stone is tooth
> For grinding raw.
>
> And grinding raw, I learn from this
> To fill my crop the way I should.
> I put down puddingstone
> And find it good.
>
> I find it good to line my gut
> With tidy octagons of grit.
> No loophole and no chink
> Make vents in it.
>
> And in it vents no slime or sludge;
> No losses sluice, no terrors slough.
> *God, give me appetite*
> *for stone enough.*

Each quatrain, through the reduction of stresses from four to two, achieves its own internal movement reflecting greater certainty. The poem circles back on itself through alliterative, taut repetitions, forging the compact, clear expression of a concise philosophy.

Kumin's later work expands in focus, becoming at times more political, and often environmentally aware. The development of this last direction coincided with her move to a New Hampshire farm where, with her husband, she raises horses. This rural life gives depth and grounding to her writing, inspiring memorable verses such as

"Homage to Binsey Poplars," "Bringing Back the Trumpeter Swan," and "Noted in the New York Times," and others about farm work, animals, and endangered species. In a central poem of middle length, "Hay," from her volume *Looking for Luck* (1992), Kumin looks back on her life to see anew important points of departure, and how she arrived:

> Interlude: The summer I was eleven
> I boarded on a dairy farm in Pennsylvania.
> Mornings we rode the ponies bareback
> up through eiderdowns of ground fog,
> up through the strong-armed apple orchard
> that snatched at us no matter how we ducked,
> up to the cows' vasty pasture, hooting and calling
> until they assembled in their secret order
> and we escorted them down to the milking barn
> where each one gravely entered her stanchion.
> There was no pushing or shoving.
> All was as solemn as a Quaker Meeting.

The bedrock meter beneath this stanza, halfway between free and formal verse, is iambic pentameter. Numerous substitutions occur; lines may drop to three stresses ("There was no pushing or shoving"). Kumin's talent for rhyme ("calling," "shoving," "Meeting") and sight rhyme ("orchard," "ducked") is also apparent. The language and rhythm are so direct, the observations so unadorned, that it is as if we are listening to good conversation. Later, we are swept up in sudden revelation as the human animal reaffirms her connection to the other animals, and the world:

> Perhaps in the last great turn of the wheel
> I was some sort of grazing animal.
> Perhaps—trundling hay in my own barn
> tonight and salivating from the sweetness—
> I will be again . . .
>
> Allegiance to the land is tenderness.

Epilogue: New Poets

It is of course early to say with certainty which of the poets born after World War II will endure as we approach a new century, but some general comments and speculation may pertain. The poets we are thinking of are not really young. On average, they are in their mid-forties and have published one to five books of verse. Moreso than in any previous generation, a number of them hold MFAs, reflecting the rise of the business that is graduate writing workshops. Many also write criticism, a fact that sets them apart from the generation of poets immediately preceding them.

There are other differences. Having grown up with the immediate inheritance of the confessional, surrealist, and free-verse poetry of the 1960s and 1970s, much of their own work demonstrates a continual questioning, rather than ready affirmation, of that birthright. Their emerging literary landscape also contains more ethnic diversity than ever before, which in time may help to generate the larger audiences for poetry that poets always seek. And as teaching positions in writing and literature were reduced in the recession of the 1980s, more and more of the poets of this generation took up work outside the academy. Whereas virtually all of their immediate predecessors have enjoyed long careers as teachers, many of the poets discussed in this epilogue work in agriculture, arts administration, business, construction, law, publishing, medicine, and social services, among other professions. Not surprisingly, they seem to be unified on one point in particular: the need to make poetry more relevant to daily life and thereby expand the audience for poetry beyond the standard audience created by the presence of writing programs in the academy.

But that might be the only major point on which they agree. The 1980s proved to be a volatile decade of reassessment in poetry. Writing programs were attacked for insulating poetry within the academy; poets were often criticized for writing only for other poets. Poetry of this sort was modest in length and technical skill, and usually hinged on references, which were often obscure, to the poet's private life. In short, one could accurately say that the dominant poetry of the time was most highly refined in its self-involvement. In that climate African-American, Asian-American, and Chicano poetry emerged in natural opposition to the status quo. Poets such as Rita Dove, Marilyn Nelson Waniek, Elizabeth Alexander, Amy Uyematsu, Maxine Hong Kingston, Rafael Campo, and Sonia Sanchez, among others, not only injected American poetry with new ethnic experience and insight, many also represented and helped to propel the explosion of women writing and publishing poetry.

In a much more obscure yet no less intense reaction, Language poets eschewed subject and audience for language as the *thing* itself. Their spirit of rebellion harkens back to Dada. As their writing primarily lends itself to analysis, they appeal more to scholars than to most writers and readers. Yet because of this analytic appeal, their obscure poems have enjoyed a certain vogue in the academy.

Reactions against the poetic norm were also embodied in the poetry and criticism of poets who sought to restore narrative to verse and revitalize traditional forms. In recent years their efforts have been referred to as a movement, interchangeably the New Narrative or the New Formalism. Yet it would be more accurate to refer to these developments as a resurgence of narrative and a return to form on the part of poets who felt increasingly restricted by the free-verse status quo. Assimilating influences as diverse as Eliot, Robinson, Frost, Jeffers, Stevens, Auden, Bishop, Larkin, Simpson, Hall, May Sarton, and Robert Penn Warren, these poets, through poems, readings, lectures, essays, and reviews revived a healthy (though frequently contentious) dialogue about poetry. Through their efforts the slight, highly personal free-verse poem diminished in significance; the long poem in its various manifestations—narrative, meditation, sequence—experienced a significant revival.

This development in particular should not be overlooked. In the 1960s and 1970s, one would have been hard-pressed to find poems of length (exceeding two pages) in any of the hundreds of literary magazines published throughout the country. Except for George Keithley's seminal book-length poem, *The Donner Party* (1972), books of poetry consisted almost exclusively of short lyrics. By the mid-1980s the situation had changed. It became increasingly unusual to pick up a magazine anywhere and not find a long poem among those published. Frequently, these poems, and many shorter lyrics, made use of traditional form. The subjects of such poems announced a change, too, turning away from mundane chronicles of one's daily life to explore the lives of others, the diverse characters of a larger community.

Andrew Hudgins's flexible pentameter in his book-length sequence *After the Lost War* (1988) carries a haunting portrait of Sidney Lanier's doomed South in the Civil War. In *Manhattan Carnival* (1981) and *City Life* (1991), Frederick Feirstein's clever rhymed couplets expose the frailty, humor, and pathos of a host of manic urban characters. Adapting Robinson Jeffers's long, long line, Mark Jarman in the book-length *Iris* (1992) creates the story of the hard life of a moderately educated Kentucky woman who finds solace in imagining how Jeffers would imagine *her* life. Other notable sequences and book-length poems of the period include Rita Dove's *Thomas and Beulah* (1986), which won the Pulitzer Prize in 1987, and her verse play, *The Darker Face of the Earth* (1994), Jim Daniels's *Punching Out* (1990), Lynn Emanuel's *The Dig* (1993), Frederick Pollack's *The Adventure* (1986), Mary Swander's *Driving the Body Back* (1986), Marilyn Nelson Waniek's *The Homeplace* (1990), Frederick Turner's science fiction epic *The New World* (1985), Robert Pinsky's *An Explanation of America* (1979), Mark Rudman's *Rider* (1995), and Vikram Seth's *The Golden Gate* (1986), which makes use of Pushkin's *Eugene Onegin* stanza through its 309 pages about gay life in the San Francisco Bay area.

Jarman's unlikely prosodic achievement in *Iris* is indicative of the experimental, formal inclinations of the time. In the poem's closing passage Iris completes a twenty-year journey, arriving at Jeffers's fabled stone house by the sea in Carmel, California. The house, now a historical landmark, offers tours to visitors:

Íris held báck a líttle as the párty éntered the smáll hoúse,

In the side garden,

In the full sunlight sweeping Carmel Bay from here to Point

Lobos, a line of iris stood,

Robust, two feet tall, their long petals curling back,

lavender, blue, and deep red-purple—

The ocean's color. Yes. She felt a secret lodge with her,

to keep, and entered the low door,

The house where pain and pleasure had turned to poetry

and stone, and a family had been happy.

We can readily see Jarman's able version of Jeffers's double pen-
tameters at work. Jarman keeps his word choice simple and locks on to
the actual movements and immediate perceptions of his character.
There is little in the way of Jeffers's philosophical speculation in this
poem. Ample substitution creates the variety necessary to sustain such
a line. We note in particular the double Ionic feet ending the first line
above ("entered the small house, in the side garden"), and yet a third
beginning the second line ("In the full sunlight"), and the clustering
of stresses, as in "deep red-purple."

The same agility and formal preoccupation is also present in many
of the period's poems of middle length (four to twenty pages). Note-
worthy examples include Emily Grosholz's "Cypress and Bitter Lau-
rel," Sydney Lea's "The Feud" and "The Blainville Testament," Chase
Twichell's "My Ruby of Lasting Sadness," David Mason's "The Night-
ingales of Andritsena," and Dana Gioia's "The Homecoming."

Gioia and Timothy Steele have also written some of the period's
best formal lyrics (though Gioia does not work exclusively in tradi-
tional form), as well as a good deal of its most influential criticism.
Gioia's first collection of essays, *Can Poetry Matter?* (1993), and Steele's
own study, *Missing Measures* (1990), of the prosodic revolution sparked
by Modernism are seminal texts for anyone who would understand
this generation's serious concerns. The roots of their own lyrics may be
traced to a host of influences including Auden, Larkin, Bishop, Hecht,
and Wilbur. Steele's method and meditative bent can be observed in
the opening stanza of his "Three Notes toward Definitions":

Culture. It's an ingredient used in making
Pineapple yogurt, Gothic cathedrals.
It's Isaac Newton's experiments with prisms—
Its opposite being, one supposes,
Fried chicken TV dinners, plastic roses,
Confessional novels brimming over
With soul and solecisms.

A supple variation of stresses from line to line (five to four to three) and emphatic end rhyme comprise the strengths of this verse.

In contrast, Gioia's iambic pentameter flows smoothly, almost without interruption:

The great offensive in the East began
this morning, as our forces overran
the enemy's positions. Total victory
is now expected within weeks! The Spring
Youth Festival will be delayed by an
impromptu demonstration of support.
Arrests continue at the Ministry.
The weekly coffee ration will remain
at sixty grams. More news in half an hour.

"News from Nineteen Eighty-Four"

At first glance there is seemingly little in the way of prosodic variety. But a closer look reveals the risky extra syllable concluding line 3. We also note the poet's method of fracturing a metrical unit with a caesura ("morning, as"; "positions. Total"). Such devices elevate the meter out of the realm of the ordinary.

Gjertrud Schnackenberg's pentameter in this excerpt from "Love Letters" is even more emphatic, befitting the breezy nature of her subject:

I don't love you because you're good at rhymes,
And not because I think you're not-so-dumb,
I don't love you because you make me come
And come and come innumerable times,
And not for your romantic overcoats,
And not because our friends all say I should,
And not because we wouldn't or we would
Be or not be at one another's throats,
And not because your accent thrills my ear—
Last night you said not "sever" but "severe,"
But then "severe" describes the act "to sever"—
I love you for no reason whatsoever.

Despite the many end stops, these lines create ever more speed and fun as they accumulate. In three books, Schnackenberg has also proved herself to be a master of internal and end rhyme.

In contrast, Molly Peacock's pared-down stresses seem urgent in their compression, and grim in substance:

DREAM COME TRUE
The little girl is shy.
She wonders why
on tiptoes, like paws,
there are laws

such as these:
she will never please
however much
she curtsies, never touch

except the dead head
she touches now and
springs away from, knocking
the flowers, ripping her stocking

on the casket that is
so much higher than she is.
She gets nothing
because there is nothing

but pale flowers on a waxed floor,
no more "Stop that!" then no more.

Her father who lies there
will be her nightmare.

The brevity and breathless enjambment of these lines remind one
of Dickinson; their tone echoes Dickinson and Sylvia Plath. Even so,
Peacock puts her own stamp on the material. In general, she avoids
Dickinson's occasional fondness for abstract thought. She also re-
fuses to overdramatize her subject, as Plath often did. The keys to
Peacock's prosody, and to her approach to subject, are clarity and
restraint. The dominant dimeter of the lines above effectively shrinks
the time frame within the poem and assigns great pressure and impor-
tance to the end rhymes. Even the use of repeated words for rhyme
and emphasis in the fourth stanza is shrewdly calculated and perfectly
executed, endowing the poem with greater resonance. Like Robert
Creeley, Peacock appears to be a miniaturist, but her range is wide and
compelling.

The same may be said of the better poems produced throughout
this generation of writers. For further examples of the variety to be
found there, we note the breadth of vision in Wyatt Prunty's work, the
pointed humor in much of Thomas M. Disch's poems; the generation
even includes a master satirist, R. S. Gwynn (we especially refer readers
to his long poem, "The Narcissiad"). These poets, like many of their
peers, compose almost exclusively in traditional forms. Yet it is impor-
tant to keep in mind that the period's better writers recognize few
boundaries, moving easily between free verse and formalism, and of-
ten inhabiting an interesting middle ground made up of free verse
and formal characteristics. Poets Bruce Bawer and David Dooley, in
their early work, are notable for such dexterity, as are more established
poets like Jane Kenyon and Liam Rector.

Kenyon's verse, though frequently in free forms, often echoes the
technical restraint of traditional patterns:

LET EVENING COME

Let the light of late afternoon
shine through chinks in the barn, moving
up the bales as the sun moves down.

Let the cricket take up chafing
as a woman takes up her needles
and her yarn. Let evening come.

> Let dew collect on the hoe abandoned
> in long grass. Let the stars appear
> and the moon disclose her silver horn.
>
> Let the fox go back to its sandy den.
> Let the wind die down. Let the shed
> go black inside. Let evening come.
>
> To the bottle in the ditch, to the scoop
> in the oats, to air in the lung
> let evening come.
>
> Let it come, as it will, and don't
> be afraid. God does not leave us
> comfortless, so let evening come.

Syntax defines the rhythm, repetition establishes the pattern of recurrence in both form and subject. Kenyon's tercets waste not a unit of sound (or sense) in this epiphany so perfectly balanced between free and formal concerns.

Liam Rector works a similar vein, though his verse—by way of Eliot and Roethke—is even more liable to cast in dramatic lighting the potential for give-and-take between free and formal verse.

> WHERE YOU GET OFF
> And where do you get off, calling me the Hyacinth Girl? Your
> taken apartment is burning; you worry that you will
>   inherit. I
> send all my funds to apartment. Your "career" has turned
>   banal;
> your apartment is burning. You smoked your first cigarette
>   in
> condemned building . . .

Rector deftly echoes the sestina and villanelle, tightening his long, prosy lines by dropping key connectives (*the*, for example) and making liberal use of repetition, alliteration, and internal rhyme:

> You always knew you'd inherit. She stares at you now,
>   staring

banal. She inherits the ground of your building—that girl
  stands
apart now, burning. Partly what she said in apartment
  was that
she was the Hyacinth Girl.

When born, you inherit what's burning. In this case,
  the banal
apartment—the building you did with that girl.

As many have pointed out, the free-verse revolution has come and gone. Though some insist on casting debates about the merits of free and formal verse in sociological and political terms, these new writers seem to have come to terms with such questions in a markedly different way. They appear to share a general agreement that both the free-verse revolution and the recent resurgence of narrative and form have expanded the possibilities for poetry. We appear to have arrived at a historical point of demarcation, a point at which polemics end and a renewed understanding and appreciation of poems and their diverse prosodies begin.

Notes

❮● *Notes to the Prologue: The Moon through the Trees*

1. Yvor Winters, *The Function of Criticism* (Denver, 1957), p. 99.
2. Robert Hillyer, *In Pursuit of Poetry* (New York, 1960), p. 34.
3. Herbert J. C. Grierson, *Metaphysical Lyrics and Poems* (New York, 1959), p. xxiv.
4. Sydney Lanier, *The Science of English Verse*, vol. 2 of *Works* (Baltimore, 1945), p. 135.
5. George Saintsbury, *A History of English Prosody* (London, 1906), 1:74.
6. Timothy Steele, *Missing Measures* (Fayetteville, Ark., 1990).
7. Paul Fussell, *Poetic Meter and Poetic Form* (New York, 1965).
8. Philip Dacey and David Jauss, eds., *Strong Measures* (New York, 1986).
9. W. K. Wimsatt, Jr., and Monroe C. Beardsley, "The Concept of Meter: An Exercise in Abstraction," *PMLA* 74 (1959): 588.

❮● *Notes to Chapter I: Prosody as Rhythmic Cognition*

1. Victor Zuckerkandl, *Sound and Symbol* (New York, 1956), p. 200.
2. Yvor Winters, *In Defense of Reason* (Denver, 1957), p. 546.
3. This is not a scansion of the line, but an attempt to analyze an important musical element, rate, or tempo.
4. Seymour Chatman, in *Style and Language,* ed. Thomas A. Sebeok (Cambridge, Mass., 1960), p. 151.
5. That horses can dance to music and dogs "count," notwithstanding. Human symbolic activity involves both physical response to the symbol and the ability to communicate the symbol's complex meanings. A horse can dance to music; it cannot tell us whether it prefers Beethoven to rap.
6. The term belongs to D. W. Prall; see his *Aesthetic Analysis* (New York, 1936), and Susanne K. Langer's *Feeling and Form* (New York, 1953), esp. pp. 54–58.
7. Story has it that the young men at Oxford paraded around the quad to the meter of *Atalanta in Calydon.*

8. See Susanne K. Langer's *Philosophy in a New Key* (New York, 1948), pp. 93–95, 201.

9. T. S. Eliot, *On Poetry and Poets* (New York, 1957), p. 32.

❧ Notes to Chapter II: The Scansion of the English Meters

1. *Poems of Gerard Manley Hopkins*, 2d ed. (London, 1930), p. 5.

2. See Otto Jespersen's "Notes on Metre," in his *Linguistica* (Copenhagen, 1933), pp. 249–74. This article appeared originally in 1900.

3. René Wellek and Austin Warren, *Theory of Literature* (New York, 1949), p.159.

4. *Poetical Works of Robert Bridges*, 2d ed. (London, 1953), p. 408.

5. Rhythmic movement here recalls Meredith's prosodic curiosity, *Love in the Valley*.

6. Robert Bridges, *Milton's Prosody*, 2d ed. (Oxford, 1921), p. 87.

❧ Notes to Chapter III: Modern Poetry in the Metrical Tradition

1. Uncommon, that is, to first-rate poetry. We have curiosities tender or tedious, such as Hood's "Bridge of Sighs" and "The Charge of the Light Brigade."

2. W. B. Yeats, *Essays and Introductions* (New York, 1961), p. 163.

3. Susanne K. Langer, *Philosophy in a New Key* (New York, 1948), p. 198.

4. I. A. Richards, *Practical Criticism* (New York, 1948), p. 198.

5. Robert Bridges, "Humdrum and Harum Scarum: A Lecture on Free Verse," *Collected Essays, Papers, Etc.,* vol. 2 (London, 1928), pp. 54–55.

6. Albert Guérard, *Robert Bridges* (Cambridge, Mass., 1942), p. 269.

7. Ibid., app. A, pp. 269–84.

8. Robert Bridges, *Milton's Prosody*, 2d ed. (Oxford, 1921), pp. 92–105.

9. Guérard, *Robert Bridges*, pp. 276–77.

10. Robert Bridges, *Collected Essays, Papers, Etc.,* vol. 15 (London, 1933), pp. 70–71n.

11. Ibid., p. 91.

12. Ibid., p. 90.

13. Robert Bridges, *The Testament of Beauty*, 2. 204–10. We have added the initial capitals and regularized Bridges's purified spelling.

14. Robert Bridges, "Wintry Delights," pp. 405–8.

15. See W. J. Stone's "Classical Metres in English Verse." Bridges includes Stone's treatise as an appendix to the first edition of *Milton's Prosody* (Oxford, 1901), pp. 113–64.

16. *Collected Poems of Edwin Muir* (New York, 1957), p. 13.

17. John Crowe Ransom, "The Strange Music of English Verse," *Kenyon Review* 18, no. 3 (summer 1956): 474.

18. John Crowe Ransom, "Criticism as Pure Speculation," in *The Intent of the Critic*, ed. Donald A. Stauffer (Princeton, 1941), pp. 110–11.

19. Ibid, p. 12.

20. John Crowe Ransom, *The New Criticism* (Norfolk, Conn., 1941), p. 259.

21. Ransom, "Criticism as Pure Speculation," p. 104.

22. John Crowe Ransom, "The Inorganic Muses," *Kenyon Review* 5, no. 2 (spring 1943): 474.

23. *The New Criticism*, p. 234.

24. See Ransom's draft of the "metrical code" in "Strange Music," p. 471.

25. Ransom, "Strange Music," p. 470.

26. Ibid.

27. Ibid.

28. Ibid., p. 466.

29. Arnold Stein, "A Note on Meter," *Kenyon Review* 18, no. 3 (summer, 1956): 451–60.

30. Ransom, "Strange Music," p. 473.

☙ Notes to Chapter IV: Nineteenth-Century Precursors

1. Wylie Sypher, *Rococo to Cubism in Art and Literature* (New York, 1960), p. 150.

2. George Saintsbury, *A History of English Prosody* (London, 1906), 3:513.

3. See Eliot's introduction to Pound's *Selected Poems* (London, 1928), pp. 6 ff.

4. Robert Graves, *The Crowning Privilege* (New York, 1956), p. 135.

5. We find good descriptive treatment in Gay Wilson Allen's *American Prosody* (New York, 1935); however, Professor Allen makes no attempt to search theoretical grounds.

6. See Donald Davie's *Articulate Energy*, pp. 85–91.

7. Ibid., p. 129.

8. Thomas H. Johnson, "The Vision and Veto of Emily Dickinson," *Final Harvest* (Boston, 1961), p. xi.

9. Saintsbury, *History of English Prosody*, 3:391.

10. Paull F. Baum, "Sprung Rhythm," *PMLA*, 74 (1959): 424.

11. Yvor Winters, *In Defense of Reason* (Denver, 1957), p. 110.

12. *The Letters of Gerard Manley Hopkins to Robert Bridges*, ed. C. C. Abbott (London, 1935), p. 246.

13. James Joyce, *Finnegans Wake* (New York, 1939), pp. 215–16.

☙ Notes to Chapter V: Imagism and Visual Prosody

1. *Literary Essays of Ezra Pound*, ed. T. S. Eliot (London, 1954), p. 3.

2. T. E. Hulme, *A Lecture on Modern Poetry*, reprinted in Michael Roberts's *T. E. Hulme* (London, 1938), pp. 269–70.

3. Ibid., p. 267.

4. Ibid., p. 270.

5. Ibid., p. 215 n. 2.

6. Ibid., p. 262.

7. See the preface to Ezra Pound, *Some Imagist Poets* (London, 1915), pp. vii–viii; also, *Literary Essays* (Norfolk, Conn., 1954), pp. 7, 13, 288, 385, and 401; and *The Letters of Ezra Pound*, ed. D. D. Paige (New York, 1950), p. 23.

8. Stanley K. Coffman, Jr., *Imagism* (Norman, Okla., 1951), p. 182.

9. H.D., *Helen in Egypt* (New York, 1961), p. 1.

10. Pound, *Literary Essays*, p. 4.

11. See Harold Whitehall's *Structural Essentials of English* (New York, 1956), esp. pp. 16–18.

12. We find this version in Williams's *Collected Earlier Poems* (Norfolk, Conn., 1951), pp. 429–30.

13. *The Autobiography of William Carlos Williams* (New York, 1951), pp. 174–75.

14. See Williams's remarks on page 217 of the *Autobiography*.

15. Williams, *Autobiography*, p. 264.

16. Ibid.

17. Joseph H. Summers, *George Herbert: His Religion and Art* (London, 1954), p. 123.

18. See R. P. Blackmur's *Form and Value in Modern Poetry* (New York, 1957), pp. 374–75.

19. Karl Shapiro, *Essay on Rime* (New York, 1945), p. 23.

❧ *Notes to Chapter VI: The "Celebrated Metric" of Ezra Pound*

1. *"Cantos" of Ezra Pound: Some Testimonies* (New York, 1933), p. 16.

2. T. S. Eliot, *Ezra Pound: His Metric and Poetry* (New York, 1917), p. 15.

3. See introduction to Pound's *Selected Poems* (London, 1928), pp. 5, 18.

4. It was Gertrude Stein who called Pound "a village explainer: all right if you're a village."

5. Ezra Pound, *ABC of Reading* (New York, 1960), p. 206.

6. *Literary Essays of Ezra Pound*, ed. T. S. Eliot (London, 1954), p. 6.

7. Eliot, *Ezra Pound*, p. 15.

8. Charles Norman, *Ezra Pound* (New York, 1960), p. 282.

9. *Autobiography of William Carlos Williams* (New York, 1951), p. 225.

10. According to Charles Norman, *Ezra Pound*, the Hungarian composer Tibor Serly "arranged" the sonata from a single voice line. Tibor added development, harmony, and sectioning.

11. Ezra Pound, *Antheil and the Treatise on Harmony* (Chicago, 1927), pp. 13–14, 47, 125, 126.

12. Pound, *Literary Essays*, p. 6.

13. Pound, *ABC of Reading*, pp. 198–99.

14. Pound, *Literary Essays*, pp. 12–13.

15. Ibid., p. 93.

16. Pound, *Literary Essays*, pp. 12–13.

17. Ezra Pound, "Harold Monro," *Criterion* 11, no. 45 (July 1932): 590.

18. John Espey, *Ezra Pound's Mauberley* (Berkeley and Los Angeles, 1955), p. 42.

19. Letter to Felix E. Schelling, July 9, 1922 in *The Letters of Ezra Pound,* ed. D. D. Paige (New York, 1950), p. 180.

20. Ibid., p. 181.

21. See Pound's *The Spirit of Romance* (Norfolk, Conn., 1951), p. 262.

22. Hugh Kenner, *The Poetry of Ezra Pound* (Norfolk, Conn., 1951), p. 262.

23. Ernst Cassirer, *An Essay on Man* (Garden City, N.Y., 1953), p. 219.

24. *Paris Review* 28 (summer–fall 1962): 47–49.

25. Caedmon Records, TC 1122.

?? *Notes to Chapter VII: T. S. Eliot and the Music of Poetry*

1. Stéphane Mallarmé, *Selected Prose Poems, Essays, and Letters,* trans. Bradford Cook (Baltimore, 1956), p. 42.

2. Susanne K. Langer, *Philosophy in a New Key* (Cambridge, Mass., 1942), p. 261.

3. T. S. Eliot, *On Poetry and Poets* (New York, 1957), pp. 24–25.

4. Langer, *Philosophy,* p. 261.

5. For example, see Bonamy Dobrée, *The Lamp and the Lute,* and E. M. Stephenson, *T. S. Eliot and the Lay Reader.*

6. Eliot, *On Poetry and Poets,* p. 18.

7. T. S. Eliot, "Reflections on *Vers Libre,*" *New Statesman* (March 3, 1917), pp. 518–19.

8. Sister M. Martin Barry, *An Analysis of the Prosodic Structure of Selected Poems of T. S. Eliot* (Washington, D.C., 1948), p. 105.

9. "[T]he meter of *The Waste Land . . .* is a broken blank verse interspersed with bad free verse and rimed doggerel." In "T. S. Eliot; or, The Illusion of Reaction," *In Defense of Reason* (Denver, 1957), p. 500.

10. "Reflections on *Vers Libre.*"

11. *Literary Essays of Ezra Pound,* ed. T. S. Eliot (London, 1954), p. 421.

12. Eliot, "Reflections on *Vers Libre.*"

13. Eliot owes to Tourneur and Middleton these passages worked into the texture of "Gerontion":

> Now to my tragic business, Look you, brother,
> I have not fashioned this only for show
> And useless property; no, it shall bear a part
> E'en in its own revenge. . . .
>> Tourneur, *The Revenger's Tragedy*

> I am that of your blood was taken from you
> For your better health; look no more upon't,
> But cast it to the ground regardlessly,
> Let the common sewer take it from distinction . . .
>> Middleton, *The Changeling*

Grover Smith, Jr., makes a full accounting of Eliot's debts to the Jacobean dramatists; see *T. S. Eliot's Poetry and Plays* (Chicago, 1956), p. 305 n. 1.

14. Ibid., pp. 50–54.

15. In Lawrence Durrell's *Key to Modern British Poetry,* we find a fascinating arrangement of the opening section of *The Waste Land* as a radio play. Durrell separates out the characters and adds stage directions and sound effects.

16. It is also the stanza of Dryden's *Annus Mirabilis* and John Davies's *Nosce Teipsum.* Eliot comments, "No one, not even Gray, has surpassed Davies in the use of the quatrain which he employed for *Nosce Teipsum,*" *On Poetry and Poets,* p. 153.

17. On Harvard Vocarium record H. F. S. 3122/3124.

18. The italics in the last line are ours and correspond to Eliot's reading. He syncopates the line by stressing the offbeats.

19. Eliot, "Poetry and Drama," in *On Poetry and Poets,* p. 88.

20. Edmund Wilson, *A Piece of My Mind* (Garden City, N.Y., 1956) p. 138.

21. In the Senecan tragedies we find iambic trimeter in the dialogue; the choruses are set to a variety of lyric meters.

22. Eliot, "Poetry and Drama," p. 92.

23. Ibid., p. 91.

24. Ibid., p. 92.

25. Donald Tovey, *The Main Stream of Music* (New York, 1959).

26. See Smith, *Eliot's Poetry and Plays,* p. 151.

27. On Caedmon record TC1045.

28. From a lecture given at New Haven and reported by F. O. Matthiessen. See *The Achievement of T. S. Eliot,* 3d ed. (New York, 1959), pp. 89–90, and the note, p. 96.

29. Herbert Howarth, "Eliot, Beethoven, and J. W. N. Sullivan," *Comparative Literature* 9 (summer 1957): 322–32.

30. J. W. N. Sullivan, *Beethoven, His Spiritual Development* (New York, 1949), pp. 127–28.

31. See Howarth, "Eliot, Beethoven." But also see Harvey Gross, "Music and the Analogue of Feeling: Notes on Eliot and Beethoven," *Centennial Review* 3 (summer 1959): 269–88.

32. Eliot, "Reflections on *Vers Libre.*"

33. Donald Davie, "T. S. Eliot: The End of an Era," in *T. S. Eliot: A Collection of Critical Essays,* ed. Hugh Kenner (Englewood Cliffs, N.J., 1962), p. 195.

⁊ Notes to Chapter VIII: Stevens, Frost, and Jeffers: Three Who Stayed Home; Hart Crane: One Who Found No Home

1. *Conversations on the Craft of Poetry,* ed. Cleanth Brooks and Robert Penn Warren (New York, 1961), p. 59.

2. Marianne Moore early recognized the similarity of these two poems. See her *Predilections* (New York, 1955), pp. 33–34.

3. Wallace Stevens, *The Necessary Angel* (New York, 1951), p. vii.

4. Ibid., p. 81.

5. Ibid., p. 73.

6. See F. O. Matthiessen, *The Achievement of T. S. Eliot,* 3d ed. (New York, 1959), pp. 89–90.

7. Thomas Mann, *Dr. Faustus* (New York, 1948), p. 54.

8. Letter to Allen Tate, June 12, 1922. *The Letters of Hart Crane,* ed. Brom Weber (New York, 1952), p. 90.

9. Letter to Gorham Munson, January 5, 1923, *Letters of Hart Crane,* pp. 114–15.

10. Eliot, "Marlowe," *Selected Essays* (New York, 1950), p. 100.

◆ Notes to Chapter IX: Auden and After

1. W. H. Auden, *The Dyer's Hand* (New York, 1962), p. 47.

2. The order of end words in the original Provençal form was 123456, 615243, 364125, 532614, 451362, 246531; the envoy, of three lines, was 25, 43, 61.

3. This is Sebastian's monologue (*Collected Poetry* [New York, 1945], pp. 370–71).

4. Aristotle, *Poetics,* I, 9.

5. William York Tindall, *A Reader's Guide to Dylan Thomas* (New York, 1962), p. 133.

6. Ibid., p. 11.

7. This does not seem one of the traditional forms of *cynghanedd croes,* but it is certainly as ingeniously effective as any specified by the Welsh court poets.

8. We are indebted to G. S. Fraser for calling this to our attention. See his *Vision and Rhetoric* (London, 1959), pp. 233–34.

9. Ibid., pp. 234–35.

10. Theodore Roethke, "Some Remarks on Rhythm," in *Conversations on the Craft of Poetry,* ed. Cleanth Brooks and Robert Penn Warren (New York, 1961), pp. 48–62.

11. Ibid., p. 48.

12. Ibid., p. 50.

13. Ibid., p. 60.

14. Ibid., pp. 61–62.

15. With important qualifications by Ralph J. Mills, Jr., in *Poets in Progress* (Evanston, Ill., 1962), pp. 20–22.

16. Roethke, "Some Remarks on Rhythm," p. 62.

17. Ibid., p. 59. Roethke is repeating, nearly verbatim, Eliot's remarks in "Reflections on *Vers Libre.*"

18. The phrase is Lowell's own; in Brooks and Warren, *Conversations,* p. 35.

19. Ibid., p. 33.

20. *Land of Unlikeness* appeared in a limited edition of only 250 copies (1944.)

21. A full exposition of the Miltonic resemblances is given by Hugh B. Staples in his *Robert Lowell, The First Twenty Years* (New York, 1962), p. 45.

22. In Brooks and Warren, *Conversations,* p. 38.

23. Lowell speaking in an interview published in *Paris Review* 25 (winter–spring 1961): 66.

24. Ibid.

25. Ibid., p. 67.

26. Ibid., pp. 70–71.

27. *Notebooks: 1967–68* (New York, 1969), pp. 159–60.

28. Donald Justice, ed., *The Collected Poems of Weldon Kees* (Norman, Okla., 1975), p. x.

29. Ibid.

30. Philip Larkin, *Collected Poems*, ed. Anthony Thwaite (New York, 1990), p. xvi.

31. Ibid., pp. xviii–xix.

32. Adrienne Rich, *When We Dead Awaken: Writing as Re-Vision.*

33. Elaine Showalter, consulting editor, Lea Baechler and A. Walton Litz, general editors, *Modern American Women Writers* (New York, 1991), pp. 450–51.

34. Sandra Gilbert, in *Conversant Essays,* ed. James McCorkle (Detroit, 1990).

35. Louis Simpson, *The King My Father's Wreck* (Brownsville, Ore., 1994), pp. 85–86.

36. Mark Jarman, "The Pragmatic Imagination and the Secret of Poetry," *Gettysburg Review* 1 (1988).

37. Louis Simpson, "Donald's Way," in *The Day I Was Older,* ed. Liam Rector (Santa Cruz, Calif., 1989), p. 65.

38. Annie Finch, ed., *A Formal Feeling Comes: Poems in Form by Contemporary Women* (1994), p. 143.

Index